The Private Side of the Canton Trade, 1700–1840

The Private Side of the Canton Trade, 1700–1840

Beyond the Companies

Edited by Paul A. Van Dyke and Susan E. Schopp

HKU PRESS
香港大學出版社

Hong Kong University Press
The University of Hong Kong
Pok Fu Lam Road
Hong Kong
https://hkupress.hku.hk

ISBN 978-988-8390-93-9 (*Hardback*)

British Library Cataloguing-in-Publication Data
A catalogue record for this book is available from the British Library.

Cover image: *China Street, with Part of the European Factories, Canton*. From a print reproduced from the same view in James Wathen, *Journal of a Voyage in 1811 and 1812 to Madras and China* (London: Black, Parry, & Co. and Nichols & Co., 1814). Courtesy of Wattis Fine Art, Hong Kong.

Digitally printed

In memory of John E. Wills Jr.,
who has been an inspiration to all of us.

Contents

Illustrations

Figures

Tables

Preface

Paul A. Van Dyke

This volume represents one step along the way in bringing private traders into clearer focus and making them more central to the discussion of the China trade. They were an intricate part of the commercial operations, filling in gaps in the flow of money and goods. The large European trading companies were as much dependent on private investments to keep their trade moving forward as were the Hong merchants. Without those investments, most of the companies would have scaled back their operations in China or they would have abandoned the trade altogether.

A number of studies have been done on the private trade of the officers of the various East India companies and also on the 'country' trade within Asia.[1] Milburn, Morse, Pritchard, Dermigny, Quiason, Krieger, Koninckx, Bowen, and numerous others have discussed various aspects of the private trade in Asia. Most of this discussion is about Europeans, with a heavy emphasis on India.[2] Before the

1. 'Country' trade is a term that was widely used by both contemporaries and historians to refer to trade that took place within Asia. Because the East India companies were royal monopolies that were granted exclusive rights to trade with Asia, private individuals were not allowed to partake in the Eurasian commerce. Private persons could trade within Asia, such as between India and China, but the products they were allowed to deal in were often also limited by the companies. Some of the companies were involved in the inter-Asian trade so the term 'country' is not a separation between company and private, but rather a distinction that specifies that those vessels stayed within Asia. Country ships were usually only allowed to carry goods from Asia to Europe if they were consigned to the companies. If that happened, then the country ship temporarily became a company ship. Because we are concerned in this study with private trade, in contrast to company trade, we will use the term private rather than country.
2. William Milburn, *Oriental Commerce; containing a Geographical Description of the Principal Places in The East Indies, China, and Japan, with their Produce, Manufactures, and Trade, including the Coasting or Country Trade from Port to Port; also the Rise and Progress of the Trade of the various European Nations with the Eastern World, particularly that of the English East India Company, from the Discovery of the Passage round the Cape of Good Hope to the Present Period; with an account of the Company's Establishments, Revenues, Debts, Assets, &c. at Home and Abroad*, 2 vols. (London: Black, Parry, & Co., 1813; reprint, New Delhi: Munshiram Manoharlal Publishers, 1999); Serafin Quiason, *English 'Country Trade' with the Philippines, 1644–1765* (Quezon City: University of Philippines Press, 1966); Louis Dermigny, *La Chine et l'Occident. Le Commerce à Canton au XVIII Siècle 1719–1833*, 3 vols. and Album (Paris: S.E.V.P.E.N., 1964); Martin

twenty-first century, Michael Greenberg, Louis Dermigny, Earl Pritchard, Jonathan Goldstein, Jacques Downs, and Anne Bulley perhaps did more than anyone to open up the discussion about private trade between America, India, and China in the late eighteenth and early nineteenth centuries. In 1951, Greenberg published his book *British Trade and the Opening of China 1800–1842*. It is one of the first studies to address the important role that private traders played in ending the British East India Company's (EIC) operations in China. While he devoted most of his discussion to the Company and saw British private traders more as adversaries to the EIC rather than as essential components that helped that enterprise survive, his work is important for bringing private traders more centrally into the discussion.[3]

From Greenberg's studies, it became evident that there was a need for better information and knowledge of private trading activities in China in the eighteenth century. In 1957 and 1958, Pritchard published two articles on 'Private Trade between England and China in the Eighteenth Century (1680–1833)'. This was one of the earliest studies to focus specifically on British private traders and to look at them as legitimate businessmen in their own right and completely separate from the Company. Pritchard brought the activities of the privately-run agency houses in India into much clearer focus so we could see how they fit into the overall operation of the China trade.[4]

From 1959 to 1964, Dermigny published two books entitled *Cargaisons Indiennes. Solier et Cie 1781–1793* and *Les Mémoires de Charles de Constant sur le commerce à la Chine*. Both of these studies contain a substantial amount of information about private trading activities in China in the eighteenth century.[5] In 1964 Dermigny also published his multivolume study *La Chine et l'Occident: le commerce à Canton au*

Krieger, *Daufleute, seeräuber und Diplomaten. Der Dänische Handel auf dem Indischen Ozean (1620–1868)* (Köln, Weimar, Wien: Bohlau Verlag, 1998); Huw Bowen, 'Privilege and Profit: Commanders of East Indiamen as Private Traders, Entrepreneurs and Smugglers, 1760–1813', *International Journal of Maritime History* 19, no. 2 (December 2007): 43–88; Earl H. Pritchard, 'Private Trade between England and China in the Eighteenth Century (1680–1833)', *Journal of the Economic and Social History of the Orient* 1, no. 1 (Aug 1957): 108–37; Earl H. Pritchard, 'Private Trade between England and China in the Eighteenth Century (Concluded)', *Journal of the Economic and Social History of the Orient* 1, no. 2 (April 1958): 221–56; Christian Koninckx, *The First and Second Charters of the Swedish East India Company (1731–1766)* (Belgium: Van Gemmert Publishing Co., 1980); H. B. Morse, *The Chronicles of the East India Company Trading to China, 1635–1834*, 5 vols. (Cambridge, MA: Harvard University Press, 1926; reprint, Taipei: Ch'eng-wen Publishing Co., 1966); Jaap. R. Bruijn, *Commanders of Dutch East India Ships in the Eighteenth Century* (Woodbridge: Boydell Press, 2011).

3. Michael Greenberg, *British Trade and the Opening of China 1800–1842* (Cambridge: Cambridge University Press, 1951).
4. Pritchard, 'Private Trade between England and China in the Eighteenth Century (1680–1833)' (August 1957): 108–37; and Pritchard, 'Private Trade between England and China in the Eighteenth Century (Concluded)' (April 1958): 221–56.
5. Louis Dermigny, *Cargaisons Indiennes. Solier et Cie1781–1793*, 2 vols. (Paris: S.E.V.P.E.N., 1959–1960); Charles-Samuel de Constant and Louis Dermigny, ed., *Les mémoires de Charles de Constant sur le commerce a la Chine*, par Charles de Constant (Paris: S.E.V.P.E.N., 1964).

XVIII siècle 1719–1833. This is a massive study of 1,450 pages which focuses mostly on the trade of the large East India companies—especially those of the French and English.[6] Chapter 3, however, is a discussion of the American trade with China, and Chapter 4 deals with privately-run agency houses. But it should be pointed out that Dermigny did not consult any of the American records, but rather gleaned that information from secondary publications and from the archives of the French and British East India companies. His study also discusses the opium trade, which of course was carried out primarily by private traders so it should rightfully be included in this historiography.

Goldstein's studies of the Philadelphian China traders (1978)—and especially his more recent book on Stephen Girard (2011)—have advanced the research on the Americans considerably. In 1979, Weng Eang Cheong published *Mandarins and Merchants: Jardine Matheson & Co., a China Agency of the Early Nineteenth Century*, which has helped to bring this private British firm into the main discussion of the trade, especially with respect to opium.[7]

In 1992, Anne Bulley published *Free Mariner: John Adolphus Pope in the East Indies 1786–1821*, which was followed by another book in 2000 entitled *The Bombay Country Ships 1790–1833*.[8] The detailed documents that Bulley discovered in the papers of the free mariner John Pope have unravelled many of the mysteries surrounding the private trade between India and China. In 1995, Bulley also assembled 'The Bombay Country Ships 1790–1833 with lists of Captains and Nominal Owners', which she updated in 1999. This unpublished list was deposited in the British Library, where it is available to consult and is a great aid in tracking down private ships and their captains. Unfortunately, private documents such as Pope's papers are very difficult to come by.[9]

In 1997, Downs published his book *The Golden Ghetto*, which was recently republished by Hong Kong University Press (2014). While Downs ends his book with a condemnation of the opium trade and defines the American experience in Canton as self-righteous and sinful, his book contains an enormous amount of data about private trade between the United States and China. If one can look beyond

6. Dermigny, *Le Commerce à Canton*.
7. Jonathan Goldstein, *Philadelphia and the China Trade 1682–1846: Commercial, Cultural, and Attitudinal Effects* (University Park, PA: Pennsylvania State University Press, 1978); Jonathan Goldstein, *Stephen Girard's Trade with China 1787–1824* (Portland, ME: MerwinAsia, 2011); Weng Eang Cheong, *Mandarins and Merchants. Jardine Matheson & Co., a China Agency of the Early Nineteenth Century* (London: Curzon Press, 1979).
8. 'Free mariner' is another term that was often used by contemporaries and usually referred to Europeans who conducted private trade within Asia.
9. Anne Bulley, *Free Mariner: John Adolphus Pope in the East Indies 1786–1821* (London: British Association for Cemeteries in South Asia [BACSA], 1992); Anne Bulley, *The Bombay Country Ships 1790–1833* (Richmond, Surrey: Curzon Press, 2000); and Anne Bulley, 'The Bombay Country Ships 1790–1833 with lists of Captains and Nominal Owners', compiled by Anne Bulley in 1995, revised 1999. Unpublished manuscript, available in a folder on the shelves of the British Library in the 'Asia and Africa Reading Room'.

the religious overtones and negative connotations, there is much to be gleaned from this impressively researched monograph.[10]

In 2004, Patrick Kin Wai Mok completed his dissertation entitled 'The British Intra-Asian Trade with China, 1800–1842'.[11] His study brings the private trade from India, Penang, and Singapore more tightly into the discussion. Up to this point, it can be seen that almost all of the research on private traders has focussed on the British, French and/or Americans. While there still remains an enormous amount of research to do on all three of those groups, we need to remember that there were many other private persons involved in the trade in Asia. For many of these other individuals, there is next to nothing written about them.

In October 2003, a seminar was hosted by Hong Kong University (HKU) on 'Sino-Indian Interactions in the 18th and 19th Centuries: Parsees, Armenians, and Muslims in Macau, Guangzhou, and Hong Kong'. Van Dyke helped to organize this event, which was jointly sponsored by HKU and the Macao Cultural Affairs Bureau. All of the private traders that were discussed in this seminar arrived in China from India.[12] It was very much a coincidental meeting because the five scholars who presented papers had only learned of each other in 2002, and were all finishing their research at about the same time. Nothing of substance had been written about these men previously, so their presentations were a breakthrough in our understanding of the extent to which these India-based groups were involved in the China trade. Since that research was done, Guo Deyan, Shalini Saksena, Carl T. Smith and Madhavi Thampi published other books and articles on the Parsees. Smith and Van Dyke also published articles on the Armenian and Muslim merchants who were involved in the trade at Canton.[13] Some of these private traders were already active

10. Jacques M. Downs, *The Golden Ghetto* (Bethlehem, PA: Lehigh University Press, 1997; reprint, Hong Kong: Hong Kong University Press, 2014).
11. Patrick Kin Wai Mok, 'The British Intra-Asian Trade with China, 1800–1842' (PhD diss., Dept. of History, University of Hong Kong, 2004).
12. The seminar took place at the University of Hong Kong in October 2003 and was entitled 'Sino-Indian Interactions in the 18th and 19th Centuries: Parsees, Armenians, and Muslims in Macau, Guangzhou, and Hong Kong Seminar'. There were only five presenters, and represented everything that had been done to date on these men.
13. The following articles were a direct result of the University of Hong Kong seminar. Carl T. Smith, 'An Eighteenth-Century Macao Armenian Merchant Prince', *Review of Culture*, International Edition No. 6 (April 2003): 120–29; Carl T. Smith and Paul A. Van Dyke, 'Armenian Footprints in Macau', *Review of Culture*, International Edition No. 8 (October 2003): 20–39; Carl T. Smith and Paul A. Van Dyke, 'Four Armenian Families', *Review of Culture*, International Edition No. 8 (October 2003): 40–50; Carl T. Smith and Paul A. Van Dyke, 'Muslims in the Pearl River Delta, 1700 to 1930', *Review of Culture*, International Edition No. 10 (April 2004): 6–15; Guo Deyan, 'The Study of Parsee Merchants in Canton, Hong Kong and Macao', *Review of Culture*, International Edition No. 8 (October 2003): 51–69; Shalini Saksena, 'Parsi Contributions to the Growth of Bombay and Hong Kong', *Review of Culture*, International Edition No. 10 (April 2004): 26–35; Carl T. Smith, 'Parsee Merchants in the Pearl River Delta', *Review of Culture*, International Edition No. 10 (April 2004): 36–49; and Madhavi Thampi, 'Parsis in the China Trade', *Review of Culture*,

in Canton before the French and English East India companies began a steady trade there in 1698 and 1699, respectfully.

Sebouh Aslanian and others have expanded our understanding of the Armenian networks in the seventeenth and eighteenth century and their connections to China.[14] However, there still remains much work to be done because we know so little about most of these men. In December 2008, Van Dyke and colleagues organized a small conference at the University of Macau on 'Americans, Macao and China 1784–1950: Historical Relations, Interactions and Connections'.[15] No new research had been completed on other private China traders such as Europeans and Indians, so there was no point in expanding the focus beyond Americans. In order to attract enough participants to make the conference worthwhile, we expanded the discussion to include all Americans such as consuls and missionaries and not just traders. At the time, there were still few people doing research on Americans in China. Some of the papers from that conference were published in *Americans and Macao: Trade, Smuggling, and Diplomacy on the South China Coast* (2012).[16]

In November 2013, Van Dyke and colleagues organized a conference entitled 'Private Merchants of the China Trade, 1700 to 1842'. It was sponsored and hosted by the Research Center for Canton Port and the Department of History at Sun Yat-sen University in Guangzhou. Between 2008 and 2013 there was an explosion of new research on private persons connected with the China trade. We were able to include not only Americans and private individuals from India such as the Armenians, but also British, French, Swedish, Italians, Russians, and Germans, as well as new research on the Chinese merchants and shopkeepers in Canton. The field was finally coming into its own, with a number of new scholars joining the research. Some of the papers from this conference are included in this volume. Van Dyke added another chapter to the book that was not presented at the conference; entitled 'Ambiguous Faces of the Canton Trade', which provides some brief examples of Armenians, Muslims and Parsees who were involved in the trade, as well as a few references to Greeks, Jews and Southeast Asians. Details about these private

International Edition No. 10 (April 2004): 16–25. Guo Deyan later published his book on the Parsees, entitled *Qingdai Guangzhou de Basi Shangren* 清代廣州的巴斯商人 [Parsee merchants in Guangzhou during the Qing dynasty] (Beijing: Zhonghua shuju, 2005). Thampi later published *Indians in China 1800–1949* (New Delhi: Manohar Publishers & Distributors, 2005); and Thampi and Saksena published *China and the Making of Bombay* (Mumbai: K. R. Cama Oriental Institute, 2009).

14. Sebouh David Aslanian, *From the Indian Ocean to the Mediterranean: The Global Trade Networks of Armenian Merchants from New Julfa* (Berkeley: University of California Press, 2011).
15. The conference was held at the University of Macau on 8–9 December 2008, entitled 'Americans, Macao and China 1784–1950: Historical Relations, Interactions and Connections'.
16. Paul A. Van Dyke, ed., *Americans and Macao: Trade, Smuggling, and Diplomacy on the South China Coast* (Hong Kong: Hong Kong University Press, 2012).

individuals is often very brief and incomplete, which makes the inclusion of these bits and pieces of information that much more important.

In 2014, Richard Grace published his *Opium and Empire: The Lives and Careers of William Jardine and James Matheson* (Montreal: McGill Queens University Press, 2014). This is the most exhaustive study that has been done on Jardine and Matheson, and covers each of them from youth to death. Having more complete accounts of these two major players fills a huge void in our understanding of the early nineteenth century. Researchers will find this book especially helpful when used in conjunction with the 263 letters from the Jardine Matheson Archive that are reproduced in Alain le Pichon, ed., *China Trade and Empire. Jardine, Matheson & Co. and the Origins of British Rule in Hong Kong 1827–1843* (Oxford: Oxford University Press, 2006). Together, these two publications are a great aid in advancing the research of private trading activities in China during the early nineteenth century.[17]

The study of Sino-American private trade is a very diverse topic, and not one that can be neatly fitted into a single field. In 2010, James Fichter published his major study on the American worldwide trade, much of which has connections to China. While this is a global history and not focused specifically on Americans in Canton, it contains a lot of relevant references and information. Fichter shows how Americans took advantage of their neutral status and expanded their global connections during years when Europeans were at war.[18] In 2015, He Sibing published his book on *Macao in the Making of Early Sino-American Relations 1784–1844*. His study presents an overview of the private American traders involved in the Pearl River Delta, and has quite a bit of new information about the American firm Russell and Company.[19]

Other scholars have written about early Sino-American trade, interactions, and relations but likewise have not specifically focused on Americans in Canton. There has been a lot of interest in the fur trade between the North American Coast and China, most of which was conducted by private traders. While these transactions were sporadic and of minor importance to the overall trading activities at Canton, they reveal other aspects of private interactions in the Pearl River Delta that are not covered in other publications.[20]

---

17. Richard J. Grace, *Opium and Empire: The Lives and Careers of William Jardine and James Matheson* (Montreal: McGill Queens University Press, 2014); and Alain le Pichon, *China Trade and Empire: Jardine, Matheson & Co. and the Origins of British Rule in Hong Kong 1827–1843* (Oxford: Oxford University Press, 2006).
18. James Fichter, *So Great a Proffit: How the East Indies Trade Transformed Anglo-American Capitalism* (Cambridge, MA: Harvard University Press, 2010), 284.
19. He Sibing, *Macao in the Making of Early Sino-American Relations 1784–1844* (Macao: Cultural Affairs Bureau of the Macao S.A.R. Government, 2015).
20. James R. Gibson, *Otter Skins, Boston Ships, and China Goods: The Maritime Fur Trade of the Northwest Coast, 1785–1841* (Seattle: University of Washington Press, 1992); Zhou Xiang 周湘, 'Qingdai Guangzhou yu Maopi Maoyi' 清代廣州與毛皮貿易 [The fur trade with Guangzhou during the Qing dynasty] (PhD diss., Dept. of History, Zhongshan University,

Recent publications by Haddad, Frank and Johnston are more concerned with social, cultural, material and visual aspects of the exchanges in the contexts of America's China trade. Haddad presents many examples of Americans involved in the trade and shows how influential the exchanges were on American thought and society. Frank has shown that the craze for Chinese objects in the United States began many decades before the first American ship sailed to China in 1784. Johnston and Frank's edited volume of *Global Trade & Visual Arts in Federal New England*, is especially insightful, with several very thoroughly researched chapters on American China traders. While the main focus of the chapters is on the United States, there are numerous references to private trading activities in Canton—many of which appear for the first time in print.[21]

The American China trade records are so massive in volume and are spread out over many cities, repositories and private collections that in order to get an overall understanding of those interactions, hundreds of primary and secondary sources need to be consulted. Some of these publications are local in focus and somewhat sentimental in tone, but there is nonetheless much to be gleaned from them. Of course, there are many popular histories that have been written about the trade as well, but I will not deal with those publications here because some of them are historical fiction, with no references provided, and others are based mostly on secondary sources, which repeat much of what we already know.

As far as the private trade of the Chinese merchants is concerned, great leaps forward have been made in recent years. In 2014, Fred Grant published his book on *The Chinese Cornerstone of Modern Banking: The Canton Guaranty System and the Origins of Bank Deposit Insurance 1780–1933*.[22] While this is not a study of private merchants trading in Canton, it nonetheless contains much relevant information about both foreign and Chinese traders involved in the commerce. With regard to

---

1999); Dick A. Wilson, 'King George's Men: British Ships and Sailors in the Pacific Northwest-China Trade, 1785–1821' (PhD diss., Dept. of History, University of Idaho, 2004); and Evan Lampe, *Work, Class, and Power in the Borderlands of the Early American Pacific: The Labors of Empire* (Lanham: Lexington Books, 2014). Although focused almost exclusively on published sources most of which are secondary, Eric Jay Dolin has also published books on the Sino-American trade. Eric Jay Dolin, *When America First Met China: An Exotic History of Tea, Drugs, and Money in the Age of Sail* (New York: W. W. Norton & Company, 2012); and Eric Jay Dolin, *Fur, Fortune, and Empire: The Epic History of the Fur Trade in America* (New York: W. W. Norton & Company, 2010).

21. John Rogers Haddad, *The Romance of China: Excursion to China in U.S. Culture, 1776–1876* (New York: Columbia University Press, 2008); John Rogers Haddad, *America's First Adventure in China: Trade, Treaties, Opium, and Salvation* (Philadelphia: Temple University Press, 2013; reprint, 2014); Caroline Frank, *Objectifying China, Imagining America: Chinese Commodities in Early America* (Chicago: University of Chicago Press, 2011); and Patricia Johnston and Caroline Frank, eds., *Global Trade and Visual Arts in Federal New England* (Durham: University of New Hampshire Press, 2014).
22. Frederic D. Grant Jr., *The Chinese Cornerstone of Modern Banking: The Canton Guaranty System and the Origins of Bank Deposit Insurance 1780–1933* (Leiden: Brill Nijhoff, 2014).

financial institutions and the handling of private merchant's debts and bankruptcies in Canton and in the United States, it is indispensable.

In 2011, Van Dyke published the first volume of the *Merchants of Canton and Macao* which was followed by a second volume in 2016. This study contains histories of numerous Hong merchant families, much of which is new information. There are also chapters on the porcelain dealers and silk workers, many of whom have had almost nothing written about them in the past. The Chinese shopkeepers who were involved in the foreign trade in Canton and Macao are usually referred to collectively as 'outside merchants'. Most of the men discussed in these two volumes had transactions with foreign private traders so their examples add to everyone's story.[23]

In 2015, Van Dyke and Mok published their book on the *Images of the Canton Factories 1760–1822*.[24] While the content is mostly concerned with paintings of the Canton factories and their historical value, there is quite a lot of new information in the volume about private traders in China. Chapter 6 is entitled 'The Rise of the Private Traders 1790–1799' and provides a brief explanation of the explosive expansion of the private trade in those years and the effects it had on the structure of trade and the management of the factories. The authors also identify some of the buildings where the Americans, Muslims, Parsees, Armenians and other private traders regularly stayed in Canton, thereby providing some background information for their trading activities.[25]

In 2016, John Wong published his book on *Global Trade in the Nineteenth Century: The House of Houqua and the Canton System*.[26] This is the first extensive study of this very prominent merchant, and is full of new insights and questions about the role China played in the establishment of international trade and commerce. With the new books published by Grant, Van Dyke, and Wong, and the chapter in this volume by Maria Mok, we now have a much clearer understanding of the Chinese side of these private exchanges.

Portuguese and Spanish merchants at Macao are of course also important for this subject—albeit they have been traditionally studied as separate from the private

23. Paul A. Van Dyke, *Merchants of Canton and Macao: Politics and Strategies in Eighteenth-Century Chinese Trade*, Vol. 1 (Hong Kong: Hong Kong University Press, 2011); and Paul A. Van Dyke, *Merchants of Canton and Macao: Success and Failure in Eighteenth-Century Chinese Trade*, Vol. 2 (Hong Kong: Hong Kong University Press, 2016).
24. Paul A. Van Dyke and Maria Kar-wing Mok, *Images of the Canton Factories 1760–1822: Reading History in Art* (Hong Kong: Hong Kong University Press, 2015).
25. Another recent publication has more detailed information about the factories that private traders rented in Canton. Paul A. Van Dyke, 'The Hume Scroll of 1772 and the Faces behind the Canton Factories', *Review of Culture*, International Edition (2017), 64–102.
26. John D. Wong, *Global Trade in the Nineteenth Century: The House of Houqua and the Canton System* (Cambridge: Cambridge University Press, 2016). Wang Shuo has also completed a recent study of Houqua. Wang Shuo 王碩, 'Wu Bingjian and His Friends: The Relations Network of a Chinese Merchant in the Early 19th Century' (PhD diss., East Asian History, University of Freiburg, forthcoming). http://www.eah.geschichte.uni-freiburg.de/staff/wang-shuo (accessed 24 December 2016).

traders at Canton. There is some logic behind this division. While the Portuguese are certainly part of the private trade discussion, the bulk of their trade with China was done through Macao and was not part of the foreign trade that was based at Whampoa. Of course, they purchased their cargos at Canton, and then had them shipped downriver, but all of this business operated under a different set of rules and administration than the trade at Whampoa. Other foreigners were not allowed to take part in the trade at Macao without the approval of the Portuguese government. Normally, the only other persons who were allowed to trade there were the Spanish from Manila, who, of course, were also Catholics.[27] Several studies have been done in recent years on Portuguese merchants who were based in Macao. George Bryan Souza has been at the forefront of this research for many decades and has several recent publications.[28]

In the eighteenth century, there were a few Portuguese ships that actually went upriver to Whampoa to trade. Before 1785, a few Spanish ships also went to Whampoa.[29] Their examples, however, are very few in number and were exceptions to normal practice. In 1785, the Spaniards from Manila began a more regular trade at Whampoa, with one or more ships arriving almost every year. But even after this trade began, most of the Spanish ships continued to go to Macao. Like the Portuguese, the Spanish merchants also had to go to Canton to purchase their cargos. The trade that they did through Macao, however, fell under the rules and administration of that city and not Whampoa.

In 2013, Ander Permanyer-Ugartemendia completed his PhD thesis on the Spanish trade with Canton and Macao in the late eighteenth and early nineteenth centuries, with a special focus on the opium trade.[30] This study includes a discussion

27. For a discussion of the differences between the trade at Macao and Canton, see William Milburn, *Oriental Commerce*, 2 vols. (London: Black, Parry, & Co., 1813); and John Phipps, *A Practical Treatise on the China and Eastern Trade: comprising the Commerce of Great Britain and India, particularly Bengal and Singapore, with China and the Eastern Islands* (Calcutta: Baptist Mission Press, 1835).
28. George Bryan Souza, 'The Portuguese Merchant Fleet at Macao in the Seventeenth and Eighteenth Centuries', in *Rivalry and Conflict: European Traders and Asian Trading Networks in the 16th and 17th Centuries*, ed. Ernst van Veen and Leonard Blussé (Amsterdam: Amsterdam University Press, 2005), 342–69; George Bryan Souza, 'Merchants and Commerce in Asia and the Portuguese Empire over the Long 18th Century', *Review of Culture*, International Edition No. 34 (April 2010): 64–76; and George Bryan Souza, *Portuguese, Dutch and Chinese in Maritime Asia, c. 1585–1800: Merchants, Commodities and Commerce* (Burlington, VT: Ashgate, 2014). There are many other scholars who have studied the trade at Macao. I will not list them all here, but, see, for example, books by Zhang Tingmao 張廷茂 (2004), Angela Guimarães (2000), and A. M. Martins de Vale (1997).
29. Paul Van Dyke is presently assembling a new list of ships at Whampoa, which will show the names and years that the Portuguese and Spanish vessels were at Whampoa. Until that study is completed, the best source available is the ship list in Dermigny, *La Chine et l'Occident* 2: 521–25.
30. Ander Permanyer-Ugartemendia, 'La participación española en la economía del opio en Asia Oriental tras el fin del Galeón' (PhD diss., Universitat Pompeu Fabra, Barcelona, 2013).

of the Spanish trade at both Whampoa and Macao and has much relevance to the private traders at Canton. Unlike the Portuguese, the Spaniards actually set up a factory at Canton in 1788 and from then on flew their national flag out front just like other Europeans and Americans.[31]

Some of the Spanish trade at Canton at this time was conducted under the auspices of the *Real Compañía de Filipinas* (RCP, 'The Royal Philippine Company') which was established in 1785.[32] This was a royally chartered company similar to the East India Companies, and as such would not be classified under private trade. There were other Spanish ships that arrived at Whampoa that were privately owned and commissioned. Spanish officers of the RCP also carried on extensive private dealings that were apart from the company's operation. Those transactions and the trade of the private Spanish ships should rightfully be included in the private trade discussion. However, except for the Spanish chief Agote's Diary, we have no records of those private transactions, and it is not always clear which ships and cargos were private and which of them belonged to the RCP.[33]

As can be seen, private and company trade is not always easy to separate. On the one hand, we could argue that it might be better to talk about the trade as a whole, private and company together. I used that approach in *The Canton Trade*, which was indeed necessary in order to understand how all the different components worked together to move the trade forward.[34] On the other hand, because we know so little about the operations of the private traders, it is important to analyse them on their own terms and within their own narratives so that we can see more clearly their motivations and limitations. When we mix the private trade discussion with that of the companies, the special circumstances and characteristics of the former tends to get subsumed and/or hidden under the narrative of the latter.

In the process of putting this volume together, the question came up as to why we did not include a discussion of the private Dutch trade at Canton. We would have welcomed such a discussion, but I was unaware of any new research on the subject. Because there is some confusion as to who these Dutchmen were who stayed in Canton and Macao after the Dutch East India Company (VOC) ceased sending ships to China in 1794, I will provide a brief summary here. For the most part, these Dutch officers were the same persons who had been taking care of the VOC trade. After that company ceased its China voyages, those men became officers of the Dutch government, and operated as consuls, assistants, bookkeepers, etc. They were civil servants on the government payroll.

31. Van Dyke and Mok, *Images of the Canton Factories*, xix, 36, and 38.
32. William Schurz, 'The Royal Philippine Company', *The Hispanic American Historical Review* 3, no. 4 (November 1920): 491–508.
33. Spain, San Sebastián: Untzi Museoa-Museo Naval (UM), Fondo Manuel de Agote (FMA), R630–638 Manuel de Agote Diarios 1787–1796.
34. Paul A. Van Dyke, *The Canton Trade: Life and Enterprise on the China Coast, 1700–1845* (Hong Kong: Hong Kong University Press, 2005; reprint, 2007).

The expense of renting the Dutch factory in Canton was largely paid for by past debts that Hong merchants owed to the VOC. The Dutch officers needed additional funds to pay their salaries and cover living expenses and other costs, which they obtained from a tax they levied on each ship in their commission. In many years after 1794, they were short on funds and had to borrow money from private merchants in Macao in order to survive until another ship arrived or until one of their debtors gave them another payment. All of this activity was carried out and managed by the Dutch government in Batavia and Holland.[35]

Some of the Dutch officers who resided in China carried on private trade on the side, which would fit nicely into our discussion. Unfortunately, no detailed records have emerged showing those transactions. Some of the Dutch ships that arrived at Whampoa after the VOC voyages ceased were privately owned and would also be counted as private trade. Perhaps one day documents from those voyages will emerge, which will then help to reveal that part of the Dutch trade.[36]

We have many records from the Dutchmen who resided in Canton and Macao from 1795 to 1830, but they mostly discuss the official trade that they handled for the Dutch government. This trade does not qualify as being 'private'. In the years when no private Dutch ships arrived, these men freighted goods on privately owned vessels including Chinese, Portuguese, American, Danish, Swedish, Prussian, and others. In fact, some of the Swedish ships that carried freight for the Dutch to and from China at this time were actually owned by the Swedish East India Company (SOIC).[37] All of this trade, however, was commissioned by the Dutch government. For all of these reasons, we have not included the Dutch in this or other studies of the private traders.

Included in this present volume are chapters by Jessica Hanser, Susan E. Schopp, and Lisa Hellman. All three scholars recently completed their PhD dissertations and all of them have parts that focus specifically on private trading activities in China. Hanser discusses private British traders involved in Canton, Schopp has a discussion of private French traders, and Hellman's study has a lot of new information about the private Swedish traders operating in the delta. All three authors are now preparing their dissertations for publication. Included in this present volume as well, is a chapter by Maria Mok, who also recently completed her PhD thesis on Chinese

35. Much of this activity of the Dutch officers who remained in Canton and Macao after 1794, is document in The Hague, National Archives (NAH): Canton 256-388, HRB 95-136, RAB 140-142 and OIC 193-198, 238A, and 238Q.
36. The Zeeuws Museum, in Middleburg, Netherlands, has two Grand Chops (Inv. Nos. G02-005 and G02-006) from a couple of these Dutch private ships, dated 1817 and 1819. However, so far, no other documents have emerged from these voyages.
37. E. S. van Eyck van Heslinga, *Van Compagnie naar Koopvaardij, De scheepvaartverbinding van de Bataafse Republiek met de koloniën in Azië 1795–1806* (Amsterdam: De Bataafsche Leeuw, 1988).

export paintings and the craftsmen who made and sold them.[38] It is wonderful to see all of these new studies coming to fruition.

Nevertheless, there remains much work to be done. Hundreds of private foreign individuals were involved in the China trade in the eighteenth and early nineteenth centuries and we only have stories written about a handful of them. We hope this volume will bring us one step closer to understanding the roles these men played in the growth and advancement of the trade, and that it will encourage others to join this new and fascinating field of the private trade in China.

38. Jessica Hanser, 'Mr. Smith Goes to China: British Private Traders and the Interlinking of the British Empire with China, 1757–1792' (PhD diss., Dept. of History, Yale University, May 2012); Susan E. Schopp, 'The French in the Pearl River Delta: A Topical Case Study of Sino-European Exchanges in the Canton Trade, 1698–1840' (PhD diss., Dept. of History, University of Macau, 2015); Lisa Hellman, 'Everyday Life in Canton: The Case of the Swedish East India Company 1730–1830' (PhD diss., Dept. of History, Stockholm University, 2015); and Maria Kar-wing Mok 莫家詠, 'Xiěshí yù xiǎngxiàng zhī jiān: Guǎngzhōu shāngguǎn jì huángbù bódì wàixiāo huà de shǐliào yìyì' 寫實與想像之間：廣州商館暨黃埔泊地外銷畫的史料意義 [Between realism and imagination: The historical meaning of Canton and Whampoa export paintings] (PhD diss., Dept. of History, Sun Yat-sen University, 2017).

Introduction

Paul A. Van Dyke and John E. Wills Jr.

Between 1750 and 1840, the world became more prosperous, more crowded, and more interconnected. State-centred patterns of distribution of resources, which were typical of many forms of empire and of the mercantilist orders of early modern Europe, were destabilized by these changes. New orders that gave more scope to private initiatives, including the new nations in the Americas and the new forms of organization, consumption, and production in Great Britain and its colonies, grew rapidly.[1] The harnessing of steam power, especially for shipping, shaped these changes, but affected the Indian Ocean and the Pacific only after about 1830.[2] From early in the 1700s, and more rapidly from about 1750, growth of trade in sailing ships shaped a world of growing population, 'domestication', 'consumerism', and a variety of new political forms.[3] The mechanisms of monopolistic trading companies and imperial sharing of power, which worked best with stability or slowly changing volumes, came under increasing strain. Revolutions, new states, and anarchic break-outs of individual trade were among the consequences. New consumer goods from distant lands were everywhere: Indian textiles, coffee, tea, chocolate, spices, sugar, and many more. After 1800, new trades and resources around the Pacific, from furs

1. For one set of guidelines into the many kinds of reading that can be brought to bear on these themes see John E. Wills Jr., 'What's New? Studies of Revolutions and Divergences, 1770–1840: A Review Article', *Journal of World History* 25, no. 1 (2014): 127–86.
2. The first steamship to arrive in China was the *Forbes* in 1830. Paul A. Van Dyke, *The Canton Trade: Life and Enterprise on the China Coast, 1700–1845* (Hong Kong: Hong Kong University Press, 2005), 46. In Wei Yuan 魏源, *Hai Guo Tu Zhi* 海國圖志 (1841) no. 52, vol. 12, p. 93, there is mention of a steamer (*huo lun chuan* 火輪船) arriving in the Pearl River Delta from India in 1828. According to the foreign sources, this reference is incorrect. We know the names of all the foreign steamships operating in Asia at this time, and there is no reference to one arriving in China before the *Forbes*. The *Hai Guo Tu Zhi* was compiled over many years and the authors did not have access to foreign records to cross-reference their information so it is understandable that they did not get everything correct. Steamers were operating in India before 1830, but not in Chinese waters. We thank Peter Purdue for bringing this reference to our attention.
3. C. A. Bayly, *The Birth of the Modern World, 1780–1914* (Oxford and Malden, MA: Blackwell, 2004), 1–198.

to whales to trepang, came into play largely beyond the reach of states, empires, and monopolistic companies.

Guangzhou, which foreign visitors called 'Canton' and we will too, was an important vortex of these changes. In the late 1700s, all the tea thrown into Boston Harbor or sipped from fine porcelain at Parisian soirées where royal scandals were retold and revolutionary ideas proclaimed, had been shipped from Canton. In sharp contrast to the trades in the Indian cotton goods that were worn in Boston, London, Paris, and many more places, where the expansion of Atlantic purchases led to very active supervision of production in India, we know of no European trader before 1800 who even visited the tea-growing areas in China. Tough-minded, realistic officials in constant communication with capital grandees and the great emperors; extremely well-organized, diligent, and honest growers, processors, and merchants; and foreign merchants who came to respect the reliability of their Chinese counterparts and to enjoy the fine quarters, food, and shopping during their stay in Canton all contributed to this set of mutually advantageous arrangements.

We have seen remarkable advances in Chinese understanding of the Canton Trade. When Wills first visited Guangzhou in 1985 he found, as elsewhere in China, a lot of energy going into the study of local and regional history, but only small steps towards studying the Canton Trade; foreign languages, foreign libraries and archives, and foreign histories all seemed daunting. Many scholars and institutions have contributed to the remarkable advances since that time, including major scholars based in Guangzhou, using archives and collections from around the world, and organizing international conferences like the one that produced these chapters.

Earlier generations of European and American scholars of the Canton Trade had good reasons to focus on the trade of the great companies and to leave the private trades for later study. European archives preserved magnificent sets of those companies' reports on trade, providing an abundance of information in uniform and systematic formats, and summarizing a very large part of the actual movements of goods. The companies tried to keep track of, and to report on, the trade of their competitors, so their records shed light on the other companies and on private traders, including Armenians, Parsees, Jews, Greeks, and South Asian Muslims as well as Chinese. Private Europeans in India—especially the British—became increasingly more active in the China trade in the late eighteenth century. Loans to Chinese merchants, coming from the companies and from networks of company servants and private traders, were an important part of the dynamics of the trade on which much research still remains to be done.

Company records tend to be impersonal in tone, written by committees to be read by committees. We are thankful for company servants who wrote in more personal veins, like William Hickey, who is discussed in Wills' essay. As we uncover more private writings, we find Charles de Constant's harsh criticisms of the Chinese in their most corrupt times, the Swedish triangle uncovered by Lisa Hellman, and a host of hints, including Wills' discussions of Poivre and Osbeck, of the importance in these relations of 'natural history', of European fascination with exotic plant life, a theme splendidly developed in Fa-ti Fan's *British Naturalists in Qing China: Science, Empire, and Cultural Encounter*.[4] The export of Chinese seeds and plants included many efforts to take tea plants and Chinese tea-production techniques to India, ending in the world-changing success of Robert Fortune just after the First Opium War (1839–1842).[5]

The companies' records give us details about the private permission trade, which employees were allowed. These data have been used extensively in the early studies mentioned above. However, trade figures about private persons in China who were not connected to the companies are few and far between.

The permissions trades surely were important for upscale goods like fine teas, top-end porcelain, and the many different export-art objects that were available to purchase in Canton. The companies rarely traded in these items. As Maria Mok shows so well in her chapter, paintings, lacquerware, porcelain, lifelike small portrait statues, and much more were mostly purchased on private accounts and were so important in cultural interchange. We get hints of a more relaxed life for those who stayed over the off-season in Macao (circa February to June). As Godden and numerous other scholars have shown, the East India Company's records contain many detailed lists of the items that employees purchased in Canton as part of the permissions trade. Many of these lists have survived from as far back as the early eighteenth century, and some of them have been published.[6]

The great diversity in the trade begins to show its many faces in Van Dyke's chapter, where we find 'Moors, Greeks, Armenians, Parsees, Jews and Southeast Asians' brought together in piecemeal fashion but with some important implications. The traditional means of defining the trade according to national flags displayed on ships has skewed our understanding of what was actually happening. Many of the private individuals who were financing those voyages were based in India or Southeast Asia. They hired Europeans to carry their cargos and to command their ships. Customs officials in China—as well as historians in the present day—have logically assigned the trade of those ships to the flags they displayed. This has kept the real owners in the shadows. Until we have more stories of these 'ambiguous faces', we will never understand the influence they had on the commerce.

Schopp brings together for the first time a discussion of the private French trade in China from 1698 to 1833. The French were among the earliest of the Europeans

4. Fa-ti Fan, *British Naturalists in Qing China: Science, Empire, and Cultural Encounter* (Cambridge, MA, and London: Harvard University Press, 2004).
5. For a smart and lively summary, see Sarah Rose, *For All the Tea in China: How England Stole the World's Favorite Drink and Changed History* (New York: Penguin, 2010). Much remains to be done in the full use of Fortune's lively descriptions of his adventurous trips to China's 'tea country'.
6. G. A. Godden, *Oriental Export Market Porcelain and Its Influence on European Wares* (London: Granada, 1979). There are quite a few lists of permission goods contained in Godden's book.

to open the China trade to private enterprise. This was partially owing to the limited duration of the various French East India companies and the gap between the second and third companies, and the often strained relations between the court of Versailles and merchants. Schopp shows that Sino-French trade began with private traders to whom the French East India Company leased its monopoly on a limited basis. She also demonstrates that for the years from 1770 to 1785, there was no French East India Company operating in China, and the trade was carried on entirely by private individuals. From 1770 to 1778, forty private French ships arrived at Whampoa, averaging a little more than four ships per year. As Van Dyke points out in his chapter, this influx of private French ships tipped the balance to the point that the private trade began to rival the company trade at Canton.

On the opposite side of these exchanges were, of course, the Chinese merchants. Mok's chapter gives us a lively account of the Chinese shopkeepers in Canton and their uncanny ability to lure customers through their doors. While some foreign visitors saw these men in a rather negative light, Mok shows quite convincingly that the majority of the visitors probably went away pleasantly satisfied with their purchases and shopping experience. Repeat sales, maintenance of quality, competitive pricing and good customer relations were all very important to these entrepreneurs in order to remain competitive. We sometimes forget that the hundred or so Chinese shopkeepers that catered to the foreign community at Canton were also private traders.

In order to pass the days, weeks, and months in Canton and/or Macao, one needed something more than just work. For many men, socializing and companionship were just as important as taking care of business. Lisa Hellman takes a look at the love life of one of the Swedish traders during his stay in China in the 1750s and early 1760s, and at the problems and concerns he faced outside of his trading activities. In her chapter and in Goldstein and Cox's chapters, we find that fortunes begotten from the China trade could disappear just as fast as they were acquired—if the money was not invested wisely.

The continued growth of the China trade in the late 1700s and early 1800s depended on the provision of credit to Chinese merchants and producers; it already was a major factor in the 'debt crisis' of 1755–1760. Jessica Hanser follows some of the private British traders based in India, and their operations in China in the 1760s and 1770s. The British plunder of India gave Englishmen and Scots new money to lend and new impatient attitudes in dealing with debtors. Chinese borrowing was at high rates of interest. High interest and high risk often went hand in hand, and when the latter gained prominence over the former, then private foreign investors were faced with considerable losses. Dealing with these private concerns in Canton was no small matter for Chinese officials, because the foreigners did all they could to mobilize forces to apply pressures on the administration of trade to honour the debts.

After the Americans entered the China trade in 1784, private trade gained a big boost. As Van Dyke shows, with the influx of Americans and the growing number of private ships arriving from India, the balance between company and private ships turned in favour of the latter from 1788 onwards. Goldstein and Cox both present examples of Americans involved in the China trade. Goldstein shows that Nathan Dunn was so impressed by the Chinese and his experience in Canton that when he returned to the United States, he opened a museum devoted to educating people about China. While this will be old news to persons familiar with the history, the contrast between Dunn in Goldstein's chapter and Warren Delano in Cox's chapter provides a more balanced understanding of the private trading experience in China.

On the one hand, Dunn much disliked the opium trade and continually spoke out against it. On the other hand, Warren Delano made much of his fortune by selling opium to the Chinese. Both of them returned home with a fortune of about $200,000, but gotten from very different means. The growth of the import of opium, almost always a private trade, was a further major factor leading from the functional mutual accommodation of the 1770s to the disasters of 1839–1842. Cox follows Delano's story up to the First Opium War, and shows how he and his associates dealt with the clamp-down on the opium trade.

What these stories show is that all of these men were welcomed at Canton as private individuals. They traded alongside the large East India companies, with equal access to the market. The products that private traders handled might be restricted in other ports that they visited, which could affect their purchasing decisions in Canton. However, while they were in China they were free to sell and purchase whatsoever they desired, so long as the items were legal. Monopolies that controlled prices, commodities and access to markets were not allowed in Canton, and everyone (except Russians and Japanese who had treaties to trade in other Chinese ports) was guaranteed equal privileges to the trade without prejudice to a person's nationality, religion or ethnicity.

In fact, it could be argued that one of the inherent problems of the trade was that it was not regulated tightly enough. Foreign investors poured money into Canton in order to take advantage of the profits that could be made from the difference between the interest rates inside and outside of China. Many foreigners were investing in the Canton junk voyages to Southeast Asia as well, which could produce profits of upwards of 40 percent per annum. While this money helped to finance growth, and kept the trade moving forward, it led to many Hong merchants going broke. Officials only gained knowledge of these activities after the fact, when they reached crisis proportions, and the government had to step in and deal with the problems that emerged. And because it was so easy to trade in contraband before 1836, with little risk of getting caught, there grew a very substantial trade in opium, which eventually led to war and the collapse of the trade altogether. All of these problems could have been avoided had there been better monitoring of these activities. The many examples that are presented in the chapters that follow show that Canton did indeed live up to its reputation, as Milburn stated:

> The commerce of Canton, immense as it is, is carried on with an astonishing regularity, and in no part of the world can business be transacted with so much ease and dispatch to the foreign merchant.[7]

We end our study by looking forward to more of the work of our colleagues represented in this volume, as well as to finding more available data on the private traders. We are just beginning to understand their importance for the financing of the growing Canton trade, and for the intricate personal and cultural exchanges of an age of divergences.

7. William Milburn, *Oriental Commerce*, 2 vols. (London: Black, Parry, & Co., 1813; reprint, New Delhi: Munshiram Manoharlal Publishers, 1999), 2: 473. See also the quote in the 1831–1832 British Parliamentary debates, where it is stated that 'Greater facilities are given to trade in the port of Canton than in almost any port in the world', *1831–2 Parliamentary Debates and Papers. Reports from Committees: eighteen volumes. Appendix to Report from Select Committee*, p. 462. See also the quote at the end of Maria Mok's chapter. There are quite a few other quotes like this in the Canton trade literature.

1
British Private Traders between India and China

Jessica Hanser

Over half a century ago, Michael Greenberg wrote that 'under cover of a legal subterfuge there had grown up at Canton a small but peculiarly compact merchant community of free traders, whose economic basis was the Country Trade with India. It therefore had standing behind it the great East India Agency houses'. But Greenberg also pessimistically claimed that 'the early history of these concerns is little known and perhaps never will be in any detail . . . here the point to be stressed is the significance of this handful of East Indian Concerns in the growth of the Canton trade'.[1] Because nineteenth-century private traders left more records than their eighteenth-century predecessors (and incited a war with China in 1839), historians after Greenberg naturally focused on those latter connections between India and China.[2]

With new data that has recently emerged, we can now look at the earlier period as well. An in-depth examination of eighteenth-century British private traders in Canton and their clients in India reveals the development of new financial and political entanglements between India and China during the second half of the eighteenth century. Private traders created a financial system connecting credit markets in India and China, and in so doing, began to draw China into the financial and political orbit of Britain's emerging empire in India.

The second half of the eighteenth century saw an increased flow of products and people from British settlements in India to Canton and Macao. Political changes in India and commercial developments in Canton encouraged new commerce and migration between India and China. As the British East India Company (EIC) gained a stronger political foothold in Bengal and Madras during the 1750s

1. Michael Greenberg, *British Trade and the Opening of China, 1800–42* (Cambridge: Cambridge University Press, 1951; reprint, 1969), 34–35.
2. Anthony Webster, *The Twilight of the East India Company: The Evolution of Anglo-Asian Commerce and Politics, 1790–1860* (Woodbridge: Boydell Press, 2009); Jurgen Osterhammel, 'Britain and China, 1842–1914', in *The Oxford History of the British Empire*, ed. Andrew Porter, Vol. 3 (Oxford: Oxford University Press, 1999), 146–69; John King Fairbank, *Trade and Diplomacy on the China Coast: The Opening of Treaty Ports, 1842–1854* (Cambridge: Harvard University Press, 1964); and Dilip K. Basu, 'Asian Merchants and Western Trade: A Comparative Study of Calcutta and Canton, 1800–1840' (PhD diss., University of California Berkeley, 1975).

and 1760s, many Company servants accumulated great fortunes. British imperial expansion in the subcontinent and territorial conquests in Bengal paved the way for the post-Plassey plunder; many Company servants (the most notorious being Robert Clive) personally enriched themselves through 'gifts' and private contracts with local Indian leaders.[3] With greater military and political power in the region, Company servants also invaded the internal trade of India. They could now access, and in some cases, monopolize, the production and trade of a variety of local goods including: cotton, salt, rice, indigo, saltpetre, and opium.[4] With all of these new commercial opportunities available to them, a growing body of Company bureaucrats and military men in India were becoming rich and looking for ways to invest their funds in Asia.[5]

At the same time that British wealth was accumulating in India, both the EIC and the Hong merchants in China urgently needed silver. The dramatic growth of the tea trade during the eighteenth century left the Company scrambling for the silver currency it needed to make advances to Hong merchants and pay for its annual tea investment. Because the Company sold no export product popular enough among the Chinese to balance the Company's tea expenditures, it was forced to export silver from Britain to China, a practice severely criticized by the British public. Reacting to pressure from home, the Company's Court of Directors optimistically sent very little silver to China in the 1770s and early 1780s.[6] They hoped that wealth being generated in their new Indian territories could be transmitted to England via China.

Since the Company had recently become the official tax collector of the richest province in India (Bengal), the Court of Directors did not think this expectation unreasonable. As a result, they pressured the Indian presidencies, particularly Bengal, to use their supposed surplus revenues to fund the China trade. The strategy might have worked had Bengal revenues ever lived up to the claims of Robert Clive and others, and had the Company managed to maintain peace in India. But military and administrative costs made it impossible for the Indian presidencies to fund the China trade independently. The East India Company's frantic correspondences and heated meetings testify to the constant bureaucratic struggle over funding the China trade.[7] Lord Cornwallis, governor-general of India, was not alone in his sentiments

---

3. P. J. Marshall, *East Indian Fortunes: The British in Bengal in the Eighteenth Century* (Oxford [Eng.]: Clarendon Press, 1976), 234–43.
4. P. J. Marshall, *Bengal: The British Bridgehead, Eastern India 1740–1828* (Cambridge: Cambridge University Press, 1987), 102.
5. P. J. Marshall, *East Indian Fortunes*, Chapter 9.
6. Huw Bowen, *Business of Empire: The East India Company and Imperial Britain, 1756–1833* (Cambridge: Cambridge University Press, 2006), 224–26.
7. H. N. Sinha, ed., *Fort William-India House Correspondence* (Delhi: Published for the National Archives of India by the Manager of Publications, Government of India, 1957), Vol. II, 1759.01.23, pp. 124–25, Vol. III, 1760.12.31, p. 61, 1761.12.23, p. 121, and Vol. V, 1768.11.11, p. 136.

when he complained privately to Henry Dundas, 'I have few greater plagues than the remittances to China, and indeed I must be candid enough to acknowledge that I think I have not managed that business well'.[8]

The Hong merchants of Canton also struggled with a similar problem. The tea trade was a capital-intensive business, and Hong merchants required large amounts of cash to pay advances each year to tea merchants, upcountry growers, suppliers, and manufacturers.[9] Unfortunately, many of the Hong merchants began their businesses severely undercapitalized. As a result, 'all of the large merchant houses in the eighteenth century were intensely focused on procuring foreign capital'.[10]As other chapters in this volume have pointed out, the Canton market was free and open to everyone but that did not diminish the need to have silver to pay for the exports. Domestic credit markets and social institutions in China could not provide sufficient capital for the eighteenth-century tea trade. Most Hong merchants lacked collateral to secure their loans. As a result, pawnshops and other better-capitalized Hong merchants would not directly lend them money.[11]

Abundant supply of capital in one place (India) and demand for it in another (China) created financial opportunity for daring private traders. East India Company servants, Company ship captains, free merchants, and 'interlopers' made their way from India to China to establish themselves as brokers and bankers for wealthy clients in India. As far as the British residents in Asia are concerned, this migration seems to have begun during the 1750s and increased from a trickle to a steady flow during 1760s and 1770s. Over twenty unlicensed private traders were identified by the Company doing business in Canton at different points between 1761 and 1780.[12] The Court of Directors wrote with concern about the 'unlicensed persons going to China' from settlements in the East Indies who stayed year-round

8. National Library of Scotland: Melville Papers, No. 3385, letter dated 1788.11.04, from Cornwallis to Dundas, p. 162.
9. John D. Wong, 'Global Positioning: Houqua and His China Trade Partners in the Nineteenth Century' (PhD diss., Harvard University, 2012), 105; Paul A. Van Dyke, *Merchants of Canton and Macao: Politics and Strategies in Eighteenth-Century Chinese Trade*, Vol. 1 (Hong Kong: Hong Kong University Press, 2011), 19–20.
10. Van Dyke, *Merchants of Canton and Macao*, Vol. 1, 221–22.
11. Paul Van Dyke, John Wong, and Ch'en Kuo-Tung, however, cite cases in which Puankequa during the eighteenth century and Houqua during the nineteenth century were willing to loan money to junior Hong merchants indirectly through the East India Company. Paul A. Van Dyke, *Merchants of Canton and Macao: Success and Failure in Eighteenth-Century Chinese Trade*, Vol. 2 (Hong Kong: Hong Kong University Press, 2016), 92; Wong, 'Global Positioning,' 104, and 107–9; and Ch'en Kuo-Tung, *The Insolvency of the Chinese Hong Merchants, 1760–1843* (Nankang, Taipei: Institute of Economics, Academia Sinica, 1990), 169–70. See also British Library (BL): India Officer Records (IOR) G/12/202, 1816.03.11, pp. 23–25 and G/12/206, 1817.03.06, p. 19.
12. H. B. Morse, *Chronicles of the East India Company Trading to China, 1635–1834*, 5 vols. (Oxford: The Clarendon Press, 1926–29), Vols. 2 and 5, passim.

in Canton and Macao.[13] To discourage this practice, they gave the following order to the supercargos at Canton:

> As the residing of any persons the year round in China on their own private affairs is a practice we will by no means admit of, you are therefore positively ordered to cause any persons so residing (if any such there be) or you apprehend have any intentions to do so to leave Canton and proceed by the first proper conveyances to the parts of India from whence they came and you are to make this our order publicly known, that no person or persons may have any pretense for staying at Canton longer than the usual season for the departure of shipping for any of our presidencies or settlements or elsewhere in India.[14]

The first warning was probably issued during the early 1760s. The problem for the Company was that private traders were guaranteed freedom to trade in Canton by the Qing government, which ran contrary to EIC interests. The Company did what it could to protect its monopoly by placing limitations on private British operating in China but with little effect.

Several of the people named in Table 1.1 came to China from India. For example, the Court of Directors believed that George Smith of Canton arrived in Bengal via Basra and then shortly thereafter moved to China.[15] Charles Crommelin also came to China via India. He was actually born in Bombay in 1717 and served as governor there from 1760 to 1769. He later moved to Canton, where he worked as a commission merchant for several years.[16] John Crichton arrived in India as a Company writer in 1755 at the age of 16.[17] He first voyaged to China in 1762 but shortly thereafter returned to India as a passenger on a Portuguese ship from Macao. After serving as supercargo of several country ships, he moved to Canton in 1768 with 'the resolution to reside'.[18]

These and other private brokers managed their clients' wealth in Canton. One wonders about the quantity and quality of information British investors in India received from their agents in China. Did commission merchants, such as George Smith of Canton, communicate regularly and honestly with their clients in India? Unfortunately, the letter books of the Canton commission merchants have not survived. We do know that these Canton brokers received cargos of goods shipped and consigned to them by Company servants in India. These shipments included

13. BL: IOR H/411, pp. 55–79. For the case and opinions of J. Wallace (solicitor-general) and George Rous on the Company's seizing of George Smith at Canton and sending him home, see entries dated 1780.01.08 and 1780.01.08, respectively.
14. Ibid.
15. Ibid.
16. Richard Pugh, 'Charles Crommelin (1717–1788) A Governor of Bombay', http://www.crommelin.org/history/Biographies/1763CharlesRussel/02-CharlesGovOfBombay.htm (accessed 5 January 2017); BL: IOR H/219, Extract of the general letter from Bengal dated 1783.10.23 and H/24, p. 116.
17. BL: IOR J/1/2, p. 358.
18. BL: IOR G/12/68, 1779.07.08, letter from John Crichton to the Hoppo, p. 6.

Table 1.1 Private Traders Who Received Notice from EIC to Quit China

Date of Warning	'Interloping' Private Traders
1761	Captain Robert Jackson, George Smith, John Spencer
1763	George Smith
1769	Capt. Robert Jackson of Macao
1771	John Crichton, Dyce, William Dallas, William Dalrymple, George Smith, Walter Cowdie, John Corsar
1773	Dr. John Laird, John Crichton, George Smith. John Corsar (sailed in Dec. 1772), William Dalrymple, Abraham Leslie
1774	Charles Crommelin, William Dalrymple, George Smith, William Hamson
1775/6	Charles Crommelin, George Smith, Thomas Dickenson
1778	George Smith, Abraham Leslie, Richard Lockyer, Thomas Dickinson, Thomas Hutton, James Frudd

Source: H. B. Morse, *Chronicles of the East India Company*, Vols. 2 and 5.

products from India and Southeast Asia such as tin, cotton, redwood, saltpetre, opium, rattans, pepper, rice, sago, arrack, catch, sandalwood, nutmeg, dragons blood (a dye), cotton, ivory, sharks' fins, putchuck, fish maws, seed pearl, coral, stick lack, yellow beads, black wood, cloves, snuff, camphor, handkerchiefs, long ells, palampores, bêche-de-mer, moco stones, birds' nests, looking glasses, clocks, lead, cuttings, window glass, raisins, gold thread, amber, stone blue, watches, cloves, cochineal, tortoise shell, and numerous other items.[19] The brokers then deposited the proceeds of their sales into the Company's treasury in Canton for bills of exchange to be remitted to them in London—usually within a year's time. Table 1.2 shows several of the large deposits made into the Canton treasury by private traders in Canton on behalf of individuals and houses of agency in India. Commission merchants 'channeled a great deal of private money into the [China] trade' and helped their clients remit their Indian wealth to Britain.[20]

By helping their clients move their money around the globe, investors in India and their agents in China financed the East India Company's tea trade. In 1787, George Smith of Canton boldly claimed that were it not for businessmen such as he, 'the yearly investment of the India Company could not have been supplied'.[21] According to Captain Rogers, the Company 'as I have been credibly informed ever looked to those private persons for their supplies of cash when their treasury was open . . . Their commanders of ships could not produce a sum equal to the Company's investment . . . As such I cannot suppose the East India Company

19. BL: IOR G/12/67, 1779.11.30.
20. Paul A. Van Dyke, *The Canton Trade: Life and Enterprise on the China Coast, 1700–1845* (Hong Kong: Hong Kong University Press, 2005; reprint, 2007), 157.
21. BL: IOR G/12/18, 1787.07.12, author George Smith, 'Narrative of the proceedings for the Recovery of Debts owing by the Chinese Merchants to British subjects', pp. 113–53 and 'General Statement of Debts Owing by Chinese Merchants to British Subjects', pp. 154–56.

Table 1.2 Brokerage Services Provided by Smith, Crichton, and Leslie

Year	Paid into Canton Treasury by Whom	To Whom Payable in England	Amount Paid
1772	George Smith and John Crichton	John Secker Esq., John Wilson, Robert Palk Esq., Gen. Richard Smith and Charles Boddam	£6,000 (approx.)
1777	George Smith	Mr. Alex Crawford of Richmond Surrey on account of Mr. Robert Crawford of Dacca	£4,225
1777	George Smith	Messieurs Rumbold, Charlton, and Raikes London on account of Messieurs David Killikan, John Robinson, Charles Crofts, Charles Grant and John Fergusson of Calcutta 'merchants and members of the commercial society there'	£3,000
1777	George Smith	John Hunter Esq.	£893 3s. 9d.
1777	George Smith and Abraham Leslie	Reverend John Thomas	£4,455 14s. 8d.

Sources: BL: IOR/R/10/9, November and December 1772, G/12/61, February 1777, G/12/62, November 1777.

have suffered by their [private traders] residences'.[22] It is not an exaggeration to suggest that no private investments meant a greatly reduced tea trade. Between 1769 and 1792, private traders deposited 27,174,113 taels into the Company's Canton treasury.[23] The prime cost of exporting Chinese tea to Britain for the same period was 43,761,711 taels.[24] The financial activities of private traders substantially supported the Company's China trade, a fact not missed by those with a vested interest in that commerce. The first American consul to Canton noted in his journal that the proceeds of private trade, much of which were deposited in the Canton treasury, had 'for a number of years rendered it unnecessary for the Company to export from Europe any specie for carrying on their commerce with the Chinese'.[25] This was made possible because Canton was a free port open to everyone including these individual commission merchants from India.

Historians have paid much attention to the problem of remittance; the EIC's monopoly on trade between Britain and Asia severely limited the ways its employees could remit their wealth home.[26] Company bills of exchange thus became the

22. BL: IOR G/12/91, Vol. 2, Captain Rogers, 'Some remarks on the heavy debt now owing by the Chinese to European subjects', 5.
23. Earl Pritchard, *The Crucial Years of Early Anglo-Chinese Relations*, 1750–1800 (New York: Octagon Books, 1970), Appendix X, 400.
24. Pritchard, *The Crucial Years*, Appendix V, 395.
25. Josiah Quincy, ed., *The Journals of Major Samuel Shaw*, 169.
26. P. J. Marshall, *East Indian Fortunes*, 220; and Amales Tripathi, *Trade and Finance in the Bengal Presidency*, 1793–1833 (Calcutta: Orient Longmans, 1956), Chapter 1.

most reliable mode of transmitting wealth from Asia to Britain, and the Company attracted money to its Canton treasury at times by offering attractive exchange rates. But bills could become a scarce commodity because the Company limited the amount of money it would receive in its Canton treasury and, during some trading seasons, refused to issue bills at all. In 1774, after receiving instructions from the Court of Directors that no bills of exchange could be drawn on the Company in London, the supercargos closed the Company's Canton treasury. Those who had expected to remit their money to London via this option were disappointed and had to find other means to move or store their wealth until the treasury opened again.[27]

George Vansittart and Ewan Law (both of whom later became Members of Parliament) were affected by this financial restriction. While in India in 1774, they had 'sent a ship from Calcutta with a cargo for China and gave orders to Mr. Shaw, the Captain and Supercargo, that after reserving a small part of the produce for a returning cargo he should pay the rest into the Company's treasury'.[28] When Mr. Shaw discovered the Canton treasury was shut, he 'lent the produce of our cargo to Mr. George Smith the 1st of October 1774 on his bond at five percent with an engagement that it should be paid into the Company's treasury in 1776 or 1777, if they would then receive it for drafts upon England'. Vansittart and Law never saw the $106,000 in profits from their India cargo because George Smith loaned it to the Chinese merchants.[29] Smith confirmed 'that the Company's cash being shut', he had no other means of employing the money sent, 'but in the hands of the Chinese merchants until such time as it should please their honors again to open the channel of remittance'.[30]

Vansittart and Law may have been genuine when they claimed they only wished to remit their Indian wealth home, but Vansittart was an unusually risk-averse investor and did not typify the attitude of most Company servants.[31] As important as the remittance problem was, many Company servants were not interested only in remitting their money to Britain as quickly as possible; they also sought high rates of return on lucrative investment opportunities in Asia. Many employed their money in marine insurance, country trade, Company bonds, and private loans to Indian and Chinese borrowers. Company servants diversified their portfolios and limited their risk by choosing a variety of moderate to high-risk investments.

Among a variety of investment options, private loans to Chinese merchants emerged as an attractive opportunity. These loans, it seemed, would yield high

27. BL: IOR G/12/60, letter from George Stratton to the Council of Fort St. George, dated 1777.07.23.
28. BL: IOR E/1/73, p. 403, letter from George Vansittart and Ewan Law to the Court of Directors, dated 1783.11.01.
29. Ibid.
30. BL: IOR G/12/18, pp. 91–112.
31. BL: IOR Mss EUR F331/19, pp. 37–43, letter from George Vansittart to Robert Palk, dated 1772.08.14.

returns with only moderate risk. Interest rates in India were often lower than in Canton, creating lucrative opportunities for arbitrage. According to a British free merchant in India, some lenders had made a business out of borrowing money at low interest rates from the Company's settlements and lending it to Chinese merchants at higher rates.[32] Company supercargos confirmed that brokers in Canton profited from the difference in the interest rates between India and China.[33] A Company ship captain claimed that 'the lenders in China have never received any more than the difference between the Indian and Chinese interest, which in general may have been 6 percent'.[34] Holden Furber suggests that interest rates in India generally ranged between 9 to 12 per cent annually.[35] One private trader claimed he never 'knew an Englishmen to receive more than 15 to 24 percent per annum'.[36] Eighteen to 20 per cent was closer to the norm. With such high interest rates in Canton, a savvy trader could make a fortune through arbitrage. Borrowing money in India and lending it in China became lucrative and routine, enough so that some British traders made it their livelihood.

The promise of high rates of return lured many Company servants to loan money in Canton. By the late 1770s, it was reported that most of the European inhabitants in India of long standing had loaned money to Chinese merchants.[37] In 1780, the EIC supercargos in Canton counted 249 different bonds amounting to $4,296,650 in Chinese debt owed to British investors.[38] During the late 1780s, more than fifty-five people claimed Chinese merchants owed them money. Of these fifty-five, at least twenty-nine were Company servants, surgeons and free merchants stationed in India and St. Helena. Fourteen of them worked as ship captains, marine servants and surgeons for the EIC.[39]

The eighteenth-century financial connections between India and China took on a political dimension when a panic in 1774–1775 led to the financial collapse of several Hong merchant houses. After Seunqua's business failed in 1774, British investors called in their loans from the rest of the Chinese merchants, and drove

32. BL: IOR H/434, letter from Smith to Dundas, dated 1786.04.15.
33. BL: IOR G/12/20, 1781.01.15, letter from David Lance and William Fitzhugh to Henry Lane. Unfortunately, the 1,290 single pages in this file have no consecutive page numbers. This letter concerning the Chinese debts is about 586 single pages into the file.
34. BL: IOR G/12/91, undated letter from Captain Rogers starting with the words 'Some remarks on the heavy Debt now owing by the Chinese to European subjects', pp. 301–14.
35. Holden Furber, *Rival Empires of Trade in the Orient 1600–1800* (Minneapolis: University of Minnesota Press, 1976), 291.
36. BL: IOR H/434, letter dated 1786.04.15, from Smith to Dundas.
37. BL: Add MS 29210, p. 343, Warren Hastings Papers, 'Debt due from Chinese merchants to Englishmen'.
38. BL: IOR G/12/68, 1780.03.18, pp. 108–9.
39. BL: IOR G/12/90, document entitled 'This Covenant and Agreement', dated 1788.02.19, pp. 62–65.

several of them out of business.[40] An anonymous correspondent of Warren Hastings, governor-general of Bengal, reported that in 1775, 'large demands were made upon them [the Chinese merchants] on behalf of gentlemen in England and going thither who wanted their money home and sent orders for its being paid into the treasury at Canton for Bills on the Court of Directors'.[41]

These sudden large demands on the Chinese merchants by their British creditors undoubtedly undermined the viability of the Chinese businesses. Yet there were longer-term structural reasons for the collapse. In fact, the financial system forged by British private traders in India and China was built upon unstable foundations. Loans at such high rates of interest, generally between 18 and 20 per cent, compromised the finances of Chinese borrowers and increased the likelihood of default. John Crichton clearly understood this problem when he proposed to the Hoppo (*hubu* 戶部, superintendent of customs in Canton) that the maximum legal interest rate in China should be capped at 12 per cent.[42]

When the brokers failed to recover their money from several insolvent Chinese merchants, and Canton officials and the Company's supercargos refused to intervene, help for private traders came quickly from India. John Crichton and several other investors in Madras met with Navy Rear-Admiral Edward Vernon who recently had arrived in India to fight the French. They hoped he would be willing to represent to the governor and Hoppo in Canton the hardships under which they laboured. As a reward, the Madras creditors 'engaged to give Sir Edward a tenth part of the amount recovered'.[43] Without waiting for permission from the Madras Company council or consulting the Company's Canton supercargos, Vernon had 'come to the resolution of sending his Majesty's frigate *Sea Horse*' to China, and ordered the Commander of

40. Frederic D. Grant Jr., *The Chinese Cornerstone of Modern Banking: The Canton Guaranty System and the Origins of Bank Deposit Insurance 1780–1933* (Leiden: Brill Nijhoff, 2014), 112. References to 'Seunqua' in the EIC records are confusing, because the name is sometimes applied to three different brothers of the Yifeng Hang 義豐行, including Cai Anqua, Cai Taiqua and Cai Tsjonqua. Cai Anqua died insolvent in late 1774 or early 1775; then Cai Taiqua and Tsjonqua took over the business and were ordered to settle the arrears that were left behind; Taiqua died in autumn 1775, and then Tsjonqua took over the business. He made some headway in repaying the debts, and continued to trade until he finally failed in 1784. The failure, however, was not triggered by the debt crisis of the early 1770s, but rather the Fourth Anglo-Dutch War which resulted in a great reduction in the VOC trade in the early 1780s which Tsjonqua was much dependent on. Thus, even though it appears in the EIC records that Seunqua's Yifeng Hang failed in 1774, it kept operating for another ten years before it was actually declared bankrupt. The collapse of the firm is much more complicated than what appears in the British records. For the story of the Yifeng Hang and the problems in nomenclature, see Van Dyke, *Merchants of Canton and Macao*, Vol. 1, Chapter 7 and Appendix 7H.
41. BL: Add MS 29210, Warren Hastings Papers, 'Debt due from Chinese merchants to Englishmen', p. 343.
42. BL: IOR G/12/68, letter dated 1779.07.08, from John Crichton to the Hoppo, p. 7.
43. Josiah Quincy, ed., *Journals of Major Samuel Shaw*, 307.

Table 1.3 British Creditors of Chinese Hong Merchants Claiming Compensation in 1787

Civil and Military Servants	Surgeons	Ministers	Governors and Lieutenant-Governors	Company Wives	Free Traders	Company Ship Captains and Marine Servants	Unidentified
M. Purling (SH)	Stephen Briggs (SH)	John Thomas (M)	Rawson Hart Boddam (BB)	Frances Montresor	George Smith (C)	R. Parks	John Burges
Henry Bazett (SH)	Gilbert Pasley (M)		D. Corneille (SH)	Mrs. William Larkins (BG)	John Hunter (FM)	Jo. Clements	J. Brasier
H. Brooke (M)	Thomas Cairns (Ship)		Matthew Bazett (SH)	Mary Church (BB)	George Smith (M)	Patrick Maitland	Robert Stewart
Ch. Desvoeux (M)	Thomas Sword (Ship)				John Blake	William Money	Tho. Thomas
G. Dawson (M)	T. Hutton (C)					James Farquharson	Andrew Reid
J. Hollond (M)	C. Gordon (C)					William Elphinston(e)	
E. Hollond (M)						James Dundas	
W. Hollond (BG)						Peter Pigou	
E. Monckton (M)						G. Stainforth Jr.	
G. Paterson (BG)						John Rogers	
G. Stratton (M)						W. Fraser	
Charles Smith (M)						William Browne	
John Sulivan (M)							
G. Vansittart (BG)							

(continued on p. 17)

Table 1.3 (continued)

Civil and Military Servants	Surgeons	Ministers	Governors and Lieutenant-Governors	Company Wives	Free Traders	Company Ship Captains and Marine Servants	Unidentified
Ewan Law (BG)							
R. Barclay (M)†							
Francis Wood (C)							
John Griffith (BB) ‡							
M. Bazett (SH)							
Charles E. Pigou (C)							
William H. Pigou (C)							

Sources: Covenant and Agreement of the Creditors, BL IOR/G/12/90, pp. 53–61; J. D. Gurney, 'The Debts of the Nawab of Arcot', Appendix 1.
Key: SH = Saint Helena, BB = Bombay, M = Madras, C = Canton, BG = Bengal
† Robert Barclay, perhaps a different one, may have served as a surgeon in St. Helena in 1770.
‡ There were a number of John Griffiths working in the East Indies at the time, so this is an educated guess.

his Majesty's frigate, Captain Alexander Panton, to deliver personally to the officials in Canton the representations of the British creditors.[44] He explained in his letter to the governor of Guangdong Province that he could not 'consistently with my duty to my sovereign and to my country see his subjects oppressed and distressed'.[45]

This was not the last time Captain Panton was dispatched to Canton. Almost a year after he had made his first representation to the Canton officials, the 'hotheads in India were taking the bit in their teeth' and resolved to solicit the help of yet another Navy Admiral, this time Sir Edward Hughes.[46] They had been encouraged by the impression of some gentlemen residing in Canton, 'that the Mandareens & Merchants were much afraid, on hearing the Business with which Captain Panton was charged; which gave sufficient proof, that if proper spirited measures should be pursued the recovery of the China Debts, may be easily accomplished'.[47] The Madras creditors believed that a 'more than ordinary interposition' was again necessary to 'forward the success of the national object'.[48] Hughes reasoned it could not hurt to dispatch Panton once more. While he spoke of moderation, this representative of the king of Great Britain made sure in his letter to the Canton viceroy to flex some British muscle, explaining to the Chinese officials that he had a strong squadron of the king's warships 'to protect His own dominions and subjects'.[49]

How far were the British creditors willing to go to recover their money? The Company's council of supercargos 'were certain' that if the viceroy persisted in refusing Captain Panton a second audience he 'would bring up his ship (and with his seamen) demand an audience at the city gate the consequence of which, might be very fatal both to them, and to the Companies affairs'.[50] British private traders hoped to send a message to the Chinese government that 'England is chiefly, if not altogether supported by its trade, which is defended by the strongest naval force in the whole world'.[51] In fact, George Smith hinted that a more aggressive strategy might have been in the works. In their thank-you letter to Admiral Hughes for his intervention, George Smith, John Crichton, and Thomas Hutton wrote that they were certain 'if a proper force could be spared and sent as he might think necessary from the representation of Capt. Panton it would have the desired effect'.[52]

44. BL: IOR G/12/68, letter dated 1779.07.20, from Sir Edward Vernon to the Council at Fort St. George, pp. 4–5.
45. BL: IOR G/12/68, letter dated 1779.08.01, from Sir Edward Vernon to the Fouyuern, p. 59.
46. Pritchard, *The Crucial Years*, 205.
47. BL: IOR G/12/68, letter dated 1780.06.01, from creditors of Chinese merchants to the president and council of Fort St. George, p. 175.
48. BL: IOR G/12/68, letter dated 1780.06.01, from creditors of Chinese merchants to the president and council of Fort St. George, pp. 176–77.
49. BL: H/168, letter dated 1780.06.14, from Edward Hughes to the 'Fu-Yuen Viceroy of the province of Canton', p. 555. See also BL: IOR G/12/68, letter dated 1780.06.13, from Edward Hughes to the President and Council of Fort St. George, pp. 181–82.
50. BL: IOR G/12/68, 1780.09.21, Consultation, p. 186.
51. BL: IOR G/12/68, letter dated 1779.07.08, from John Crichton to the Hoppo, p. 16.
52. BL: IOR G/12/18, 1787.07.12, George Smith, 'Narrative of the proceedings . . .', pp. 91–112.

The Court of Directors in London read about the events in Madras and Canton with great alarm. The British Navy was being hired out by private traders in India and China to provoke the Chinese government. They worried how this event might be perceived by the Chinese:

> However careful the Captain of the Man of War sent to China at different times upon this business may have been not to give offence to the Chinese government, by any intimation of hostility, the appearance of sending a Man of War to a Chinese port upon such an occasion, is too plain an intimation of threat to admit of a double construction, and the consequences flowing from it, are apparent.[53]

Luckily for the East India Company, Governor Li Zhiying chose to de-escalate the crisis. He reported to the Qianlong emperor that Captain Panton had come to Canton as a country trader to deliver silver to the East India Company—not as a British Navy admiral in a warship to threaten the Chinese government.[54] This was a bit of a stretch of the truth, but not entirely without merit. The last time that the *Sea Horse* had arrived (September 1776) it did indeed bring a shipment of ninety-seven chests of silver coin for the Company and was thereby exempted from all the regular ports fees and duties.[55] In 1779, however, the *Sea Horse* brought no money for the Company and its mission was to demand the repayment of British debts.

The Court of Directors found Abraham Leslie's behaviour even more 'outrageous', 'alarming', and 'mischievous'.[56] At the same time that this early experiment with gunboat diplomacy was underway, Abraham Leslie had also been making use of military resources from India to pry his money from Chinese hands. Leslie began his career in Madras as a Company surgeon. In 1773, his private business concerns brought him to China where he acted as a broker for John Hunter, a former private trader who became a Director of the East India Company in 1781 and served as a Member of Parliament for Leominster between 1784 and 1797. Leslie was desperate to recover the money of his powerful client.[57] Rather than contracting with the British Navy, he decided to employ his own private band of Indian lascars to occupy the warehouses of several of his Chinese debtors. The council of supercargos recorded that 'Mr. Leslie today took possession of Yngshaw Hong, and put some of

53. BL: IOR G/12/19, 1781, Extract of instructions to be sent to Canton for regulating the activities of country ships, pp. 76–89. Here, the Court of Directors is referring to the Flint Affair in which a Company servant sailed to Tianjin to present a petition to the emperor concerning trade difficulties in Canton and the desire to trade at other ports. Flint was imprisoned for three years, and the Chinese person who translated his petition into Chinese was executed.
54. Taiwan, Taipei: National Palace Museum, 軍機及宮中當, 26992. Memorial of Li Zhiying and Tu Ming'e to the Qianlong emperor, dated 45/05/12 (15 May 1780).
55. BL: IOR G/12/59, 1776.11.09, pp. 166–70, R/10/8, 1776.10.25, p. 69.
56. BL: IOR G/12/19, 1782, 'Extract of the instructions proposed to be sent to the Company's supracargoes in China', paragraph no. 7, p. 145.
57. R. G. Thorne, ed., *The House of Commons, 1790–1820* (London: Published for the History of Parliament Trust by Secker and Warburg, 1986), 656; and BL: IOR G/12/72, letter dated 1781.04.21, from Leslie to the Canton Council, pp. 74–76.

his Black people into it'.[58] It was reported that Leslie had 'broken open the doors' and 'sets at the Door of the Hong, with a guard of two or three Lascars with Pistols and Cutlasses to defend what he calls, his right to the Premises'.[59] The Hoppo ordered Leslie to retire 'from that place, & return to his factory, which he positively refused to do'; instead, he kept the Chinese hongs by force of arms.[60] Not only had Leslie taken over properties that had been 'seized on by Government for the Emperor's duties', but he also kept a guard of six or seven lascars at each of these properties.[61]

Conclusion

During the eighteenth century, China was by no means part of the emerging British empire, formal or informal, but it was on the borderlands of that empire. Within a rapidly changing commercial and political context, British private traders, investors in India and their agents in China, created new connections between the subcontinent and the southeast coast of China. According to Holden Furber, the second half of the eighteenth century saw a commercial revolution in the Indian Ocean in which trade was reoriented eastward towards China. British private traders reigned supreme in this new commercial system.[62] But this revolution was not merely commercial. Rather, a new predominantly British financial system linking India and China was forged, which ran parallel to other existing networks of Indian-based commission merchants such as those of the Portuguese, Muslims, Armenians, and later, Parsees. However, with these new financial connections came political entanglements. Investors in India and their British agents in China used the coercive power of the British state (without its permission or knowledge) and their own private Indian militia to enforce their contracts with Chinese merchants. Before the rise of aggressive agency houses such as Jardine, Matheson & Co., and the expansion of the nineteenth-century opium trade, eighteenth-century British private traders in search of personal gain drew China into the financial and political orbit of Britain's burgeoning Asian empire.

58. BL: IOR G/12/68, 1780.09.22, Consultation, p. 195.
59. BL: IOR G/12/68, 1780.09.24, Consultation, p. 195.
60. BL: IOR G/12/66, 1779.10.09, Consultation, p. 17.
61. BL: IOR G/12/19, extract letter dated 1780.12.16, from the Select Committee to the EIC: debt negotiations and general affairs, pp. 126–27.
62. Holden Furber, *John Company at Work: A Study of European Expansion in India in the Late Eighteenth Century* (Cambridge: Harvard University Press, 1948), 161–62.

2

Ambiguous Faces of the Canton Trade

Moors, Greeks, Armenians, Parsees, Jews, and Southeast Asians

Paul A. Van Dyke

> Canton, 1815: Parsees – or Persian merchants, Hindoos, Armenians, Malays, Moormen or turks, from Arabia, and a few Jews – all these are here from various part of India by means of the large country ships . . . the Parsees, who are a handsome race, gather, & stand by themselves in circles, or walk in couples. Other asiatics from necessity mingle with them being of cap – and turbaned races – & resort to the Parsee factory while here from the ships on business. The Hindoos & Lascars squat about every where. chattering like monkeys. These with Malay & Manila men are under guardianship of the Comp[an]y, and Country Ships. Serangs – or chiefs – and their officers.[1]

An examination of the China trade done by the British Parliament in the early 1830s concluded that 'Greater facilities are given to trade in the port of Canton than in almost any port in the world'.[2] Yet, when we read accounts of the China trade in history books, rarely do we find mention of such ethnic diversity and economic fluency as these statements suggest.[3] This multicultural environment was made possible by Qing policy which guaranteed that the trade be opened to everyone, with no restrictions on race, religion, or nationality. The only exceptions were the Russians and Japanese who had treaties with China to trade in other Chinese ports, and were therefore not allowed at Canton.

Europeans and Americans have captured the attention of most historians, resulting in the private Asian traders, as well as Armenians, Turks, and Jews, being marginalized and left out of the conversation. These omissions are partially the result of historians being more interested in the trade of the European East India companies and Americans, but it is also the result of few records surviving from

1. Phillips Library, Peabody Essex Museum (PEM): Bryant P. Tilden Journal 1815–1816, typescript, pp. 95–96.
2. *Reports from Committees*. 18 vols. *East India Company's Affairs*. Session 6 December 1831–16 August 1832, Vol. X, Part II, 'China Trade', pp. 457–64. This quotation is on p. 462.
3. Of course, I am only talking about documented histories, and not novels. There are historical novels that include much diversity in their discussions, but in order to advance the history, the stories must be documented. Very little research has been done on these individuals for reasons discussed in the preface.

those individuals. For many of them, the only information we have comes from other sources.

In recent years, our knowledge of private traders involved in the China trade has made giant steps forward. We now have brief introductory histories of the Armenians, Muslims, and Parsees in Canton and Macao in the eighteenth and nineteenth century;[4] we have quite a few biographical studies of American China traders;[5] and we have a number of new studies on European merchants involved in the trade.[6] While there is much more research that needs to be done in all of these

4. The following publications were the result of a seminar held at the University of Hong Kong in October 2003 entitled 'Sino-Indian Interactions in the 18th and 19th Centuries: Parsees, Armenians, and Muslims in Macau, Guangzhou, and Hong Kong Seminar'. Carl T. Smith, 'An Eighteenth-Century Macao Armenian Merchant Prince', *Review of Culture*, International Edition No. 6 (April 2003): 120–29; Carl T. Smith and Paul A. Van Dyke, 'Armenian Footprints in Macau', *Review of Culture*, International Edition No. 8 (October 2003): 20–39; Carl T. Smith and Paul A. Van Dyke, 'Four Armenian Families', *Review of Culture*, International Edition No. 8 (October 2003): 40–50; Carl T. Smith and Paul A. Van Dyke, 'Muslims in the Pearl River Delta, 1700 to 1930', *Review of Culture*, International Edition No. 10 (April 2004): 6–15; Guo Deyan, 'The Study of Parsee Merchants in Canton, Hong Kong and Macao', *Review of Culture*, International Edition No. 8 (October 2003): 51–69; Shalini Saksena, 'Parsi Contributions to the Growth of Bombay and Hong Kong'. *Review of Culture*, International Edition No. 10 (April 2004), 26–35; Carl T. Smith, 'Parsee Merchants in the Pearl River Delta', *Review of Culture*, International Edition No. 10 (April 2004): 36–49; and Madhavi Thampi, 'Parsis in the China Trade', *Review of Culture*, International Edition No. 10 (April 2004): 16–25.
5. I list here just a few of the many studies that have short histories of, and biographical data about, American China traders. Jonathan Goldstein, *Philadelphia and the China Trade 1682–1846: Commercial, Cultural, and Attitudinal Effects* (University Park, PA: Pennsylvania State University Press, 1978); Jonathan Goldstein, *Stephen Girard's Trade with China 1787–1824* (Portland, ME: MerwinAsia, 2011); Jacques M. Downs, *The Golden Ghetto: The American Commercial Community at Canton and the Shaping of American China Policy, 1784–1844* (Bethlehem: Lehigh University Press, 1997; reprint, Hong Kong: Hong Kong University Press, 2014); John Rogers Haddad, *America's First Adventure in China: Trade, Treaties, Opium, and Salvation* (Philadelphia: Temple University Press, 2013).
6. I just list here a few of the new studies about private European merchants involved in the China trade. There are many other studies as well. Richard J. Grace, *Opium and Empire: The Lives and Careers of William Jardine and James Matheson* (Montreal: McGill Queens University Press, 2014); Jessica Hanser, 'Mr. Smith Goes to China: British Private Traders and the Interlinking of the British Empire with China, 1757–1792' (PhD diss., Dept. of History, Yale University, May 2012); Susan E. Schopp, 'The French in the Pearl River Delta: A Topical Case Study of Sino-European Exchanges in the Canton Trade, 1698–1840' (PhD diss., Dept. of History, University of Macau, 2015); and Lisa Hellman, 'Everyday life in Canton: the case of the Swedish East India Company 1730–1830' (PhD diss., Dept. of History, Stockholm University, 2015). For a very detailed study of some of these private Englishmen involved in the China trade, see Anne Bulley, *Free Mariner: John Adolphus Pope in the East Indies 1786–1821* (London: British Association for Cemeteries in South Asia [BACSA], 1992); Anne Bulley, *The Bombay Country Ships 1790–1833* (Richmond, Surrey: Curzon Press, 2000); and Patrick Kin Wai Mok, 'The British Intra-Asian Trade with China, 1800–1842' (PhD diss., Dept. of History, University of Hong Kong, 2004).

groups, there is at least some representation of these men in the historical literature. However, there are still many shadowy figures who were involved in the trade—most of them from India—for which we have little knowledge.

In this study, I bring together bits and pieces of data about these ambiguous traders. The men often show up identified by generic terms such as Moors (usually referring to Muslims), Armenians, Greeks, Persians (often referring to Parsees), and Jews, with no further explanations about them. Most of the entries provide no names, and sometimes the same people are referred to as being Moors, Armenians, and/or Jews at the same time, which blurs their true identities. Of course, they were all real people with real names, real homes, and real families. Despite their obscured identities, they were important players in Canton's rise to prominence in the late eighteenth century.

The first thing we need to make clear is that just because a ship arrived in China with an English or French captain and was flying a flag of those nations, it does not mean that those ships were commissioned by those persons or nationalities. The following extract explains this more clearly.

> 1831–1832: The country trade between India and China is almost entirely in the hands of the British mercantile houses at Calcutta and Bombay; there is scarcely any trade with Madras. The country trade is principally in the hands of British merchants, but the Parsees of Bombay are also personally engaged in it, and the capital of the Hindoo merchants of Calcutta is employed therein. The country trade of India competes largely with the Chinese in the trade from the British possessions in India, and the Malay Islands, to China.[7]

Many of the private ships that arrived at Canton's downriver anchorage of Whampoa were actually commissioned by Armenians, Muslims, Parsees, or other traders based in India. Occasionally, a ship might also show up in China under commission of a ruler in Southeast Asia. In September 1790, for example, the *Marquis de la Fayette* arrived at Whampoa with a French crew, flying a Moorish flag, but consigned to the King of Achin.[8] The vessel originated in the French colony of Mauritius but it was not carrying a French cargo.

There are many other examples. The *Success Galley* arrived at Whampoa in September 1780, with a British flag and British commander. However, it belonged to the Nabob (Nawab) of Arcot.[9] In July 1791, the ship *Wallajah* arrived at Whampoa from India via Manila. The ship was commanded by the English captain Eardley Wilmot Mitchell and was equipped with a mostly English crew. The English officers

7. *Affairs of the East India Company. Reports from Committees: 1831–2*, vol. 6 (London: The House of Commons, 1832), 462.
8. Rigsarkivet (National Archives), Copenhagen (RAC): Ask 1206, 1790.09.12, p. 36v; British Library (BL): India Office Records (IOR) L/MAR/B/437F and L/MAR/B/420D.
9. BL: IOR G/12/70, pp. 242–43, L/MAR/B/489A.

in Canton recorded the *Wallajah* to be an English country ship, but it arrived flying the 'the colors of the Nabob of Arcot'.[10]

On 1 October 1789, the ship *Kes Russool Muchoy* (also spelled *Fiey Ressool Mucky*) arrived at Whampoa. The captain was George M. Nelson of Bombay and the vessel displayed English colours. The owner of the ship and sponsor of the voyage was the Nabob of Surat. The Dutch recorded the name of the ship as 'Nabobs Ship'. The British, French, and Americans all mentioned that this ship was a private British vessel from India, but it was not actually British.[11]

There was a tendency in the eighteenth century—as there is among historians today—to identify ships according to the flags they displayed. It makes sense that historians would repeat what contemporaries wrote in their records, but the outcome is a much-distorted view of history. As is shown from examples above and below, the sponsors of many of these private vessels in China were often Asians and not Europeans. Unfortunately, most of the historical records only contain information about the captains and the flags of the vessels, with little or no mention of the owners or sponsors.

Because of these omissions and because of the practice of defining ships according to their flags, the British and Americans have appeared as the dominant private traders at Canton in the late eighteenth and early nineteenth centuries. This has been the case from the beginning. In the English East India Company's (EIC) Diaries and Consultations from the eighteenth and early nineteenth centuries, for example, all of the trade of the private ships was compiled and grouped according to the flags of those vessels and/or whether they were country ships (remaining in Asia) or ships bound for Europe. The Dutch East India Company (VOC) grouped the private ships in the same way.

It was problematic and time consuming to collect all of the details about the sponsors of every private ship at Whampoa. Not only would some of those persons be reluctant to provide that information, but it also took a lot of time to collect. By the late 1780s, there were usually twenty to forty or more private ships at Whampoa each year.[12] Getting the names of the vessels and captains was difficult enough, not to mention collecting information about owners and sponsors. There was actually

10. BL: IOR G/12/101, 1791.07.08, p. 9, G/12/102 List of Ships for 1791, pp. 69–71; and Universiteits Bibliotheek (University Library), Ghent (GHL): Ms 1985, VOC *dagregister*, 1791.07.08, p. 45.

11. National Archives, The Hague (NAH): Canton 251 pp. 187–90, Hoge Regering van Batavia (HRB) 80 and 82 Ship List for 1789; La Courneuve, Affaires Étrangères Archives Diplomatiques (AEAD): 8MD Asie 19 p. 219r Ship List for 1789; BL: IOR G/12/96, 1789.10.01, p. 44, G/12/97, pp. 31–33, L/MAR/B/450G, L/MAR/B/452J; and Josiah Quincy, ed., *The Journals of Major Samuel Shaw, the First American Consul at Canton: With a Life of the Author* (Boston: Wm. Crosby and H. P. Nichols, 1847; reprint, Documentary Publications, 1970), 297.

12. Dermigny, *La Chine et l'Occident: Le Commerce à Canton au XVIII Siècle 1719–1833*, 3 vols. and Album (Paris: S.E.V.P.E.N., 1964), Vol. 2, 521–25.

nothing to be gained from having the latter information. The companies needed an overall picture of what products were being imported and exported on private ships, but details about their owners was unimportant. Because contemporaries classified private ships in this manner, it is not surprising to see historians doing the same.

Even though this study is concerned primarily with the trade at Whampoa, there was also a similar trend going on at Macao. Almost every history about the commerce in that port defines it in terms of Portuguese and/or Spanish investments. Those were the only two flags that were allowed in the port, but they do not tell the whole story. The following reference is taken from the British Parliament's review of the trade in the early 1830s, which was assembled from numerous interviews taken from long-time residents of Canton and Macao.

> There is a good deal of intercourse between Manilla and Macao; the vessels sail under the Spanish and Portuguese flags, but it is understood that they belong to the Chinese; they import the produce of the Eastern Archipelago.[13]

Macao also recorded the vessels according to their flags and/or 'nominal' owners so it is understandable that the histories written about that port would show the Portuguese and Spanish being the main sponsors of the trade. The statement above, however, suggests that Chinese financiers were behind much of this commerce.

As far as Whampoa is concerned, while it is very helpful to have all the names of the private vessels and their commanders, without data about the *real* sponsors we are left with a similar distorted picture. We are still far from being able to fill this knowledge void, but I would like to at least push the discussion into that direction so that we begin to think about including these ambiguous individuals whenever the opportunity arises. I begin with a few references to Armenian and Moorish (Muslim) ships in China. Carl T. Smith and I have already published several articles on the Armenians and Muslims involved in the trade so I will not repeat those references here.[14] I will rather discuss new information that we did not include in those studies.

It is not always straightforward identifying private vessels or their sponsors. In 1722, for example, the ship *London* arrived at Whampoa to trade. The ship was from India, and was said to be Armenian-owned.[15] The *London* arrived at Whampoa again in 1723 and the British officers in Canton recorded it as follows.

> 1723, Jul 23: This day an Armenian ship came up the River. She was here last year & went to Batavia & is return'd from Batavia. She is about 300 tonns & has brought here about 1000 peculls pepper a little spice & some tinn.[16]

---

13. *Reports from Committees*. 18 vols. *East India Company's Affairs*. Session 6 December 1831–16 August 1832, Vol. X, Part II, 'China Trade', pp. 457–64. This quotation is on p. 462.
14. Smith and Van Dyke, 'Armenian Footprints in Macau', 20–39; Smith and Van Dyke, 'Four Armenian Families', 40–50; and Smith and Van Dyke, 'Muslims in the Pearl River Delta, 1700 to 1930', 6–15.
15. BL: IOR L/MAR/B/646A.
16. BL: IOR G/12/24, 1723.07, p. 25.

> 1723, Jul 23: Arrived the *London* under Armenian Colours of about 300 tons from Batavia belonging to Madras Capt. Constantine a Greek Com[mander]. & Supra Cargo loaden with pepper &ca.[17]

> 1723, Jul 23: Arrived the *London* of 300 tons, from Batavia, "under Armenian Colours", belonging to Madras, a Greek Company, and Supercargo, laden with pepper &ca.[18]

On the morning of 23 July 1723, one of the British officers aboard the EIC ship *Duke of Cambridge*, which was anchored at Whampoa, recorded that: 'att 9 AM came in a Moors ship ye *London* from Batavia belonging to Madras'.[19] When the *London* arrived at Batavia on its return passage from Canton in January 1723 and again on its voyage to Canton in June 1723, the Dutch recorded it as being a *Greix* (Greek) ship with a *Greix* captain.[20] They made no mention of the *London* being Armenian or Moorish. In their general letters sent to Holland the Dutch clarified that the ship *London* had arrived at Batavia on 17 January 1723, and that the captain was the Greek Joan Constantino.[21]

In the Diaries and Consultations of Fort St. George, the following entry appears on 3 July 1722: 'Ship London Seignr. John Constantine Pilot sail'd for Canton'.[22] What these entries seem to suggest, is that the *London* arrived in China displaying an Armenian flag and seems to have been owned by Armenians in India. It was commanded by the Greek captain John Constantine from Madras. The crew may have been made up of Lascars, which, if true, would account for it being recorded as a Moors' ship. The Dutch in Batavia recorded the ship as being 'Greek', which raises the question of what flag it actually sailed under after it left China. Was it Greek or Armenian?

Another example is the ship *New Mode*, which arrived at Whampoa in 1727 with Dutch officers aboard. Some sources mention that the ship was flying an Armenian flag while others say it displayed a Malabar flag.[23] Because of the presence of Dutch officers, the *New Mode* was suspected of being a scout ship commissioned by the VOC to try out the China trade. The English in Canton mentioned that 'She

---

17. BL: IOR G/12/21, 1723.07.23, p. 42.
18. BL: IOR G/12/8, 1723.07.23, p. 1422.
19. BL: IOR L/MAR/B/700B, 1723.07.23.
20. Arsip Nasional Republik Indonesia (ANRI): Batavia Castle *dagregisters* (DR) 2555, 1723.01.17, p. 8, 1723.06.29, p. 226.
21. '17 jan. kwam ter rede de Londen uit Canton onder den Grieksen kapitein Joan Constantino met een lading thee'. W. Ph. Coolhaas, ed., *Generale Missiven van Gouverneurs-Generaal en Raden aan Heren XVII der Verenigde Oostindische Compagnie*. 1713–1725, Vol. 7 (The Hague: Instituut voor Nederlandse Geschiedenis, 1979), 650.
22. *Records of Fort St. George. Diary and Consultation Book of 1722* (Madras: Government Press, 1930), 1722.07.03, p. 85.
23. BL: IOR G/12/26, 1727.10.05, pp. 23–24, L/MAR/B/665B; Stadsarchief (Municipal Archive), Antwerp (SAA): IC 5704, 5705, 1727.10.01–31; GHL: Ms 1848–1849.

is said to be freighted by the Chinese that live at Batavia'.[24] There were a number of Armenians who were active in the trade at Batavia, and who could have joined up with the Dutch and Chinese there to sponsor a voyage to China, but in this case, it is unclear who actually owned the ship and cargo.

In 1749 another ship arrived at Whampoa that belonged to the Armenian Goodje Marker of Surat and it also sailed under an Armenian flag. It was referred to in some sources as an Armenian ship and in other sources as a Moorish ship.[25] The majority of the trade that Armenians conducted in Canton was done by freighting goods on other ships. In August 1754, the private English ship *Success Galley*, under command of Mr. Duncan, arrived at Whampoa from Bengal. The Danes mentioned that the ship was an 'Engelske Moor Skib' (English Moorish ship).[26] In August 1765, the private English ship *Cecil* arrived at Whampoa under command of the Englishman Brown, but the supercargos who were in charge of the merchandise aboard were Moors.[27]

In 1775, the private English ship *Aurora* arrived at Whampoa under command of the Englishman Janson (also spelled Jameson), but it was under commission of the Macao-based Armenian Matheus Johannes.[28] In the late eighteenth century, Johannes had ships sailing out of Macao as well, which he owned, but they displayed a Portuguese flag (because he had become a naturalized Portuguese).[29]

Matheus Johannes died in Canton in 1794 and his brother Lazaro took over managing his ships and trade.[30] In March 1800, the Dutch mentioned that some Portuguese ships belonging to Lazaro left Macao bound for Borneo.[31] Armenians in Macao continued to freight goods on English ships as well. On 20 June 1800, for example, seven Armenians left Macao for Canton. The Dutch mentioned that they had interests in the private English ship *Peggy*, which was commanded by Captain

24. The quotation is from this source BL: IOR G/12/26, 1727.10.05, pp. 23–24. See also BL: IOR L/MAR/B/665B; GHL: Ms 1848–1849; and SAA: IC 5704, 5705, 1727.10.01–31. The latter source mentions that the ship sailed under an Armenian flag.
25. The following sources mention that it was an Armenian ship. Gothenburg Maritime Museum (Sjöfartsmuseum) (GMM): SMG 6131 *Lovisa Ulrica* Journal; BL: IOR L/MAR/B/607B, L/MAR/B/614A, L/MAR/B/619A; and NAH: Canton 314, doc. No. 18, dated 1749.11.30. The latter source mentions that there was a ship at Whampoa belonging to the Armenian merchant Goodje Marke of Surat. The following sources mention that it was a Moors' ship. Archives Nationales, Paris (ANP): 4JJ 132.44, 1749.08.18, p. 68; BL: IOR L/MAR/B/322A, L/MAR/B/596A-B, L/MAR/B/603A, L/MAR/B/626D; NAH: VOC 8721, report dated 1750.03.22, p. 153, and Canton 17, undated letter addressed to Batavia. On the 11th page it shows the number of ships at Whampoa in 1749.
26. RAC: Ask 1024, 1754.11.26–27, p. 67r.
27. NAH: Canton 227, p. 1764.
28. NAH: Canton 84, 1775.09.21, p. 108, 1775.10.22, p. 122.
29. Smith and Van Dyke, 'Armenian Footprints in Macau', 20–39; Smith and Van Dyke, 'Four Armenian Families', 40–50.
30. Smith and Van Dyke, 'Four Armenian Families', 43–45.
31. NAH: Canton 97, 1800.03.31.

Fleming. The *Peggy* had arrived in China from India and, by July, it was loaded and ready to depart for Pegu and Bengal.[32]

Private traders often remained behind in Macao or Canton in order to purchase the goods they wanted for the next season. In this way, when the ships finally arrived in the early fall, they would be assured of having enough cargo to load them. The following entries from an EIC ship captain at Macao show two private traders doing just that.

> 1712, Jul 14: After visited the Hoppo's Deputy who told us that he had already sent advise, and that he did not doubt but that the Hoppo would comply with any reasonable demand, after which wee visited Capt. Sofaer who is an Armenian belonging to Madras, and has wintered att ye port his stock being so large could not gett gold sufficent to dispatch him, he advised that one Mr Jones belonginge to Madras was onn the same dilemma with himselfe, and that he was now att Canton and did live with Anqua, it was agreed to write him directly to bee informed how the shipps the former season came off, and likewise any other advise that he thought meight bee advantagious to us, which was immediately put into execution, att night returnd on board.[33]

> 1712, Jul 25: Anqua of Canton with Mr Edward Jones came to Maccou he brought a chopp for each shipp for a free trade. This day the said Anqua dined on board the *Statham* with ab^{t} 8 or 10 other Chinese Hoppo's Deputy and after came on board our shipp. He would not medle with any business but referd it till the morn an appointed att Capt. Sofars house to meet.[34]

The records do not tell us how Captain Sofars or Edward Jones managed to ship their merchandise to India. They may have consigned space aboard one of the Portuguese ships at Macao or perhaps one of the French ships that arrived at Whampoa that year. Because Sofars was an Armenian captain, it seems logical that he would have had his own ship. However, we have no references to Armenian ships being at Whampoa in these years so it is unclear. What is clear is that Sofars and Jones had remained behind in China to prepare their shipments, some of which was gold; the former man rented a house in Macao and the latter man stayed in Anqua's factory in Canton. A French journal from 1716 also mentioned that Armenian vessels had visited Amoy in recent years.[35]

As the reference above shows, these private traders were active in the illegal trade in gold. All of the East India companies were involved in buying gold, as were Portuguese traders in Macao, so these private ships posed considerable competition to them.[36] In 1731, for example, the EIC officers in Canton reported the following.

---

32. NAH: Canton 97, 1800.09.30, Canton 264, HRB 111, pp. 167–71, HRB 113 Ship Lists for 1800; and BL: IOR G/12/135, pp. 42–44.
33. BL: IOR L/MAR/B/112B, 1712.07.14.
34. BL: IOR L/MAR/B/112B, 1712.07.25.
35. Le Gentil, *Nouveau Voyage au tour du Monde*, 3 vols. (Paris: Flahault, 1727), 1716.08.28, p. 265.
36. For examples of the Portuguese in Macao dealing in gold, see George Bryan Souza, *The*

1731, Aug 17: when ever four thousand shoos of gold hath been demanded in one season it hath risen to so great a price that but little proffit could be made by it in Europe & that he [Mr. Naish] believes the demand this year is att least as much as below mentioned vizt.

For our Hon[ble] Masters about		2200
our commanders	£10000	300
The French gentlemen		1200
Supra Cargo's of the *Canton Merchant* from Madras		700
Supra Cargo's of the *Nassaw* from Bombay		600
Supra Cargo's of the *Shauhallom* from Bengall & Suratt		600
The Madras ship expected		600
The Armenians Portugeeze at Maccao		800
Shoos [shoes/ingots of gold]		7000

If therefore it be allowed a demand of 4000 shoos hath carried gold up to so great a price as but little proffit could be made thereby in Europe, what are we then to expect when at least 7000 shoos are demanded, & at a time when gold is generally allowed to be more scarce than usual at many places where it is generally purchased for this markett?[37]

1731, Aug 19: Mr. Middleton said he does conceive that what Mr. Naish said last consultation with relation to the great price of gold & the particular demands of the gentlemen from all parts amounting to seven thousand shoos could only be meant as an inducement for us to lay out a great part of our remaining silver in wrought silks which he readily will concurr in when to his masters advantage lett the price of gold arise from what cause it will and as there is a large Moor ship arriv'd since our last meeting she perhaps may want twice as much gold as the Madras ship still expected.[38]

The *Canton Merchant*, *Nassaw*, *Shauhallom* (or *Shallum*) and the 'large Moor ship' mentioned in the entry above were all private vessels from India. The ship expected from Madras was probably the *Catherine*, which was also a private ship. Of course, the Armenians and Portuguese in Macao were also private traders, and the reference to 'French gentlemen' probably included some private trade as did the trade of 'our commanders'. Of the 7,000 shoes of gold that were exported in 1731, more than half of them were purchased on private accounts, and most of those men were from India. Thus, unlike the tea trade which the companies dominated, private traders were formidable opponents in the gold trade. This was true throughout the first half of the eighteenth century. In terms of monetary value, at 120 taels per shoe,

---

Survival of Empire: Portuguese Trade and Society in China and the South China Sea, 1630–1754 (Cambridge: Cambridge University Press, 1986), see index for page numbers; and A. J. R. Russel-Wood, 'An Asian Presence in the Atlantic Bullion Carrying Trade, 1710–50', *Portuguese Studies* 17 (2001): 148–67.

37. BL: IOR G/12/31, 1731.08.17, p. 69.

38. BL: IOR G/12/31, 1731.08.19, p. 70.

the 7,000 shoes came to 840,000 taels. By the early 1760s, the price of gold in China became more equal with that of silver, which resulted in many people abandoning that trade.[39]

Private traders from India regularly freighted goods on Portuguese ships based in Macao, as the following example shows.

> 1733, Jun 21: [at Malacca] (pg 3) Found at anchor here a large Portegueze Ship, call'd *Nostra Senhorpena de Francia*, Capt Manuel de Corea, she saild from Maccao the 24th of February last, freighted by the Armenians for the Coast of Cormandell, being so late in the season she put for the Streight of Sunda, & went to Batavia, in hopes of disposing of some of her cargo there, being a very deep ship, but not being able to effect that, & apprehensive of meeting with bad weather when out of the Streights of Sunda, they came to the place the 7th instant, where they design to continue till the middle of November, & then proceed for the Coast of Cormandell.[40]

The Portuguese ships were much involved in the carrying trade throughout the eighteenth century, and this sometimes included the ships from Lisbon. In January 1779, for example, the Dutch mentioned that the Portuguese ship *Mariana Vittoria* was about ready to leave Macao for Lisbon and most of the cargo was being freighted by private English and Armenian traders.[41]

Unfortunately, we have very few records from the hundreds of private voyages that were made between India and China in the eighteenth and early nineteenth century. Other foreigners in Canton usually paid little attention to these vessels. Even when we do have information about a ship sailing under an Asian flag or sponsor, the references are often unclear. The ship *St Louis*, for example, arrived at Whampoa sometime around July 1725 from the Malabar Coast. One source mentioned that the ship was French with a French crew.[42] Another source mentioned that the ship sailed under a 'Malabar flag', which means it was probably commissioned by one of the Indian traders.[43] In October 1725, the ship *Jesus, Maria, Joseph* arrived at Whampoa. It was said to be French but also sailed under a Malabar flag.[44]

Many ships that arrived at Whampoa were simply recorded as being 'Moors', which usually meant that they were under commission of a Muslim trader in India and were manned by Lascars. However, many of the references are unclear. As the examples above show, Armenian ships were sometimes called Moorish ships. Other 'Moors' ships anchored at Whampoa in 1699, 1704, 1715, 1722, 1723, 1724, 1725, 1726, 1727, 1731, 1738, 1739, and 1744. Besides the *St Louis* in 1725, the other

39. Paul A. Van Dyke, *Merchants of Canton and Macao: Politics and Strategies in Eighteenth-Century Chinese Trade*, Vol. 1 (Hong Kong: Hong Kong University Press, 2011), 18–19.
40. BL: IOR G/12/35, 1733.06.21, p. 3. For a more complete study of the Portuguese trade at Macao, see Souza, *The Survival of Empire*.
41. NAH: Canton 87, 1779.01.17; and BL: IOR G/12/64, 1778.08.06, p. 5.
42. ANRI: DR 2559, 1726.01.26.
43. SAA: IC 5922 List of Ships in Canton in 1725; and GHL: Ms 1923.
44. SAA: IC 5922 List of Ships in Canton in 1725; GHL: Ms 1923; and BL: L/MAR/B/235B, L/MAR/B/36C.

ship names that are known include the *Fesserbonne* (1738), captain Golzeby; the *St Domingo* (1739), captain Coja Maroot Joseph; and the *Phatta Salam* (1744), captain Abu Backer. The *Fesserbonne* encountered a typhoon in the lower delta and arrived without masts.[45]

The names of the captains in the latter three ships appear to be of Indian origin, and not European. But it was just as common to have a European captain commanding an India-based ship. In all of these examples there is no mention in the records of the owners or sponsors. The ships are simply recorded as Moorish and probably sailed under an Asian flag. They could have been Muslim, Armenian, Hindu, or Parsee. Another ship at Whampoa in 1699 was said to be an 'Arab' ship.[46] Was it the same as the Moors ship that was in port that year?[47] On 2 January 1797 about half a dozen private ships left Whampoa and one of them was said to be flying 'Arab' colours.[48]

All we can say about these references to Moors and Arabs is that the ships were commissioned by private traders based in Asia. Some of these ships were said to have originated in India, but it is unknown where the other ships came from. This confusion is not limited only to Indian-based ships but to others as well. Some of the East India companies' ships flew one flag but were actually under commission of another nation. The Dutch regularly commissioned Portuguese ships based in Macao and Chinese junks based in Guangzhou and Amoy to carry cargo for them to Batavia. From the 1780s to the early years of the nineteenth century, the Dutch also commissioned several Prussian and Swedish East India companies' ships and American vessels to carry their freight. These vessels might be owned by Portuguese, Chinese, Prussians, Swedes, or Americans and may have flown those respective flags, but they were working for the Dutch.[49]

In 1704, the ship *Queen* arrived at Whampoa and it was said to be from Persia and bound for Persia.[50] When Persia or Persians are mentioned in the Canton records it is often a reference to Parsees. In this case, however, the ship appears to have been privately owned by persons in India but it was commissioned by EIC officers to sail to China.[51] Wills also shows in his chapter that the EIC ship *Hampshire* was hired

45. RAC: Ask 879a, Ask 999; BL: IOR G/12/44, pp. 114–15, G/12/45, pp. 119–20, L/MAR/B/404B; ANP: 4JJ 131.31–32; and GHL: Ms 1928.
46. Saxe Bannister, trans., *A Journal of the First French Embassy to China, 1698–1700* (London: Thomas Cautley Newby, 1859), 140 and 148–49.
47. BL: IOR L/MAR/A/CXXIII.
48. BL: IOR L/MAR/B/407A, 1798.01.02.
49. E. S. van Eyck van Heslinga, *Van Compagnie naar Koopvaardij, De scheepvaart verbinding van de Bataafse Republiek met de koloniën in Azië 1795–1806* (Amsterdam: De BataafscheLeeuw, 1988).
50. BL: IOR L/MAR/B/715B.
51. *Records of Fort St. George. Letters to Fort St. George 1703–1704* (Madras: Government Press, 1931), letter no. 115, dated 1704.08.19, pp. 116–18; and *Records of Fort St. George. Diary and Consultation Book of 1722* (Madras: Government Press, 1930), 1704.04.30, p. 37, 1704.06.14–15, pp. 48–49.

out to private traders in India for a voyage to Canton in the fall of 1701. After the vessel returned to India in early 1702, it was again employed by the Company.[52] Thus, even when a ship appears as though it might be a private or company vessel, we find out that it was actually working for someone else.

In October 1784, the ship *Pallas* arrived at Whampoa as a private English ship. When it left, however, it sailed away under an American flag.[53] In September 1780 the *Eliza* arrived at Whampoa under English colours, but was then sold to the Portuguese supercargo Miranda at Macao. After it was unloaded, Miranda took possession of the ship and renamed it *Marquis de Angeja*. The inbound cargo was English and the outbound cargo was Portuguese.[54]

In 1778, there was another private ship at Whampoa named *Eliza*, but it is unclear whether it was the same vessel as above. This ship was owned by the private English merchant George Smith.[55] On 26 January 1779, that vessel left China bound for Bombay, and the Dutch mentioned that it was being freighted by Armenian merchants in Canton.[56]

In October 1789, the American ship *Atlantic* arrived at Whampoa. After unloading the cargo, the owner auctioned the ship off for 6,600 Spanish dollars to a Parsee buyer.[57] The inbound cargo was American and the outbound cargo was Parsee's. In October 1798, the private ship *Dragon* arrived at Whampoa under English colours. After it was unloaded, it was sold to an American.[58]

By the late eighteenth century, many of the private ships from India had adopted Indian names. They might have an English captain and sail under an English flag but were named after famous Indians and often manned with Lascars, which suggests they may have been owned and/or commissioned by Asians. The names include *Muxadavad*, *Sabajang*, *Bahaar*, *Fattee Shaw*, *Istambolle*, *Dadaley*, *Shaw Ardisier*, *Shaw Byram Gore*, *Sullimanny*, *Ganjavar*, *Soloman Shaw*, *Sultan*, *Kes Russool Muchoy*, *Fazeallum*, *Thantum Tazbux*, *Nurmaddah*, *Boman Yaid*, *Shaw Muncher*, *Nabab Wallajak*, *Lowjee Family*, *Travancore*, *Fuz Kaddreee*, *Shaw Jehangir*, *Shaw Hormahie*,

52. Anthony Farrington, *Catalogue of East India Company Ships' Journals and Logs 1600–1834* (London: British Library, 1999).
53. NAH: VOC 4426, letter dated 1785.01.31, par. 73, VOC 4426 and 4428 Ship list for 1784, Canton 246 pp. 229–32; Quincy, ed., *The Journals of Major Samuel Shaw*, 182; Kenneth Scott Latourette, 'Voyages of American Ships to China, 1784–1844', in *Transactions of the Connecticut Academy of Arts and Sciences* 28 (April 1927): 237–71; BL: IOR G/12/80 pp. 57–58, L/MAR/B/257A, L/MAR/B/482J, L/MAR/B/544-I-M.
54. BL: IOR G/12/70, 1780.10.30, p. 220, G/12/71 p. 78, L/MAR/B/285LL, L/MAR/B/408A, L/MAR/B/490C, L/MAR/B/469G, L/MAR/B/172G, L/MAR/B/1H, L/MAR/B/259B, L/MAR/B/499D, L/MAR/B/499D.
55. For George Smith's story, see Jessica Hanser's chapter in this volume.
56. NAH: Canton 88, 1779.01.26.
57. Rhys Richards, 'United States Trade with China, 1784–1814', *The American Neptune* 54: Special Supplement (1994); NAH: Canton 251 pp. 187–90, HRB 80 & 82 Ship List for 1789; BL: IOR G/12/97 pp. 31–33, L/MAR/B/124B, L/MAR/B/530E.
58. BL: IOR G/12/123 Ship List for 1798 pp. 15–17.

Zoroaster, *Fattahoo Rhamoun*, *Koddah Buckers*, *Cabalamban*, *Shaw Kekescherra*, *Dores Navegante*, *Morad Buz*, and *Zenobia*. We know that some of these ships were commissioned by Indian merchants, and many of them made voyages to China consecutively year after year.[59]

In the latter half of the eighteen century, most of the private ships from India had English captains and sailed under a British ensign. After 1749, it is rare to find references to ships with a Moorish flag at Whampoa. That fact, however, does not mean that Indian merchants ceased trading at Canton. The vessels and cargos were rather disguised under a British flag, which brought them more security at sea and in China because they were then considered to be under the administrative protection of the EIC.[60] But as the American Tilden pointed out in 1815, 'Country English ships . . . Many of the Parsees are owners of both ships and cargoes, but they are sailed under British colors'.[61] On a voyage between India and China, which typically took between six to eight months from beginning to end, it was common to expect at least 10 per cent profit on your investment.[62]

From the early eighteenth century to 1773, East India companies dominated the commerce at Canton. When the second French East India Company ended in 1769, that trade was opened to private traders. As Schopp has shown in her chapter, from 1770 to 1778 many French ships arrived at Whampoa, which pushed up the total number of private vessels in port to rival those of the companies. From 1788 and after, the number of private ships at Whampoa equalled or surpassed the number of company ships.[63] The 1790s saw a huge influx of private traders at Canton. At that time, there were around 50 to 80 ships in port each year and about half of them were privately owned and commissioned.[64]

---

59. Paul A. Van Dyke's unpublished ship list, forthcoming.
60. 'The Americans [at Canton] have frequently found it difficult to obtain a security merchant. It is less difficult for the country ships from the circumstance of their being British, for it is known that they are under the Company's [EIC's] representatives'. *Reports from Committees*, 18 vols. *East India Company's Affairs*. Session 6 December 1831–16 August 1832, Vol. X, Part II, 'China Trade', pp. 457–64. This quotation is on p. 462.
61. PEM: Bryant P. Tilden Journal 1815–1816, typescript, p. 97. The British Parliament also understood this relationship with Indian investors. 'The country trade [in China] is principally in the hands of British merchants, but the Parsees of Bombay are also personally engaged in it, and the capital of the Hindoo merchants of Calcutta is employed therein.' *Reports from Committees*, 18 vols. *East India Company's Affairs*. Session 6 December 1831–16 August 1832, Vol. X, Part II, 'China Trade', pp. 457–64. This quotation is on p. 462.
62. 'A fair average gain for the commander on a voyage [between India and China] is 5,000 £, the capital employed being about 50,000 £.' *Reports from Committees*, 18 vols. *East India Company's Affairs*. Session 6 December 1831–16 August 1832, Vol. X, Part II, 'China Trade', pp. 457–64. This quotation is on p. 462.
63. I am assembling a new and more complete list of ships at Whampoa, but until that is finished, use Louis Dermigny, *La Chine et l'Occident*, 2: 521–25.
64. Paul A. Van Dyke and Maria Kar-wing Mok, *Images of the Canton Factories 1760–1822: Reading History in Art* (Hong Kong: Hong Kong University Press, 2015), Chapter 6 'Rise of the Private Traders 1790–1799'.

The total volume that was exported by company and private ships each year is a different story. We do not have accurate tonnage figures for the hundreds of private vessels that traded at Canton, but we do know that they were generally smaller than those of the companies.[65] According to Dermigny's tonnage figures the companies dominating the overall volume of trade at Canton up to at least 1800. In the early years of the nineteenth century, however, the volume handled by private ships began to surpass that of the companies.[66] This outcome was partially owing to an increase of private ships arriving and partially owing to other East India companies abandoning the China trade. By 1807, the French, Dutch, Swedish, Danish and Imperial East India companies had all ceased sending ships to China, and then the British EIC was, for the most part, the only company that remained.[67]

Many private traders did not have ships but simply arrived with a bag full of money or pockets full of precious stones.[68] They were nonetheless welcomed at Canton just like everyone else so long as they could prove that they were there to trade and had means of shipping their merchandise home. With regard to Jews, they were often closely connected to the Armenians in China. In 1748, Noble mentioned that he had seen 'multitudes of Armenians at Canton; and I am much mistaken if there was not many Jews among them. They flocked always together, and here, as everywhere in Europe, they distinguished themselves from the people of China. Their beards, features, and complexion, confirmed my conjecture.'[69]

65. 1831–1832: 'The country ships are very fine merchantmen of from 500 to 700 tons; a few are as large as 1,000 tons; they are manned with Asiatics, but officered by Europeans. Before sailing from Bengal to China, they are obliged to enter into a bond to conform to the regulations of the Company's supracargoes.'

'The Company's ships carry 30 or 40 guns, and 130 men; 26 guns, and 135 men. Chests of tea taken in large ships are stowed more rapidly, less liable to be broken, and less damaged. There is no difference with respect to liability to damage between a large and a small vessel, if the latter be dry. The merchant must, in a pecuniary point of view, give the preference to the smaller vessel, but there are many advantages in those of a larger size; the cargo is packed better, the vessel is more readily loaded, and the tea would come home better, though it is not a cargo that is much damaged. A vessel of 600 tons is better as a merchant vessel than one of 1,200, except with regard to the port-charges at Canton, which are heavier in proportion on the smaller than on the larger vessel: the cargo is not safer in large ships, and the insurance is not less. The difference of port-charges does not counterbalance the disadvantages. The most economical vessel would be one of 450 tons, navigated by 18 or 19 men. The most advantageous size would be one of 500 or 600 tons, the American size.' *Affairs of the East India Company. Reports from Committees: 1831–2*, 462.

66. Dermigny, *La Chine et l'Occident*, 2: 521–25.

67. For a summary of the decline of the companies and the rise of the private traders in Canton in the late eighteenth century, see Van Dyke and Mok, *Images of the Canton Factories*, Chapter 6 'Rise of the Private Traders 1790–1799'.

68. For some examples of Armenians arriving with just a few items to trade, see Smith and Van Dyke, 'Armenian Footprints in Macau', 20–39; and Smith and Van Dyke, 'Four Armenian Families', 40–50.

69. Charles Frederick Noble, *A Voyage to the East Indies in 1747 and 1748* (London: T. Becket and P.A. Dehondt, 1762), 244.

Other references provide more specific details about a few of these men. On 19 July 1753, the private French ship *St Jean Baptiste* arrived at Whampoa from Surat.[70] The English officers mentioned that there were two supercargos connected to this ship, Le Rouy and Jacobs, and that the latter man was a Jew.[71] In October 1760, the Dutch mentioned that a Jewish trader by the name of Shabatay had arrived in Canton in the previous year with many pearls and precious stones. He was a resident of Baghdad and had gained passage to China from Surat aboard Captain Fisher's ship (possibly the EIC ship *Drake*). Travelling with him were two writers and three slaves.[72]

With the proceeds from the sale of his pearls and precious stones, Shabatay purchased 200 chests of porcelain. In October 1760, he asked the Dutch officers in Canton for permission to send his cargo, his servants and their luggage to Batavia, aboard one of the Dutch ships. He wanted to find passage to the VOC factory in Persia, and from there he would return to his home in Baghdad.[73]

More Jews arrived in the years that followed. In their annual trade report dated 31 December 1762, the Dutch mentioned that there were Armenians and Jews remaining in China (Canton or Macao) year-round.[74] On 24 May 1763, the Dutch in Canton received a letter from Father Le Bon in Macao. In the letter Le Bon mentioned that

> On their arrival, the Jews had been greatly humiliated and the people [in Macao] had wanted to throw them into prison, although the Chinese Hoppo, being the Mandarin of Macao, had speedily acted on their behalf, and had forced the Portuguese to receive them.[75]

I have found nothing more about this incident in the records, but another reference suggests that these Jews may have gone upriver to Canton to trade. In their trade report dated 24 December 1763, the Dutch mentioned that the Chinese officials were anxious for all foreigners to leave Canton after their ships left. They said that the English would be allowed to stay longer because they had a ship in port. The Dutch, French, Danes, Swedes, Armenians and Jews were all forced to leave Canton for Macao, after their ships had departed.[76] There is no mention of what ships the Armenians and Jews were connected to. The private ship *Sabajang* was in port this year and had arrived from India via Manila so they may have been connected to

70. BL: IOR G/12/57 p. 37, L/MAR/B/614B, L/MAR/B/602-I, L/MAR/B/397B, L/MAR/B/572B, L/MAR/B/622E, L/MAR/B/800A, L/MAR/B/603B.
71. BL: IOR G/12/57, p. 37.
72. NAH: VOC 4386, *dagregister*, 1760.10.06, p. 78.
73. NAH: VOC 4386, *dagregister*, 1760.10.06, p. 78.
74. NAH: Canton 223, 1762.12.31, p. 192.
75. Paul A. Van Dyke and Cynthia Viallé, comp., *The Canton-Macao Dagregisters*, 1763 (Macao: Macao Cultural Institute, 2008), 24 May, p. 59.
76. NAH: Canton 278, letter dated 1763.12.24, p. 15. In 1753, the supercargo Jacobs, of the private French ship *St Jean Baptiste*, was said to be a Jew as well. BL: IOR G/12/57, p. 37.

her. This vessel sailed under an English flag and was consigned to the private trader George Smith, who also remained in China and had many connections with traders in India.[77] As Hanser has shown in her dissertation, there were a couple of George Smiths active in the trade in Canton so the references to that name, here and above, are not necessarily all referring to the same person.[78]

Another example of a private trader without a ship is the Armenian Anthony Baptist Stamme (also called Jan Baptist Stamme). In September 1760, he applied for passage aboard one of the Dutch ships. He had 11,000 taels in cash, was living in the house of the Hong merchant Poankeequa (Pan Zhencheng 潘振承) in Canton, and had given that merchant some money to invest. Stamme wanted to go either to Cape Hope, or directly to Amsterdam, if possible. In the end, however, he arrived at Macao too late to board the Dutch ships and had to find other means of getting to his destination.[79]

I have not found references confirming whether or not Shabatay actually made it to Baghdad by the plan above. In their annual trade report dated 11 January 1761, the Dutch mentioned that there were *Armeniaanen* (Armenians, plural) and a *Jood* (Jew, singular) who remained in China at the end of the season.[80] If this portrayal is correct, then it would suggest that either Shabatay or Stamme stayed behind to take care of trade in the upcoming 1761 season.

Stamme seems to have had relatives living in Europe to whom he transferred money from China. On 25 December 1759, he gave the Danes at Canton a bottomry loan of 1,800 taels to insure the voyage of the ship *Princess Louisa*. If the ship and cargo arrived safely in Copenhagen, then the Danes were to pay his agent in Amsterdam, Frantsis Namtala Stamma, the 1,800 taels premium plus 30 per cent interest. The payment was due three months after the safe arrival of the ship and was to be paid in British pounds. Issuing bottomry bonds was an effective way for private traders in Asia to transfer their funds to Europe, and earn interest on their money at the same time.[81] From 1764 to at least 1768, there was an Antonio Stamme based in Marseille who may have been related to persons above. He had numerous financial transactions with the Swedish supercargos trading at Canton.[82]

From the references above, and from other Dutch records, we learn that there were a few Jewish traders in residence in Canton and/or Macao from at least 1759

77. NAH: Canton 224, pp. 222–26, Canton 278, report dated 1763.12.24, pp. 2–3 and 107; BL: L/MAR/B/486D, L/MAR/B/438J, L/MAR/B/535D, L/MAR/B/776A, L/MAR/B/98C, L/MAR/B/390C, L/MAR/B/582D.
78. Hanser, 'Mr. Smith Goes to China'.
79. NAH: VOC 4384, report dated 1761.01.11, pp. 539v–540r, VOC 4386, *dagregister*, 1760.09.11, p. 66.
80. NAH: VOC 4384, report dated 1761.01.11, p. 261.
81. RAC: Ask 1144, 1759.12.25, pp. 140r–41r.
82. Stockholm, Nordic Museum Archive (NM): Godegårdsarkivet. Ostindiska Handling F17: 1–7 (hereafter referred to as NM: F17), digital pp. T1_00052, T1_00209, T1_03274–3276, T1_06038–6039.

to 1767.[83] Unfortunately, we do not have an exact number or their names, but there were only a few men. For most of these years, the Dutch referred to the Jews in the plural form (*Jooden*) so except for 1761, there was probably more than one in other years. As shown in the example above, Jews were usually recorded together with Armenians, which is logical considering their close business connections and that they seemed to have associated closely in their daily activities.

In trade reports from 1768, 1769, 1770, and later, the Dutch mentioned that a few Armenians remained in China each year, but there are no further mentions of Jews in Canton.[84] In the late 1760s, however, there was man by the name of Pereira who was active in Macao and whom the Dutch referred to as an English-Portuguese Jew. On 21 January 1770, the Dutch reported that he had served as an agent for the Nabob of India for the past five years. He left Macao for Europe on the EIC ship *Neptune* which departed on 27 January 1770.[85]

In 1771, Benyowsky referred to a Jewish agent in Macao, but he did not provide a name.[86] In 1769, William Hickey, who often got people and events mixed up, mentioned that there was a private trader from Madras by the name of General De Castro who had arrived in China in September. Hickey did not have a very good impression of this man, but mentioned that Castro 'was, or had been a Jew' and was 'in the service of the Nabob of Arcot'.[87] If this is true, then Castro may have been the replacement for Pereira.

In September 1771, the English mentioned that there was a man by the name of Castro in Canton who was seeking passage to Macao. In a later reference this man was identified as the 'free merchant' Daniel de Castro. After arriving at Macao, he was joined by his wife and two servants and then all of them departed for India aboard the EIC ship *Horsendon* in February 1772.[88]

All of these entries from 1769 to 1772 showing Castro and a Jew being in China could be referring to the same person. Daniel de Castro shows up in the Danish records from 1777 to 1780 loaning money to the Danish Asiatic Company (DAC)

83. NAH: Canton 226, 1765.01.04, p. 178, Canton 227, 1766.01.04, p. 165, Canton 228, 1766.12.26, p. 142, Canton 229, 1767.12.31, p. 170.
84. NAH: Canton 230, 1768.12.22, p. 168, Canton 231, 1769.12.10, p. 144.
85. NAH: Canton 79, 1770.01.21. On 15 July and 20 September 1696, the Dutch in Batavia received letters from the 'Jewish merchant Pedro Pereira' in Surat, which may have been the same Pereira family from India that shows up in Macao in the late 1760s. ANRI DR 2516, 1696.07.15, p. 544 and 1696.09.20, p. 757; and BL: IOR L/MAR/B/98E, 1770.01.27. Pereira was of course a common Portuguese name in Macao, but this Jewish family seems to have been based in India. Jorge Forjaz, *Famílias Macaenses*, 3 vols. (Macao: Fundação Oriente, Instituto Cultural de Macau, 1996); and A. M. Martins do Vale, *Os Portugueses em Macau (1750–1800)* (Macao: Institvto Portvgvês do Oriente, 1997).
86. S. Pasfield Oliver, *The Memoirs and Travels of Mauritius Augustus Count de Benyowsky* (London: T. Fisher Unwin, 1898), 386 and 388.
87. Alfred Spencer, ed., *Memoirs of William Hickey (1749–1775)* (New York: Alfred A. Knopf, 1921), 221–22.
88. BL: IOR R/10/7, 1771.09.22, p. 44, R/10/9, 1772.02.02, p. 14.

to help finance their voyages to China. In a couple of those year, he loaned money to the DAC in concert with Moses de Castro and Pelling & Petrie of Madras. In some of these transactions the Danes received the money while they were still in Canton, but the transactions seem to have been done indirectly via other agents in China.[89] I found no mention of these men actually being in China in those years. The Danes did not mention any of these men being Jews, but their names and other references above suggest that they may have had Sephardic connections.[90] Unfortunately I have been unable to confirm any of these assumptions, nor have I been able to clearly link the Castros to Benyowsky's reference. Nevertheless, the entries are relevant for this study because even though we may not be able to prove their ethnicities we know that all of them were private traders who helped to finance the China trade.

While these entries are brief and unclear, they nonetheless show that it was not necessary to own or commission an entire ship to become involved in the China trade. Carl Smith and I have provided other examples of Armenians and Muslims in Canton and Macao.[91] Another entry provides us with more details about how these itinerant traders operated.

In 1778, the Armenian merchant Babtiste Basilion and a Greek trader from Madras named Wandy Metree sailed to Manila in a small vessel (sloop) loaded with their cargo. Upon arriving in the Philippines, they found a depressed market and were unable to sell their goods for a profit. They decided to wait until the market recovered and rented accommodation in the city.

In the meantime, news arrived from Europe that Spain and Great Britain were at war. Because Basilion and Metree had come from Madras, they were suspected of having English connections. Consequently, the Spanish governor ordered them to leave immediately or be imprisoned. The two men had much difficulty trying to find passage from Manila to Macao and pleaded with the governor to grant them more time. The governor responded by saying that if they did not leave within eight days, they would be put to death.

The two men hastily purchased the small vessel *Santa Rita* for 4,000 Spanish dollars, and hired Manoel Roderico, a native of Macao, to command her. They hired some Chinese and Indian sailors to man the ship. The governor insisted that they take a French priest with them to Macao, who had been imprisoned for the past three months on suspicions of being a spy. They left Manila on 16 August 1780 flying Spanish colours because no other European flag was permitted at Manila at

89. RAC: Ask 234, doc. No. 17, Ask 235, doc. No. 25, 27, 38, Ask 237a, doc. No. 66, Ask 1183, 1780.12.21, p. 137r.
90. The Dutch did not mention any Jews being in Canton in 1770 or 1771, but they sometimes missed men and ships that were in port. It is also possible that they did not know that Castro had Jewish connections. NAH: Canton 232, 1770.12.12, p. 180, and Canton 233, 1771.12.23, p. 168.
91. Smith and Van Dyke, 'Armenian Footprints in Macau', 20–39; Smith and Van Dyke, 'Four Armenian Families', 40–50; Smith and Van Dyke, 'Muslims in the Pearl River Delta, 1700 to 1930', 6–15.

this time and because they were carrying a passport from the Spanish governor. Upon arriving in the delta near Macao the *Santa Rita* was captured by the English captain Tasker as a prize of war.[92]

This was a very unfortunate affair for Basilion and Metree. The two men were travelling with their treasures, and gaining passage aboard any ship that would have them. All they owned were 'three chests of treasure, three chests of [edible] birds' nests, some Sapanwood, and other articles'.[93] Basilion and Metree were not Spanish and the cargo was not Spanish, but because they flew a Spanish flag and were carrying a Spanish pass they became victims of Captain Tasker's opportunistic ambitions, and lost their ship and cargo as casualties of war.[94]

We learn from other references that Captain Tasker had not been issued a Letter of Marque from the British crown, and therefore he had no right to forcefully take possession of the *Santa Rita* in the name of Britain. Consequently, he was ordered to hand over the booty to Captain Panton of the British warship *Sea Horse* (the same captain and ship as mentioned in Hanser's chapter), which was lying upriver waiting to escort the tea fleet home. The EIC officers recorded the value of the confiscated goods to be $8,299.[95] Panton deposited this amount into the EIC's treasury at Canton and was given a 'one year after sight' Bill of Exchange, which was 'made payable to himself'.[96]

Tasker handed the ship back to Basilion and Metree, but not before he had forced them to sign a ransom note stating that they owed him 2,000 Spanish dollars for the return of the vessel. When the two men arrived back in India, they appealed to an Armenian acquaintance in London to help them solve this matter with Tasker and to recover the money and possessions that had been handed over to Panton.[97] Unfortunately, I have found no reference indicating how this matter was resolved.

In 1803, another Armenian ran into a similar situation like Basilion and Metree, but fared much better. On April 13 of that year, the private French ship

92. BL: IOR H/155 Miscellaneous Series 1780–1, letter dated 1780.09.29, pp. 1–7 and G/12/70, 1780.11.08, pp. 223–30.
93. BL: IOR G/12/70, 1780.11.08, p. 225. The Dutch officers in Macao mentioned that the men had brought with them 12,000 Spanish dollars, and some birds' nests. NAH: Canton 89, 1780.09.08.
94. BL: IOR G/12/70, 1780.09.13, p. 157. For more about this story of Babtiste Basilion and Wandy Metree losing their ship at Macao, see Ina Baghdiantz McCabe, 'No Network is an Island: Collaboration and Competition between Trade-Diaspora in the Early Modern Period', in *Diaspora as a Resource. Comparative Studies in Strategies, Networks and Urban Space*, ed. Waltraud Kokot, Christian Giordano and Mijal Gandelsman-Trier (Berlin: Lit Verlag, 2013), 143–70, 160–64.
95. This source says that the $8,299 came from the sale of the birds' nests, and does not mention any other items or money. BL: IOR G/12/19, pp. 129–31.
96. BL: IOR G/12/70, 1780.11.08, pp. 223–30.
97. BL: IOR G/12/19, pp. 129–31, G/12/70, 1780.11.08, pp. 223–30. The Dutch said the ransom was $3,000. NAH: Canton 89, 1780.09.08. The testimony from the two men, however, confirmed that it was $2,000. McCabe, 'No Network is an Island', pp. 160–64.

Paix, commanded by Captain Fallouard, arrived at Whampoa from Manila. The owner of the vessel was Nazar Jacob Shamier, an Armenian from Fort St. George, and he was aboard the ship when it arrived in China.[98]

Shamier had purchased the *Paix* in Manila in November 1802 and hired the French captain to sail her to China. Consequently, when the ship arrived at Whampoa it was flying a French flag. Because it was rumoured that Britain and France were about to declare war, Shamier feared that he might be attacked by the British after he left China. Being born and raised in Fort St. George, he declared himself to be a British subject and pleaded with the EIC officers in Canton to help him procure an English captain so that he could sail back to India under a British flag.

In the end, the EIC committee asked Shamier to give them a sworn statement that he was the rightful owner of the vessel. He was then allowed to sell the *Paix* to the Englishman James Farquharson (captain of the EIC ship *Alfred* which was lying at Whampoa at the time). Farquharson presented the Bill of Sale to the EIC committee showing that he was the new owner, and the ship was then allowed to leave China under a British flag.[99]

What the examples of Basilion, Metree, Shamier and others above clearly show is that the flags only tell us who the commanders were, or in the *Santa Rita*'s case, the pass they possessed. The identity of the owners and the cargos had nothing to do with the flags. Chinese Hoppos (customs superintendents) also recorded the ships arriving at Whampoa according to their respective flags, and issued passes to go up and downriver as if the ships were from those nations. However, if we wanted to analyse the composition of the trade and establish what parts of the commerce belonged to whom, it makes no sense to call the *Santa Rita* and the *Paix* Spanish or French ships, respectively.

By the early nineteenth century, Parsees had emerged as a dominant group of Indian traders involved in the commerce.[100] Parsees have been credited with establishing one of the earliest banks in Canton, which by 1819 was already in existence. Banknotes issued by the Parsee owners of the 'Canton Bank' were written in both English and Chinese which made them accessible to everyone.[101] While the extent to which Chinese merchants made use of these notes is still uncertain, the fact that they were written in that language shows that the Parsee owners were at least attempting to make this type of currency popular in China.

Many of these individuals from India had ships at Whampoa every year, for which we have few details. Some of these men were prominent players in the trade. In 1785 and 1786, the Moorish merchant Rustumjie Dadaway, and from 1798 to

98. BL: IOR G/12/144, 1803.04.13, p. 55.
99. BL: IOR G/12/145, 1803.10.26, pp. 23–24 and 1803.11.02, p. 32.
100. Guo, 'The Study of Parsee Merchants in Canton, Hong Kong and Macao'.
101. Otto Chun-Cheung Lam, 'The 1819 Bank Note and Parsee Bankers in China', *The Numismatic Chronicle* 164 (2004): 209–18.

1800 Mohamed Dadaway, were actively involved in the trade and the usury market at Canton.[102] Sadooden Shack Ally Coor was the supercargo of the private English ship *Milford* in 1799.[103] He and Dosalbhoy Maneckjee also loaned money to the EIC.[104] In 1798, the Muslim merchant Samsooden, who was in charge of the private ship *Shaw Jehangir*, was listed as one of the creditors of the failed Hong merchant Monqua (Cai Wenguan 蔡文官).[105] Mahomed Hussein and Edeljee Bowanjee were also loaning money to Chinese merchants at this time, as was the Armenian Matheus Johannes.[106] Names that end with 'jee' or 'boy' are usually references to Parsee traders. Another example is in the 20 September 1828 issue of the *Canton Register* which states that: '*Died*. At Macao, on the 6th current C. Cachatoor Esq. an Armenian merchant, one of the oldest foreign residents in Canton.'[107]

As Hanser, Schopp, Wills, and Hellman have also shown in their chapters, private traders were very much involved in loaning money to Chinese. Because those exchanges carried greater risk, it was perhaps natural that interest rates on loans to Hong merchants were higher—often at 20 per cent per annum. One could potentially make even more profits by loaning money to the operators of the Canton junks, to help finance their voyages to Southeast Asia each year. Many of the junks were owned and/or sponsored by the Canton Hong merchants, so a private foreign trader could invest some money in a normal business loan of 20 per cent interest and other money in marine (bottomry) insurance at 40 per cent per annual voyage. As long as the investments were spread out over several merchants and/or vessels, those loans had the potential of producing a much higher rate of return than what one could make by buying, selling and shipping merchandise. It is thus not surprising to see these private traders from India being much involved in those exchanges throughout the eighteenth and early nineteenth century. As early as the 1720s, many of the Hong merchants were already indebted to 'certain Armenians'.[108]

Except for the detailed figures that Hanser shows in her chapter, very few other data survive from these private transactions. From the many disparate studies that have now been done on the private traders, we can now say for certain, that much of the tea trade of the East India companies would not have happened without those

102. NAH: VOC 4428, letter dated 1785.12.09, par. 33, Canton 247, general report dated 1786.01.24, p. 178, Canton 292, letter dated 1798.12.31, par. 8, p. 17, Canton 264, letter dated 1801.02.22, par. 12.
103. BL: IOR G/12/126, 1799.09.21, p. 141.
104. BL: IOR G/12/126, 1799.08.30, p. 129, 1799.12.29, p.237.
105. NAH: Canton 261, p. 74; Van Dyke, *The Canton Trade*, Plate 3; and Paul A. Van Dyke, *Merchants of Canton and Macao: Success and Failure in Eighteenth-Century Chinese Trade*, Vol. 2 (Hong Kong: Hong Kong University Press, 2016), 116.
106. NAH: Canton 261, p. 74; Van Dyke, *The Canton Trade*, Plate 3.
107. *The Canton Register*, 1828.09.20.
108. Van Dyke, *Merchants of Canton and Macao*, Vol. 1, 17. For detailed discussions of these private loans to Chinese merchants, see Van Dyke, *The Canton Trade*; and Van Dyke, *Merchants of Canton and Macao*, Vols. 1 and 2.

investments; many foreigners would not have gone to China without the attraction of earning a high rate of return; and much of the trade between Canton and Southeast Asia would have been hindered owing to a lack of investment capital. However, we need to keep all of this in perspective, because if China had operated like many other major seaports of the eighteenth century where monopolistic companies controlled access to markets, and placed limitations on the persons who could trade in those places and the types of transactions and products that could be exchanged, much of this activity in Canton would have disappeared.

The private investments that fuelled the trade were only made possible because China maintained a consistent open-door policy that welcomed and treated all foreigners more-or-less equally, regardless of whether they were large or small operators, what religion they believed in, or where they came from (except Russians and Japanese). While there were many restrictions at Canton that foreigners were unhappy with, the fact remains that all of them could go there and trade in whatever products they wanted—so long as they were legal items. Unlike many other ports in Asia, private traders in Canton could sell and purchase all of the same products as the East India companies, and in whatever quantities they wanted. Even when a restriction was introduced such as the silk quotas in the early 1760s, which stipulated that no more than 80 piculs per ship could be exported each year, all vessels—company and private alike—were treated alike.[109]

Most of the references above to Indian traders cannot be found in any history books. There are sure to be many more of these men that are still waiting to be discovered. The entries show that the picture we have been presented with in previous histories, of Europeans and Americans dominating the private trade, is much distorted. Many of those ships were actually commissioned by Muslims, Hindus, Parsees, Greeks, Jews, Armenians, and Southeast Asians under cover of a European flag. If we had complete transparency of all the particulars concerning these private ships at Whampoa and Macao, we would likely find a good percentage of them being financed by persons from India, Southeast Asia and/or overseas Chinese. Given that the Chinese authorities opened the trade to non-Chinese regardless of nationality (except Japanese and Russians), and guaranteed them access to the market in Canton, this should not be surprising. The examples of Basilion, Metree, and Shamier are not exceptions. They are simply a couple cases out of many—most of which did not get recorded.

This ends my survey of the bits and pieces of information about these men, but it is really just the beginning. Hopefully new studies will be able to bring out more examples of these ambiguous merchants, and make the links between them and the ships they financed, so that, in time, we may gain a fuller picture of their importance to the history of the China trade.

---

109. For a summary of the silk quotas, see Van Dyke, *Merchants of Canton and Macao*, Vol. 2, 181–84.

3

French Private Trade at Canton, 1698–1833

Susan E. Schopp

Recent studies of private merchants in the Canton trade (circa 1700–1842) have confirmed the importance of their role in the commerce, which includes not only the eras of the various European East India companies but also periods of exclusively private trade. This chapter explores the forms of private trade in which the French engaged; identifies distinctive features of that trade; places the trade in the overall context of France's China trade; argues that private traders were a legitimate part of Sino-French trade at the very start; and provides brief biographical sketches of traders who were active during the period from 1770 to 1785, when France became the first nation having an East India company to abolish the company's monopoly and to open overseas trade, including that with China, to the private sector.

The Forms of Private Trade

The French private trade at Canton took several different forms. The first, which was distinctive of the first Compagnie des Indes ([French East] India Company), consisted of trade conducted by members of the private sector to whom the Compagnie leased its China trade monopoly.[1] The second was that conducted by persons who were not in the employ of an East India company and/or not assigned to a Company ship. These merchants may be divided into two groups: legitimate and illegitimate. To the legitimate group belonged individuals who were active during eras when trade was open to the private sector. The illegitimate group consisted of interlopers, who were active during an era when their nation had an East India company, but who lacked the company's permission to trade. They were therefore regarded as violators of the company's monopoly.

The third form of private trade was the 'privilege' trade (known in French as *port-permis*, and not to be confused with the term *privilège*, indicating a trade monopoly). The privilege trade was carried out by persons in the employ of an East India

1. The name of the French East India Company, as it is generally called in English, underwent several changes in the course of its history (for example, *Compagnie française pour le commerce des Indes orientales*, *Compagnie des Indes orientales*, *Compagnie française des Indes*, etc.). All French-to-English translations in this chapter are the author's.

company and sailing on one of the company's ships, and was one of the perquisites (or 'perks') of company ship officers and crew.

The fourth form of private trade was non-Europe (or 'country') trade (*commerce d'Inde en Inde*), which by traditional definition was carried out in regions east of the Cape of Good Hope—that is, in the same regions where the East India company monopolies applied. This geographical limitation was intended to prevent direct competition with the Europe trade carried out by those companies. In actual practice, however, the distinction between Europe and non-Europe trade could be blurry. Depending on the era, this fourth group, whose members were buying and selling on their own account, could include company employees operating with the company's permission, as well as individuals operating independently of an East India company.

1698–1718: Private Sino-French Trade under the First Compagnie

Direct maritime trade between China and western Europe became possible in 1684, when the Kangxi emperor lifted the Qing dynasty's ban on both outbound and incoming seagoing trade.[2] The Canton trade was subsequently open to all nations (except Russia and Japan), and was governed by regulations established by the Chinese authorities.

The French entered the trade fourteen years later with the voyage of the 500-ton *Amphitrite* to Canton in 1698. The Compagnie's trade monopoly applied to the vast region stretching eastward from the Cape of Good Hope around the globe to Cape Horn—that is, from the Indian Ocean and the seas of East Asia across the Pacific Ocean all the way to the straits of Magellan and Lemaire (the latter just southeast of Tierra del Fuego). The monopoly thus extended to all the major seas and oceans except the Atlantic.[3]

For the next two decades after *Amphitrite* set sail on her first voyage to China, Sino-French trading voyages were carried out not by the Compagnie itself, but by

2. Gang Zhao, *The Qing Opening to the Ocean: Chinese Maritime Policies, 1684–1757* (Honolulu: University of Hawai'i Press, 2013), 1. The lifting of the ban followed the Qing conquest of Taiwan in 1683.
3. The royal edict creating the Compagnie specified the extent of the monopoly: 'Déclaration du Roi portant établissement d'une Compagnie pour le commerce des Indes orientales, 1 Sept 1664': Article 27 'La dite Compagnie pourra naviguer et négocier seule, à l'exclusion de tous nos autres sujets, depuis le Cap de Bonne Espérance, jusque dans toutes les Indes et mers orientales, même depuis le détroit de Magellan et Lemaire, dans toutes les mers du Sud pour le temps de cinquante années consécutives, à commencer du jour que les premiers vaisseaux sortiront du Royaume, pendant lequel temps il est fait très expresses défenses à toutes personnes de faire la dite navigation et commerce à peine contre les contrevenants de confiscation de vaisseaux, armes, munitions et marchandises applicables au profit de la dite Compagnie'. France and Dernis, *Recueil ou collection des titres, édits, déclarations, arrêts, règlemens et autres pièces concernant la Compagnie des Indes orientales établie au mois d'août 1664: Précédé d'un Avertissement historique . . . par le sieur Dernis* (Paris: Impr. Boudet, 1755), 1: 60, http://gallica.bnf.fr/ark:/12148/bpt6k1102726?rk=85837;2 (accessed 15 February 2017).

private traders with whom the Compagnie signed limited agreements, thereby leasing its monopoly. There already existed a precedent for a similar practice in French trade in the Indian Ocean. In an effort to ease the financial burden on the Compagnie, in 1681 the Compagnie's mastermind, Jean-Baptiste Colbert, announced the decision to allow private merchants to engage in the East India trade, paying to use Compagnie ships to transport their private-trade goods. The new policy was made official by a judgment dated 6 January 1682, and the Compagnie was given the right to terminate it in five years.[4] Two private merchants, Robert Pocquelin and Vitry-la-Ville, were the first to take advantage of the new arrangement, sending goods on the two Compagnie vessels *Heureuse* and *Royale* to Surat in the spring of 1682 and paying freight and other fees. When the return cargoes were sold after the ships returned to France, they realized a 300 per cent profit.[5]

For the China voyages, the agreements signed by private merchants with the Compagnie specified the terms of trade, and typically included one or more of the following: the permitted destination (China); the time period during which the voyage must be carried out; the number of voyages allowed; and a provision for payment to the Compagnie of a certain percentage of the proceeds from the sale of the cargo. For example, the 1698 agreement that *Amphitrite*'s Jean Jourdan signed with the Compagnie allowed him to fit out two successive voyages. It also required him to take two Compagnie clerks on each of those voyages, and to give the Compagnie 5 per cent of the profits realized from the sale of the trade goods. The agreement also let Jourdan, upon the return of each of the two vessels to France, make use of the Compagnie port facilities at Port-Louis and of its sales rooms at Nantes.[6]

Carrying out the agreements, however, did not always go smoothly. Voyages could be unprofitable; whereas the first voyage of *Amphitrite*, for example, yielded a 50 per cent dividend to investors, the ship's second voyage (1701–1703) incurred a considerable loss.[7] On other occasions, problems arose when partners found

4. See Paul Kaeppelin and François Martin, *Les origines de l'Inde française. La Compagnie des Indes orientales et François Martin: étude sur l'histoire du commerce et des établissements français dans l'Inde sous Louis XIV, 1664–1719* (Paris: A. Challamel, 1908), 134–37. Pocquelin was also a director of the Compagnie, while Vitry-la-Ville became a director sometime between 1677 and 1684.
5. Jules Sottas, *Une escadre française aux Indes en 1690. Histoire de la Compagnie royale des Indes Orientales, 1664–1719* (Paris: Plon-Nourrit et Cie, 1905), 72; Kaeppelin, *Les origines de l'Inde française*, 139. For a very brief reference in English, see Holden Furber, *Rival Empires of Trade* (Minnesota: University of Minnesota, 1976), 204.
6. For further details pertaining to the terms of the agreements, see Philippe Haudrère, *La Compagnie française des Indes au XVIIIe siècle*, 2 vols. (Paris: Les Indes Savantes, 2005), 27–28, and Marion Veyssière, 'Les voyages français à la Chine: Vaisseaux et équipages, 1720–1793' (Diplôme d'archiviste-paléographe, Ecole nationale des chartes, Paris, 2000), 68–80.
7. On *Amphitrite*'s first voyage to China: E. W. Dahlgren, *Les relations commerciales et maritimes entre la France et les côtes de l'Océan Pacifique (commencement du XVIIIe siècle)* (Paris: H. Champion, 1909), 148, and for the second voyage, see p. 156. The loss amounted to 100,000 écus.

themselves in serious disagreement, as was the case in the 1702 voyages of the *Chancelier* and *Saint-François*. The voyages were sponsored by the Compagnie de la Chine of Paris and the Compagnie de la Chine of Saint-Malo. But while China was the focus for the former, the principal interest of the second, led by the Saint-Malo merchant Noël Danycan, was the Pacific, then known as the 'mer du Sud' (Southern sea).[8] That Danycan established himself in Saint-Malo was not surprising; mariners from that city were instrumental in expanding French knowledge of navigation across the Pacific, and Danycan had founded the Compagnie royale de la mer du Sud (Royal Company of the South Sea) in 1698 to trade along the coasts of Chile and Peru.

Nevertheless, the first Compagnie continued for the duration of its existence to rely on private traders for its China voyages. The last departure from France was that of the *Comte Amelot* in 1715, and the last ship to return to France was that of the *Comte de Toulouse* in 1718.

As in other European East India companies, the French company was subject to restructuring over the course of its history, and the year after the return of the *Comte de Toulouse*, one of the most major reorganizations occurred. By the Edict of Reunion of May 1719, the Compagnie des Indes was subsumed into the Compagnie d'Occident, which was subsequently renamed the Compagnie des Indes and is regarded as the second of the three French East India companies.

1719–1769: Private Sino-French Trade under the Second Compagnie: Privilege and Non-Europe ('Country') Trade

The new second Compagnie began to exercise its China trade monopoly within a year of the 1719 reorganization. In March of 1720 it fitted out the vessels *Maure*, *Prince de Conti*, and *Galatée* and sent them to China.

For the next half century, legitimate Sino-French private trade took the form of privilege trade (*port-permis*) and non-Europe trade. The *port-permis* allowed the officers and crew of Compagnie vessels to purchase a certain quantity of goods in China on their own personal account and have them shipped home to Europe at no extra charge.[9] Although the privilege trade has often been treated as simply a perquisite (or 'perk') of the captain and crew of an East India company ship, it constitutes a form of trade that qualifies as private, although its place in the history of that trade has often been overlooked.

---

8. Dahlgren, *Les relations commerciales et maritimes*, 152–62. For a detailed study of the role of Saint-Malo, see André Lespagnol, *Messieurs de Saint-Malo: une élite négociante au temps de Louis XIV*, 2 vols. (Rennes: Presses Universitaires de Rennes, 1997).
9. These voyages are those of 'Europe' ships; that is, vessels that were fitted out in Europe and that made the round-trip voyage to China and back. They are to be distinguished from 'country' ships, which traded within the region(s) stretching eastward from the Cape of Good Hope.

The amount or volume of privilege goods that an individual was allowed was determined by his rank; the higher the rank, the greater the allowance.[10] In the case of the English and initially the Swedish, the allowance was stated in tonnage, while in the case of the French and later of the Swedes, it was stated in sums of money.[11] As for the Dutch, their regulations specified, in addition to the types and quantities of goods permitted, the exact dimensions of the chests in which private-trade merchandise was to be carried.[12]

The French Regulations of 1733 (*Règlements touchant la marine de la Compagnie des Indes*), which set forth the rules for the Compagnie's shipping operations, listed the amounts in piastres according to rank. The captain, for example, was allowed 3,300 piastres, while an ensign ad honores was permitted 55.[13] The piastres had to be purchased in Europe.[14] This required the individual to have the means to buy them 'up front'—a requirement that often necessitated borrowing. In the case of large loans, the interest rate was high, and rose higher during times of war. The lender would later be reimbursed for the funds advanced and enjoyed a share in the profit.[15] The piastres were carried on board the vessel, and upon the ship's arrival at her destination, were turned over to the director of the Compagnie's *comptoir*, or trading station. At Canton, they were turned over to the *Conseil de direction*, or governing council.[16] The Conseil then used the piastres to purchase the desired trade goods, which were subsequently transported home to France at no charge, along with the cargo purchased on the Compagnie's account.[17]

The goods were sold, as the regulations required, at the Compagnie's annual sales auction in Lorient, along with the cargo purchased on the Compagnie's account.[18] Afterward, the individual received cash for the sale of his goods; payment was usually made some four months after the sale.[19]

10. Livres replaced piastres as the currency quoted in 1739. Haudrère, *La Compagnie française des Indes*, 393. For a comparison with other compagnies, see Louis Dermigny, *La Chine et l'Occident: le commerce à Canton au XVIIIe siècle 1719–1833*, 3 vols. and Album (Paris: S.E.V.P.E.N., 1964), 234.
11. In 1748, the Swedes instituted the practice of 'privilege money'. Christian Koninckx, *The First and Second Charters of the Swedish East India Company (1731–1756): A Contribution to the Maritime, Economic, and Social History of North-Western Europe in Its Relationships with the Far East* (Kortrijk, Belgium: Van Ghemmert, 1980), 327.
12. Jaap R. Bruijn, *Commanders of Dutch East India Ships in the Eighteenth Century* (Woodbridge, Suffolk [England]: Boydell Press, 2011), Chapter 12.
13. *Règlement touchant la Marine de la Compagnie des Indes, arresté en l'assemblée d'Administration du 16 septembre 1733* (Paris: L'Imprimerie royale, 1734), 19.
14. Haudrère, *La Compagnie française des Indes*, 392.
15. Philippe Haudrère, email message to author, 26 January 2017.
16. *Règlement touchant la Marine*, 1734, 20.
17. *Règlement touchant la Marine*, 1734, 21.
18. *Règlement touchant la Marine*, 1734, 21.
19. *Règlement touchant la Marine*, 1734, 21.

It was through the *port-permis* that the real money of a voyage could be made, for wages were relatively low. The Regulations of 1733 set the captain's monthly wage, for example, at 100 livres for the period when he was in port on the Compagnie's account immediately before and after the voyage, and at 200 livres while he was at sea; for a first lieutenant, at 60 livres in port and 120 livres at sea; for a chaplain, at 15 livres in port and 30 at sea.[20]

The *port-permis* system underwent occasional modifications during the 1730s and 1740s, including the amounts allocated.[21] There also existed for officers a second or 'small' (*petit*) *port-permis* of a much lesser amount. A captain's allowance, for example, was 300—not 3,300—piastres.[22] Members of the crew (as opposed to the officers) were entitled to an advance for the purchase of tea in China; the advance was equivalent to approximately two months' wages. Once again, the amount was in proportion to the individual's rank. For a master caulker and a sailmaker, for example, this amounted to 12 piastres each; for a cooper, 8 piastres; for a seaman, 6 piastres; for a soldier, 3 piastres; and for a ship's boy, 2 piastres.[23] The Canton Conseil was charged with handling the purchase of goods, which were subsequently transported to France along with the Compagnie's cargo.[24]

The third form of legitimate French private trade was the non-Europe (or 'country') trade, which like the privilege trade, was a form of private trade that was practiced not just by the French, but by other East India companies as well. Unlike the privilege trade, however, where the goods were carried on a company's Europe ships, the merchandise was transported on non-Europe ships—that is, on vessels that were active only east of the Cape of Good Hope. Furthermore, the goods were prohibited from being traded in Europe, where they would have constituted direct competition with the company. Thus, the non-Europe trade was a type of regional commerce that was carried out at ports in the Indian Ocean and Asia, but not in Europe. In actual practice, however, the distinction between non-Europe and Europe traders, and between non-Europe and Europe vessels, was sometimes a fuzzy one. This issue is not limited to the French; it was characteristic of other European nations having East India companies, too.[25]

20. *Règlement touchant la Marine*, 1734, 16–18.
21. Modification was not unique to the French; the privilege system in other nations also underwent changes.
22. *Règlement touchant la Marine*, 1734, 22–23. Officers of vessels sailing to Pondicherry and Bengal were also granted the same amount. On the elimination of the smaller port-permis, see Haudrère, *La Compagnie française des Indes*, 393.
23. *Règlement touchant la Marine*, 1734, 23–25.
24. *Règlement touchant la Marine*, 1734, 25.
25. A good example of the blurry line between private trade and company business as illustrated by individuals working for the Swedish East India Company may be found in the activities of two Swedish traders, Johan Abraham Grill and Michael Grubb. See the chapter in this volume by Lisa Hellman.

Regional and coastal trade in Asia predated the arrival of the Europeans, and was thus neither new nor European in origin. The French and other Europeans made use of routes that already existed, while also creating new routes of their own.[26] French non-Europe trade in India may have existed, on a very small scale, as early as 1700.[27] Furthermore, two French ships coming from Surat are recorded as arriving at Canton [Whampoa] in 1700.[28] This, however, pre-dates the era of the second Compagnie. French non-Europe ships arrived at Canton every decade of the second Compagnie's existence, from the 1720s through the 1760s, though with the possible exception of the 1740s, there were only one to two arrivals per decade.[29] The majority sailed from Pondicherry, which was the Compagnie's main establishment east of the Cape of Good Hope. A few others arrived from other ports; one came from Isle de France (Mauritius), one from Surat, and one via Siam (Thailand) and Tringano (in Malaysia).[30]

One of the distinctive developments in the French non-Europe trade occurred in the 1720s. Under the second Compagnie, the Compagnie itself was initially responsible for both the Europe and non-Europe trade.[31] In 1722, however, financial pressures led it to open its non-Europe trade to its employees, with several restrictions. The employees were forbidden to use Compagnie vessels to ship their goods, and they were prohibited from trading in ports where the Compagnie had a presence or *comptoir*.[32] Thus Canton, while open to the Compagnie's Europe trade, was at first off-limits to French private traders.

This restriction was subsequently removed, however, and French non-Europe trade to Canton is considered to have begun with the vessel *Saint-Joseph*, which departed Pondicherry for China in 1724.[33] The management of the French

26. Dermigny, *La Chine et l'Occident*, 769.
27. Lakshmi Subramanian, ed., *The French East India Company and the Trade of the Indian Ocean: A Collection of Essays by Indrani Ray* (Calcutta: Centre for Studies in Social Sciences, 1999), 94–95.
28. Two vessels identified simply as 'French' in British records arrived in China from Surat in August and September 1701, respectively. Susan E. Schopp, 'The French in the Pearl River Delta: A Topical Case Study of Sino-European Exchanges in the Canton Trade, 1698–1840' (PhD diss., University of Macau, 2015), 269; and Paul A. Van Dyke, 'Unpublished ship list'.
29. Manning, *Fortunes à Faire: The French in Asian Trade, 1719–1748* (Aldershot, Hampshire, Great Britain: Variorum, 1996), 236; Schopp, 'The French in the Pearl River Delta', 269; Van Dyke, 'Unpublished Ship List'.
30. Pondicherry (India) and Alfred Martineau, *Correspondance du Conseil supérieur de Pondichéry et de la Compagnie* (1726–1730) (Pondicherry: Société de l'histoire de l'Inde française, 1920), Vol. 1; Dermigny, *La Chine et l'occident*, 780–81; Manning, *Fortunes à Faire*, 236; Alfred Martineau, 'Quatre ans d'histoire de l'Inde française, 1726–1730', *Revue de l'histoire des colonies françaises* (3rd trimester 1919): 5–72; Schopp, *The French in the Pearl River Delta*, 242–64; and Van Dyke, 'Unpublished ship list'.
31. Alfred Martineau, *Dupleix et l'Inde française, 1722–1741* (Paris: Honoré Champion, 1920), 37.
32. Martineau, *Dupleix et l'Inde française*, 37, 43. Employees were required to ship on Moorish (Indian) or Armenian vessels.
33. The 1723–1724 *Saint-François* may have visited Macao, but what happened to her has yet to

establishment at Pondicherry, known as the governing council (*Conseil supérieur*), was responsible for fitting her out.[34] However, in addition to carrying goods on the Compagnie's account, she was allowed to carry goods of private traders as well, as freight.[35] She thus served simultaneously as a Compagnie and a private-trade ship.

This arrangement, however, did not prove profitable to the Compagnie, so in 1728 it discontinued the practice. The Europe vessels subsequently resumed departing from, and returning to, France.[36] Regional trade between Pondicherry and Canton became the domain of private vessels in the non-Europe trade.

Fluidity of a vessel's identity was not limited to the 1720s, however, as the case of the 1771 *Marquis de Narbonne* showed. She was initially fitted out in France for a voyage to Isle de France (Mauritius) as a Europe ship. But after arriving at Isle de France, she was then consigned on a private basis to Canton, thus becoming a non-Europe vessel.[37] At other times, the Europe-to-non-Europe transformation took place in conjunction with overwintering. If a ship failed to depart before the change of the monsoon, she busied herself in regional trade until the monsoon changed again in her favour and the prevailing winds enabled her to make the voyage westward to Europe.

Beginning in the 1760s, the non-Europe trade developed rapidly, and its growth is closely related to the considerable rise of the private Europe trade that occurred in the latter decades of the century.[38] This growth coincides with the increasing importance of trade with China, as can be seen when one identifies which routes were dominant in the non-Europe trade before, and then after, the mid-eighteenth century. In the first half of the 1700s, it was possible to identify three routes of importance in non-Europe trade: (1) routes leading westward from India across the Indian Ocean; (2) routes along the coast of India; and (3) routes heading eastward from India to Southeast Asia and, to a lesser degree, to China.[39] From the 1760s,

---

be determined. Manning found only one recorded arrival at Canton in the years 1723–1727 of a French vessel from Pondicherry: that of the *Saint-Joseph*. Manning, *Fortunes à Faire*, 186.

34. Martineau, 'Quatre ans d'histoire', 29–30; Martineau, *Dupleix et l'Inde française*, 43; Dermigny, *La Chine et l'Occident*, 780; Haudrère, *La Compagnie française des Indes*, 230. Martineau gives the starting date for the Compagnie ships to depart from Pondicherry as 1726, but in fact, the first voyage from Pondicherry, that of the *Saint-Joseph*, departed for Canton in 1724. See Dermigny, *La Chine et l'Occident*, 780; Manning, *Fortunes à Faire*, 186; and Van Dyke, 'Unpublished ship list'.
35. Martineau, *Dupleix et l'Inde française*, 43; and Manning, *Fortunes à Faire*, 82, and 185.
36. Martineau, *Dupleix et l'Inde française*, 43; and Haudrère, *La Compagnie française des Indes*, 230, and 699.
37. Archives Nationales d'Outre-Mer, Aix-en-Provence, France (ANOM): C.1.11, ff 100r–103r; *Bulletin de la Société des archives historiques: Revue de la Saintonge et de l'Aunis* 19, no. 2 (1899): 104; and Dermigny, *La Chine et l'Occident*, 843, and 856. Dermigny notes that this practice was quite legal.
38. Dermigny, *La Chine et l'Occident*, 770.
39. Dermigny, *La Chine et l'Occident*, 781.

however, the route from India to Canton, which had previously been the least significant, became all-important.

1770–1785: The First Period of Wholly Private Sino-French Trade

In 1769, France became the first of the nations having an East India company to suspend its company's trade monopoly and to open its entire East India and China trade to all French subjects.[40] This initial period of fully open trade lasted until a short-lived third Compagnie was created in 1785. During these fifteen years from 1770 to 1785, the management of the French establishment at Canton assumed several different forms to handle this private trade. Under the Compagnie, the comptoir had been managed by a *Conseil de direction*, or governing council, that consisted of a head and four supercargoes; they reported to the Compagnie's directors in Paris and to the Compagnie's shipping director at Lorient. Though not part of the Conseil, the Canton staff also included two clerks (*commis*), two junior clerks (*sous-commis*), and a surgeon (*chirurgien*).

After the Compagnie's loss of its monopoly in 1769, the *conseil* form of management was carried over to a new *Conseil royal*, or royal council, whose creation was ordered by the French monarch, Louis XV. The members of the new Conseil, which consisted of a head and three supercargoes, were one fewer in number than the Compagnie's Conseil and were also paid lower salaries than their predecessors. The persons who composed the new Conseil continued to work as private traders. Their additional staff consisted of three clerks and a surgeon.

The Conseil continued to function until 1776, but was plagued with problems; so in February of that year, the king ordered the creation of a consulate to look after French interests.[41] Consulates were not new; indeed, French consular history dates back to twelfth-century trade with Italy.[42] Furthermore, precedents already existed

40. The trade monopoly was suspended by an act of the Conseil d'Etat (Council of State): 'Arrest du Conseil d'Etat du Roi, Concernant le Commerce de l'Inde, Du 13 Août 1769', *Recueil de pièces utiles pour l'instruction de l'affaire de la Compagnie des Indes*. Place of publication not identified: n.p., n.d., http://gallica.bnf.fr/ark:/12148/bpt6k1042673v?rk=21459;2 (accessed 15 February 2017). The second half of the eighteenth century witnessed increasing challenges to the legitimacy of the various East India companies.

41. See Centre des Archives diplomatiques de La Courneuve, formerly known as the Archives des Affaires Etrangères (AAE), La Courneuve, France: 15MD Chine 16, f°11r-18v. See also Henri Cordier, 'Le Consulat de France à Canton au XVIIIe siècle', *T'oung Pao* 9 (1908): 50. 'C'est pour suivre le même plan que l'on propose à Sa Majesté d'ériger aussi en Consulat le Conseil de Direction que la Compagnie des Indes entretenoit ci-devant à Canton, et de composer ce Consulat d'un Consul et d'un Chancelier pour rendre la justice à ses sujets, et maintenir la paix et la bonne harmonie entre eux et les sujets des autres puissances de l'Europe qui y font le commerce conformément au projet d'ordonnance cy joint'.

42. Anne Mézin, *Les consuls de France au siècle des Lumières (1715–1792)* (Paris: Ministère des Affaires étrangères, Direction des archives et de la documentation, 1998), 3.

in the form of French consulates in the Levant. An even closer model existed in the French consulate at Surat, north of Bombay.

On 20 October 1776, Pierre-Charles-François Vauquelin, a 24-year veteran of the Compagnie, was appointed consul; he arrived in China in the autumn of the following year. In addition to the consul, the staff was to include a vice-consul, a chancellor, and an interpreter, though at any given time, one or two of these offices might not be filled. The consulate continued to exist until 1785, when it was rendered redundant by the creation of the third and last French East India Company.

Meanwhile, in 1779, French trade at Canton was interrupted by France's support of the thirteen North American colonies in their fight for independence from Britain; there were no voyages to China during the years 1779–1782. Trade resumed in 1783 when the French monarch, Louis XVI, was informed that the supply of goods from India and China to the ports of his kingdom was insufficient to meet both the domestic and foreign demand. He authorized a trading expedition under the prominent Saint-Malo merchant Pierre-Jacques Grandclos-Meslé.[43] Four ships, supplied by the French navy, departed in the spring of 1783, arriving at Whampoa in late August and early October that same year. An additional four vessels, acting independently and not part of the authorized expedition, also arrived at Whampoa to trade in early September, early October, and mid-November.[44]

Table 3.1 shows the number of French vessels calling at Canton in the first period of wholly private trade (1770–1785). France's commercial activity, including that in the Canton Trade, was disrupted during periods of warfare. This is evidenced in the absence of voyages from 1779 to 1782, when France was supporting the patriot cause in the American Revolution.

Profiles of French Private Traders at Canton, 1770–1785

The French private traders at Canton, like their predecessors in the Compagnie's employ, constituted a small, privileged elite. The majority came from Brittany, primarily from Nantes, Saint-Malo, and Lorient, or the surrounding areas.[45] A number of them, such as Mr. Thimothée or Pierre-Charles-François Vauquelin, had previous experience as employees of the Compagnie des Indes; they had already worked as merchants or clerks or served as supercargoes, usually in China, but occasionally in other Compagnie locations as well. Thimothée already had some twenty years'

43. Centre des Archives diplomatiques de La Courneuve, France: 8MD Asie 17, ff°132r–133r, Arrêt du Conseil d'Etat du Roi, concernant le commerce de la Chine, du 2 février 1783 (1). Also reproduced in Henri Cordier, *La France en Chine au dix-huitième siècle: documents inédits publiés sur les manuscrits conservés au dépôt des affaires étrangères, avec une introduction et des notes* (Paris: E. Leroux, 1883): 167–69.
44. Dermigny, *La Chine et l'Occident*, 1021–22.
45. These characteristics often apply to non-Canton French traders, whether private or not, and to employees of the Compagnie. See Haudrère, *La Compagnie française des Indes*, 543, for further detail, including a breakdown that includes non-Canton traders.

Table 3.1 Number of French Private Vessels Calling in China by Year, 1770–1785

Year*	Ships	Year	Ships	Year	Ships	Year	Ships
1770	2	1774	7	1778	4	1782	0
1771	3	1775	3	1779	0	1783	8
1772	3	1776	5	1780	0	1784	4
1773	6	1777	7	1781	0	1785	1

* The year shown is the year of arrival at Whampoa.

Sources: British Library (BL): IOR G/12 China Factory Records; SHDL (Service historique de la Défense, Lorient) http://www.memoiredeshommes.sga.defense.gouv.fr: *Présence française dans le monde: Compagnie des Indes, Armements des navires* (accessed 2013–2016); Dermigny 1964; Van Dyke, 'Unpublished ship list'; Veyssière 2000. In addition to the vessels noted above, in 1775, a fourth vessel, the warship *Etoile*, loaded an export cargo at Whampoa. BL: IOR G/12/58, 1775.09.06, pp. 71–72.

experience in the China trade by 1770. Vauquelin, who first came to China in 1749, had also served as a Compagnie administrator of the Isle Bourbon (Réunion) in the Mascarenes.[46]

The French Canton traders typically had a relative, usually a father or uncle, who had ties to the Compagnie or to a related sector. Among those with relatives having ties to the Compagnie was Paul-François Costar, who was the son of a former secretary-general of the Compagnie.[47] The younger Costar became an assistant to Thimothée in 1771 when the latter was promoted to head of the new royal Conseil; Costar was later appointed chancellor of the consulate after the 1782 resignation of Jean-Charles-François Galbert. Private trader Charles-Henri de Vigny was related to former supercargo Joseph-Julien Duvelaër. Duvelaër had started his career with the Compagnie in Pondicherry in the mid-1720s, and then moved to Canton, where he subsequently spent almost three decades.[48] His brother, Pierre, also served the Compagnie in India and then China. The experience of the relatives was often, though not necessarily, in China. François Terrien, for example, arrived in Canton in 1774 and had an uncle who was a coffee-plantation owner in Saint-Domingue.[49]

Other private traders had relatives in sectors such as shipping or banking. The brothers Gilles and Hipolyte Sebire offer a prime example. As sons of Saint-Malo merchant Dominique-François Sebire, they were also nephews of Guy Jean Dessaudrais Sebire, one of Saint-Malo's most important merchants and shipowners.

46. Service historique de la Défense, Lorient (SHDL): 2P 34–I.11.
47. ANOM: C.1.13, f°144; also cited in Dermigny, *La Chine et l'Occident*, 867n1.
48. ANOM: C.1.10, ff°9r–12v, and 28; Martineau, 'Quatre ans d'histoire', 29, and 31; and Haudrère, *La Compagnie française des Indes*, 550.
49. Hervé du Halgouët, 'Pages coloniales. Relations maritimes de la Bretagne et de la Chine au XVIIIe siècle. Lettres de Canton.' *Mémoires de la Société d'histoire et d'archéologie de Bretagne* 15 (1934): 331–441. See 385–86.

The latter, with his business partner Le Breton du Blessin, fitted out eight vessels that departed France for Canton between 1771 and 1776.[50]

Blood relatives were not the only type of tie that characterized French Canton traders; another was marriage into families with a history of Compagnie employment or activity in related sectors. For example, François Rothe's second wife, Jeanne Hay, was the sister of Canton trader Joseph-Marie Hay and of Compagnie ship officer Michel Hay.[51]

A smaller number of traders shared the distinction of belonging to families with Irish Jacobite ties. As Jacobites, the families had supported the cause of James II of England and VII of Scotland, whose support of Roman Catholicism led to his deposition by William of Orange in 1688. At the time, the French monarch was James's cousin, Louis XIV, and a number of the Jacobites sought refuge in France, both then and during subsequent waves of persecution. Examples of traders in this group include François Rothe, his brother Edmond, and the Hays.

The following biographical sketches introduce seven of the individuals who took a major part in Sino-French private trade during the period 1770–1785. The sketches are intended to illustrate the range of experience and backgrounds that private traders brought to Canton, and are presented in alphabetical order by the trader's surname: Julien Bourgogne, Charles de Constant, François and Edmond Rothe, Gilles Sebire, François Terrien, and Mr. Thimothée.

Julien Bourgogne arrived in China in the 1770s.[52] Bourgogne was a native of Lorient and had connections to the Montigny family, who were also of Lorient, and to whom he was related by blood. The Montignys had a strong presence in the Canton trade, especially in the latter half of the 1700s. François-René de Montigny du Timeur arrived in China in 1745 and remained for over three decades; his younger brother, Montigny de Montplaisir, was there from 1752 to 1783.[53] Montigny

50. Additional partners joined Dessaudrais Sebire and Le Breton du Blessin for the two voyages in 1776 and 1777. Paul Paris-Jallobert, *Anciens registres paroissiaux de Bretagne: Saint-Malo*, Fasc. 7, Vol. 8 (Rennes: Plihon et Hommay, 1901), 382; Dermigny, *La Chine et l'Occident*, 848–50, 863; and Veyssière, 'Les voyages français à la Chine', 104.
51. ANOM: C.1.12, f°37r.
52. Charles-Samuel de Constant and Louis Dermigny, *Les mémoires de Charles de Constant sur le commerce à la Chine* (Paris: S.E.V.P.E.N., 1964), 48n5, and Marie-Sybille de Vienne, *La Chine au déclin des Lumières: l'expérience de Charles de Constant, négociant des loges de Canton* (Paris: H. Champion, 2004), 48n55. Both Dermigny and Vienne believe Bourgogne to have arrived around 1772, while Paul A. Van Dyke stated in email correspondence with the author on 26 January 2017 that the earliest references he found in the British and Dutch records to Bourgogne's presence in China and/or Macao were early 1777. From that year to 1792, Bourgogne appears numerous times in those records. Van Dyke also found that Bourgogne was not mentioned in any of the lists of foreigners in China before 1776. The omission of his name from these lists, which were assembled by the Dutch each year at the end of the season, suggests that Bourgogne may have arrived in China with the ships in late 1776 or 1777.
53. Montigny du Timeur arrived in China on the 1745–1746 *Philibert*; see SHDL: 2P–II.12. See also SHDL: 1P 305 L. 70, f° 95, as well as Dermigny, *La Chine et l'Occident*, 868. Regarding Montigny de Montplaisir, the younger brother, the dates of his employment in China are

du Timeur also had private-trade interests in both the Ile de France (Mauritius) and the Ile Bourbon (Réunion).[54]

Bourgogne served as an agent for some of the most important figures in the merchant and shipping communities in Lorient. (This type of agent is not to be confused with the *agent royal*, or royal agent, that was later appointed in 1786; see below). Among the individuals who entrusted Bourgogne to handle large sums of money for the purchase of trade goods at Canton were François Rothe (below) and Foucaud, two major fitters-out of ships employed in the French Canton trade. Both men had been clients of Montigny du Timeur, who together with Charles-Henri Vigny, owned a trading firm in Canton and served as agents for most of the major shipowners and merchants in Lorient and Saint-Malo, including Dessaudrais Sebire, Beaugeard, François Rothe, and Foucaud.[55] In 1777, Montigny returned to France to live. He ultimately left his share of the management of the trading company to Bourgogne, who inherited his clients in France and thus became their agent.[56]

In addition to his activities as agent, Bourgogne was among those who lent money to Hong merchants in Canton; his name appears on the list that Philippe Vieillard, who was then the French consul, drew up in 1785 of individuals who had lent money to Canton Hong merchants.[57] Bourgogne's activities extended beyond the French community, as his dealings with the Imperial Company in 1783 show. The Imperial Company, or *Société impériale asiatique de Trieste et Anvers*, was founded in 1775 by William Bolts and Charles de Proli. Though nominally Austrian, it served as a cover for a multitude of private traders (in this case, interlopers) who represented a range of nationalities, especially British. It is not to be confused with the earlier Ostend Company (1722–1732), although the two are related. The multilingual Bolts was a former employee of the English East India Company in India, and worked for the Company for about a decade (1759–1768) before resigning and then being expelled; he subsequently became a private trader.[58] Proli was a banker from Antwerp; his father, who was also a banker, had been one of the backers of the Ostend Company. The short-lived Imperial Company (1775–1785) sent eight vessels to Canton in the years from 1779 to 1785. One of them was the *Prince de Kaunitz*, which was formerly the French merchantman *Superbe*; the *Superbe* had made a trading voyage to Canton in 1774.[59]

---

given as 1752–1783 in Haudrère, *La Compagnie française des Indes*, 550n80. See also SHDL: 1P 305 L.70, f°95. Montigny de Montplaisir subsequently worked for the third Compagnie des Indes in the late 1780s; see Dermigny, *La Chine et l'Occident*, 868n4.

54. ANOM: C.1.11, f 67.
55. For further detail, see Dermigny, *La Chine et l'Occident*, 871.
56. Dermigny, *La Chine et l'Occident*, 874.
57. ANOM: C.1.15, ff 69–70; and Dermigny, *La Chine et l'Occident*, 899.
58. N. L. Hallward, *William Bolts: A Dutch Adventurer Under John Company* (Cambridge [England]: Cambridge University Press, 1920), 4, 67, and 93.
59. There were two vessels bearing the name *Prince de Kaunitz*; this is the larger of the two, rated at 1200 or 1300 tons. Dermigny gives the figure of 1200 tons for the larger *Kaunitz*, and 500

The *Prince de Kaunitz* arrived at Canton in 1779 with a handful of inexperienced individuals, including the adolescent Charles de Constant, to carry out trade; they turned to Julien Bourgogne for assistance.[60] In 1780, Bourgogne joined forces with a Scot, John Reid, to form a private-trading business in Canton.[61] Reid was the younger brother of Andrew Reid, who had served as supercargo on a previous voyage of the *Prince de Kaunitz*.

Charles de Constant was born in Geneva; his family members were French Huguenots who had fled France for the Netherlands and Switzerland, respectively, in the sixteenth century. His entry into the China trade came through an uncle who worked for the Imperial Company. The uncle obtained an appointment as an apprentice for the young Charles, who arrived in Canton for the first time in 1779 and spent most of the next thirteen years there. During his first two periods of residence (1779–1782 and 1783–1786), he was associated with the Imperial Company, and in the third (1789–1793), with the French.

In the latter post, he was the last of the French company's employees to serve at Canton in that company's long history. His voyages to and from China reflect the multinational nature of his experience, for as has already been noted, he arrived in Canton for his first stay in China on the Imperial Company's ship *Prince de Kaunitz*. Then in 1786, at the end of his second period of residence in China, he sailed on the English East India Company ship *Atlas* to return to Europe. In 1789, he returned to China on the French ship *Dauphin*, and returned home for the final time on the *Etrusco*, which was initially registered under the Tuscan flag.

Lively, sociable, and quick with a pen, de Constant recorded his observations of people, places, cultures, and customs, as well as of trade goods and business practices. In the latter, his experience working for the Imperial company as well as for the French gave him a wider knowledge than employment in just one company would have allowed.

Although the commercial guide to Canton that he envisaged writing was never realized, his correspondence to family and friends, and as well as his notes and observations on business, contain a wealth of information that sheds light on life in the Canton hongs and on trade between China and western Europe during most of the years between 1779 and 1793. His descriptions of his colleagues are valuable, despite—or perhaps because of—their subjective nature, as few such personal details exist elsewhere.[62] Regarding Julien Bourgogne, for example, whom he considered a

---

tons for the smaller one, while Veyssière notes 1300 tons for the *Superbe*. Dermigny, *La Chine et l'Occident*, 965 and 967; and Veyssière, 'Les voyages français à la Chine', 274.

60. De Constant and Dermigny, *Les mémoires de Charles de Constant*, 1964: 342.
61. Dermigny, *La Chine et l'Occident*, 968.
62. Two other sources of comments on individual traders are the personal correspondence of François Terrien (Archives départementales de Loire-Atlantique, Nantes: E 1245) and of Pierre-Louis-Achille de Robien (Archives départementales des Yvelines, Montigny-le-Bretonneux: E 3056).

good friend, he notes that he was very helpful and was well regarded by the other Europeans in Canton, but that he had the tiring ability to talk without saying anything. He also noted that Bourgogne consumed large quantities of tobacco that took a long time to prepare.[63] The correspondence also reveals transformations over time in de Constant's attitude toward China. The hope and sense of adventure and discovery that shine through his early letters gradually gave way to disappointment, criticism, and resentment of China and her people.

François Rothe provides a notable example of a trader who rose from an entry-level position with the Compagnie to its highest ranks, and who subsequently made a successful transition to private trade in the period from 1770 to 1785. His life illustrates how a trader could capitalize on his earlier experience with the Compagnie and on his connections to the shipping and banking sectors.

Born in Wexford, Ireland, around 1700, Rothe arrived in France by 1730, having fled Ireland as a Jacobite. His family belonged to a branch of one of the most eminent in the Irish aristocracy.[64] He entered the service of the Compagnie des Indes in 1730, starting out as a clerk and soon rising in rank. In 1735 he became a principal merchant at Canton, a post he retained until 1739. In that year, he sailed home on the Compagnie ship *Penthièvre*,[65] and then in November married Catherine MacHugh.[66] He returned to Canton on the 1741 *Duc de Chartres* as a supercargo.[67] From 1741 to 1754, he was a first supercargo, and served as the head of the Canton Conseil.[68] He had ties to the Indian Ocean private trade network as well; his 1753 voyage to Pondicherry was only one of a number of intra-Asian voyages that he made.[69]

After returning to France to live in 1754, he became a *directeur surnuméraire* in charge of the Compagnie's sales at Lorient.[70] In 1758, he remarried; his new wife was Jeanne Anne Hay, the sister of the Canton traders Michel and Joseph Hay.[71] Two years later, in 1760, he was named director of the Port of Lorient, and served in that capacity until 1764. When the Compagnie lost its trade monopoly in 1769,

63. De Constant and Dermigny, *Les mémoires de Charles de Constant*, 48.
64. Patrick Clarke de Dromantin, *Les réfugiés jacobites dans la France du XVIIIe siècle: L'exode de toute une noblesse "pour cause de religion"* (Pessac: Presses universitaires de Bordeaux, 2005), 446.
65. SHDL: 2P 28–I.13.
66. The marriage ended with her passing ten years later, in 1749. Thierry Claeys and Yves Durand, *Dictionnaire biographique des financiers en France au XVIIIe siècle* (Paris: Editions SPM, 2009), 2: 913–15.
67. SHDL: 2P 29–II.20.
68. ANOM: E 358.
69. ANOM: C.1.10, f°81r.
70. ANOM: E 358.
71. Claeys and Durand, *Dictionnaire biographique*, 2: 921; Dermigny, *La Chine et l'Occident*, 361; and Haudrère, *La Compagnie française des Indes*, 136. Dermigny, *La Chine et l'Occident*, 361n10 asks whether the captain of the *Gloire* was part of the Hay family; ANOM: E 358 provides an affirmative reply.

he quickly became active in the private sector, fitting out the ships *Dauphin* in 1773, *Superbe* in 1774, and the *Sévère* in 1775.[72]

Rothe's younger brother, *Edmond Rothe*, arrived in France in 1730 and spent ten years in Paris as well as several months in Spain conducting business.[73] In 1743 he sailed to Canton, where he remained until 1758.[74] He served as supercargo on the 1770 *Pondichéry*, which was fitted out by his brother, François. Like his brother, he obtained French nationality. He died in 1772.[75]

Gilles Sebire was a member of a well-connected family of merchants from Saint-Malo. The second of seven sons of merchant Dominique-François Sebire, he had two brothers, Hipolyte and Jean-Baptiste, who were also traders at Canton.[76] Their uncle, Guy-Jean Dessaudrais Sebire, was one of Saint-Malo's most prominent merchants, and between 1771 and 1776 fitted out eight vessels for Canton with his business partner Alain Le Breton de Blessin.[77]

Despite his connections, Gilles Sebire was not spared the consequences of changes in alliances between merchants and traders acting as their agents. In 1777, as was noted in connection with Julien Bourgogne (above), the merchant Montigny returned to France from Canton.[78] Montigny had previously assigned his share of the profits of the cargo of the two ships *Duc de Fitz-James* and *Pondichéry* to the six clerks in the Canton comptoir; among them were Sebire and François Terrien. When Montigny suddenly changed his mind and assigned his share to one of his relatives, Bourgogne, Gilles Sebire, and the other clerks found themselves written out of the agreement—and thus the profits—altogether.

Efforts to recover their shares proved unsuccessful. Sebire returned to France later that same year. At the time of his departure, he was one of three French nationals living in the French hong.[79]

He returned to China in 1783, making the outbound voyage from France on the Imperial Company's ship *Comte Zinzendorf*.[80] Traveling on the same vessel was Charles de Constant, who was Gilles's junior by a little more than a decade.[81] During

72. Rothe fitted out the *Superbe* and the *Sévère* with partners René Foucaud and Pierre Bernier.
73. Claeys and Durand, *Dictionnaire biographique*, 2: 914.
74. Claeys and Durand, *Dictionnaire biographique*, 2: 914; and GeneaNet, Promethée: 'Dans ses lettres de naturalisation (A.N. P. 2595 ff°123–25), il dit être arrivé en France en 1730, avoir vécu à Paris 1730–40, avoir fait du commerce en Espagne, avoir embarqué en 1743 avec son frère François directeur de la Compagnie des Indes pour faire le commerce en Chine 1743–58. De retour en France fin 1758'. http://gw.geneanet.org/pierfit?lang=fr&p=edmond&n=de+rothe (accessed 15 January 2017).
75. http://gw.geneanet.org/pierfit?lang=fr&p=edmond&n=de+rothe (accessed 15 January 2017).
76. Paris-Jallobert, *Anciens registres paroissiaux*, 382.
77. They were joined by additional partners in fitting out the last two vessels. See Alain Romain, *Saint-Malo au temps des négriers* (Paris: Karthala, 2001), 210.
78. Dermigny, *La Chine et l'Occident*, 873.
79. Cordier, 'Le Consulat de France', 58.
80. Vienne, *La Chine au déclin des Lumières*, 56.
81. Vienne, *La Chine au déclin des Lumières*, 56; de Constant and Dermigny, *Les mémoires de*

the voyage, the more experienced Gilles readily tutored the younger man in mathematics, geography, and accounting, knowledge that the latter would need in the trade at Canton.[82] In 1785, just two years later, the then-acting French consul in Canton, Philippe Vieillard, proposed Sebire as his deputy, but the position went instead to Paul-François Costar.[83]

François Terrien offers an example of a young neophyte in the private trade. He arrived in Canton for the first time at the age of 21 in late 1774, with no prior experience working for the Compagnie des Indes. Unlike Gilles Sebire, who was only two years his senior and who came to Canton the same year, Terrien lacked Sebire's strong personal connections, although he did have a relative who was active in French trade in the Caribbean.[84] A number of Terrien's letters home to his cousin Augustin Dubréseuil, who was his confidant, have survived, and they reveal a young man plagued with homesickness and preoccupied with the difficulties of making a fortune. His chief pleasure in Canton was reading the books that his cousin sent him from France.

To make the fortune that lured both private and company traders to China, a trader needed funds, whether his own or borrowed from others, in order to purchase goods. Family and close friends were one source; members of the business community and shipping sector were another. Terrien had arrived in Canton with 2,510 *livres* in silver and goods, and quickly began to worry that the sum would not last him to the end of the year (1775) for living expenses, much less to build the basis of a fortune.[85] He was not alone in writing home and asking for money to invest; the need for funds, coupled with specific requests for money, were a recurring theme in personal correspondence. In 1768, for example, Compagnie trader Pierre-Louis-Achille de Robien commented in a letter to his brother, 'Who here [in Canton] has this amount of his own? Very few. Almost everyone works with money other than their own and makes only a 5% profit. One must have a considerable amount of money for this modest sum to produce significant wealth'.[86] In December 1789, Charles de Constant wrote home, 'I wish that you could get me some money', and then went on to explain how to go about sending it to him.[87]

Charles de Constant, 109.
82. Vienne, *La Chine au déclin des Lumières*, 56.
83. Cordier, 'Le Consulat de France', 65.
84. Du Halgouët, 'Pages coloniales', 386.
85. Archives départementales de Loire-Atlantique: E 1245. Letter dated Canton, 1 January 1775. 'J'ai apporté avec moi 2.510 livres en argent et en effets et je ne sais pas si cela me suffira pour me défrayer jusqu'à la fin de 1775'.
86. Archives départementales des Yvelines: E 3056. Letter dated Canton, 6 January 1768. 'Quel est celuy qui a icy cette somme en propre? Très peu de personnes. Presque tous travaillent sur d'autres fonds que les leurs et ne retirent sur les dits fonds que 5 p%. Il faut avoir de bien gros fonds à faire valoir pour que ce modique somme puisse vous faire un capital considérable'.
87. De Constant and Dermigny, *Les mémoires de Charles de Constant*, 77. Dated 6 December 1789. 'Je désire bien que vous ayés réussi à me procurer quelque argent'.

As Terrien discovered, in addition to funds, a trader needed supporters, who were often major shipowners or fitters-out or merchants from Lorient or Saint-Malo. The more important the backer, the more lucrative the opportunities a trader was likely to have after arriving in Canton, while young men arriving with lesser backing scrambled to find additional funds to invest. Terrien explained in a letter to his cousin shortly after he arrived in Canton:

> The supercargoes are obligated in some way to receive the young men whom the ship-owners send them. Now you know that a nephew of Mr. Dessaudrais Sebire arrived last year. Mr. de Vigny brought with him a young man who had been mentioned to him before he knew that I was persisting with my plan to go to China. Mr. de Robien, whose home I wouldn't enter for all the gold in the world, has two young people, one of whom is a protégé of Mr. Rothe, and the other was left to him by Mr. Dumont [a former Canton supercargo].[88]

Following a pattern that was common among both Compagnie employees and private traders, Terrien spent more than one period of residence in China. He made a trip home to France in the late 1770s, then in 1783 returned to Canton, where he remained after the creation of the third Compagnie des Indes in 1785. But unlike most of his compatriots, he never returned home to France to live. In 1787, he committed suicide in Canton. Charles de Constant attributed his death to the miseries that Terrien suffered as a result of the temporary bouts of insanity and the accompanying unreasonable behaviour of Mr. Desmoulins, who at the time was the head of the French *comptoir* at Canton.[89]

Mr. *Thimothée* served in Canton under both the second Compagnie and as a private trader.[90] His brother served for 25 years as head of the Compagnie's archives in France, while his nephew came to Canton in 1768 as an *enfant de langue* to learn Chinese.[91] At the time of the suspension of the Compagnie's monopoly in 1769, Thimothée was a member of the Canton *Conseil de direction* (governing Council). He was the only member of that Conseil to stay on and to become a member of the new *Conseil royal*, and became head of the latter in 1772.[92]

His years with the Compagnie seem to have been relatively uneventful. This changed, however, in the early 1770s, when the Conseil found itself plagued with

---

88. Archives départementales de Loire-Atlantique: E 1245. Letter dated Canton, 1 January 1775. 'Les supercargues sont obligés en quelque façon de recevoir les jeunes gens que les armateurs leur envoyent: or, vous saurez que l'année passée il vint un neveu de M. Dessaudrais Sebire. M. de Vigny avait amené avec lui un jeune homme dont on lui avait parlé, avant qu'il sut que je persistais dans le projet de passer en Chine. M. de Robien, chez qui je n'eusse pas entré pour tout l'or du monde, a deux jeunes gens dont l'un est protégé de M. Rothe et l'autre lui a été laissé par M. Dumont. Voilà déjà quatre jeunes gens fort au fait'. The nephew was Gilles Sebire.
89. Vienne, *La Chine au déclin des Lumières*, 275.
90. His surname appears in the French documents with variant spellings ('Thimothée' and 'Thimotée').
91. ANOM C.1.11, f°47r; C.1.13, f°4r, and ff°40r–41r.
92. ANOM: C.1.11, ff° 87v–89r.

dissension, which arose largely from jealousy on the part of one of its members, de Robien.[93] In November of 1774, Thimothée resigned, and left Canton the following January to return to France.

Two years later, when the Canton consulate was created in 1776, Thimothée was appointed consul. But he turned down the position, citing among his reasons the low remuneration, and noting that he knew from experience that he would need to draw from his own fortune to fully cover the necessary expenses.[94] In 1769, the last year that the Compagnie des Indes was still in possession of its trade monopoly, the salary of the head of the Compagnie's Canton Conseil was 12,000 livres.[95] Since then, however, salaries had gone steadily downward, and the amount now being offered the consul was just half of what it had been in 1769: namely, 6,000 livres.[96] It was, nevertheless, slightly higher than the 4,000 livres that the head of the royal Conseil had been offered in 1771.[97]

So in 1776, Thimothée declined the appointment of consul. The position was subsequently filled by Pierre-Charles-François Vauquelin, who served until his death in 1782. The post once again became vacant, and Thimothée applied for it. But his application was unsuccessful, and his career in the China trade was effectively over.[98]

Post-1785: The End of the Compagnie and the Return to Private Trade

In 1785, to the dismay of the private sector, a new Compagnie des Indes was created. But the new company was short-lived. In April 1790, an act of the Assemblée nationale (French National Assembly) stripped it of its trade monopoly, and three years later, in 1793, the Compagnie itself was abolished.

Meanwhile, in 1786, the year following the creation of the third Compagnie, the king ordered that an *agent royal*, or royal agent, be posted at Canton, along with an interpreter. The royal agent is not to be confused with the Canton-based commercial agents (such as Julien Bourgogne and others) of the period from 1770 to 1785, who acted on behalf of merchants and shipowners in France. The function of the royal agent was to 'be limited to informing me [the French monarch] of what goes on in China in political affairs and in commercial matters, and to carry out the orders that will be given to him'.[99] The agent was completely separate from the Compagnie.

---

93. ANOM: C.1.12, ff°87r–91r, and 111r–149r.
94. Centre des Archives diplomatiques de La Courneuve: 8MD Asie 16, f°83; and f°186.
95. Dermigny, *La Chine et l'Occident*, 866.
96. Dermigny, *La Chine et l'Occident*, 867n5. See also Cordier, 'Le Consulat de France', 55.
97. ANOM: C.1.11, f°110v.
98. In the end, no consul was appointed; instead, Philippe Vieillard was named vice-consul. Cordier, 'Le Consulat de France', 59.
99. The king's instructions concerning the agent were as follows: 'Son service se bornera à me rendre compte de ce qui se passera en Chine tant pour les affaires politiques que pour celles

The abolition of the third Compagnie in 1793 marked the end of trade under a French East India Company. Subsequent French trade with China once again became, and this time remained, private. The return to private trade was delayed, however, by domestic events in France and the Napoleonic wars. With the exception of three non-Europe vessels that called at Canton in 1802–1803, Sino-French trade was halted for the next two-and-a-half decades (1793–1818).[100]

Trade resumed in 1818 with the voyage of *Fils de France*, an 810-ton ship that was owned by the merchant Thomas Dobrée of Nantes.[101] There then followed a period of seven years (1819–1825) with no voyages. In 1826, however, the *Fils de France* came once again to Canton. Her arrival, along with that of a second vessel the same year, was soon followed by additional voyages. Between 1826 and the end of the Canton Trade period in 1842, fifty French merchant vessels called in China.[102] The number of arrivals per year ranged from one in 1831, 1832, and 1834 to as many as eight in 1833, and included at least one ship—the *Héros* from Le Havre—that circumnavigated the globe.[103]

Conclusion

Private trade played a legitimate and important role in the French Canton trade at the very start, when merchants in the private sector were responsible for French commercial voyages to China. During the years of the second Compagnie des Indes (French East India Company), when the Compagnie ceased leasing its China-trade monopoly and took over the responsibility for voyages to Canton, private trade was practiced in the form of privilege (*port-permis*) and non-Europe ('country') trade. The period of wholly private trade that followed the suspension of the second Compagnie's monopoly in 1769 marked the first time that a nation possessing an East India company suspended that company's monopoly and opened trade in China and elsewhere to the private sector. The large number of merchant voyages from France to Canton during this fifteen-year period (1770–1785) shows that private

du commerce, et à exécuter les orders qui lui seront addressés.' Quoted in Henri Cordier, 'La mission de M. le chevalier d'Entrecasteaux à Canton en 1787: d'après les archives du Ministère des Affaires étrangères'. In *Bulletin de géographie historique et descriptive* (Paris: Imprimerie nationale, 1911), 3: 411–12.

100. The three vessels were *Diana, Saint-Jacques*, and *Paix*.
101. Archives municipales de Nantes: 8Z 403–11, 502, and 508.
102. BL: IOR G/12/241, G/12/245, G/12/247, G/12/251, and G/12/254; *The Canton Register* 1836.02.16, 1836.08.09, 1836.09.27, 1836.10.25, 1836.12.13, 1837.09.05, 1837.09.19, 1837.10.03, 1837.10.17, 1837.10.31, 1837.11.14, 1837.11.21, 1837.12.05, 1838.10.30, 1838.11.20, 1839.01.29, 1839.02.12, 1839.04.16, 1839.07.02, 1839.10.22, 1840.06.09, 1840.09.22, 1840.11.03, 1840.12.08, 1841.02.16, 1841.03.23, 1841.10.12, 1841.12.14, 1841.12.28, 1842.01.04, 1842.02.22, 1842.07.12, and 1842.11.29. In addition to the 50 merchantmen, there were three arrivals of French frigates between 1838 and 1842.
103. Edmond Le Netrel, *Voyage of the Héros: Around the World with Duhaut-Cilly in the Years 1826, 1827, 1828 & 1829*, trans. Blanche Collet Wagner (Los Angeles: Glen Dawson, 1951).

traders were capable of taking advantage of the new opportunities offered. In the number of vessels sent to China, they rivalled, or even surpassed, the Compagnie's record for years when France was not at war. Although a third Compagnie was created in 1785, its abolition eight years later (1793) marked the end of the era of the company model. Private trade, and the individuals who conducted it, proved to play a significant role as a catalyst in the changes of attitudes toward, and conditions of, trade—an evolution of thought and of trading patterns that was a major factor in the demise of the East India companies, not only in France but in other European nations as well.

Where the Chinese government was concerned, it was unimportant whether the French nationals came as representatives of the Compagnie or as individuals seeking a fortune of their own. Provided that they were engaged in some form of legitimate trade, they were allowed to go upriver and to stay at Canton as long as they had a ship in port.

4

Trading with Traders

The Wonders of Cantonese Shopkeepers[1]

Maria Kar-wing Mok

Introduction

If one word were sought to describe the work of foreign traders in eighteenth- and nineteenth-century Canton, it would be 'shopping'. They came to trade, to buy, and to sell, but most of their time was spent loading ships with staple commodities such as herbs, tea, silk, and porcelain for their home markets. Foreign trade with China dates back many centuries to the Han and Tang dynasties. A few centuries later, marine technology had advanced and a change in economic and political factors at home encouraged Europeans to traverse the seas to China as well. Navigation from the west was largely determined by the monsoon winds, which meant they could only traverse the South China Sea in an easterly course during the months of June to October, and depart on a westerly course from November to February.

In the early eighteenth century, everyone who went to China from the west had to abide by the monsoon season. In 1757, along with the change of policy of the Qing government, an Imperial decree prohibited all foreign trade other than that conducted at Canton. The only exceptions to this rule were the Japanese and Russians who were not allowed there, but had special arrangements to trade in other Chinese ports. All other foreigners, regardless of race, religion, ethnic background, language, etc., were welcomed and guaranteed access so long as they came for peaceful and legitimate trade. No prior license or agreement was required, they just arrived with some trade goods and permission was granted to go upriver. As the city officially became the centre of foreign trade and activity, it became the hub where foreign traders could enjoy a stable and safe place to conduct business. Hence, this is where our discussion begins.

Traders were not the only foreigners in Canton. From time to time there were also military officers, diplomats, ambassadors, surgeons, missionaries, and others. But

1. This chapter is part of the author's doctoral thesis at Sun Yat-sen University, Guangzhou. Maria Kar-wing Mok 莫家詠, 'Xiěshí yù xiǎngxiàng zhī jiān: Guǎngzhōu shāngguǎn jì huángbù bódì wàixiāo huà de shǐliào yìyì' 寫實與想像之間：廣州商館暨黃埔泊地外銷畫的史料意義 [Between realism and imagination: The historical meaning of Canton and Whampoa export paintings]. (PhD dissertation, Department of History, Sun Yat-sen University, 2017).

when it came to shopping, traders by far made most of the transactions. They were a diverse crowd from very different backgrounds and included Europeans, Americans, and numerous others such as Armenians, Parsees, Muslims, Hindus, etc. They came to China to shop in bulk, either for large trading enterprises bearing such household names as the English, Dutch, Danish, French or Swedish East India companies (EIC, VOC, DAC, FEIC, and SOIC, respectively), or, in the case of private traders, for private companies and individual investors. These shopping activities formed the core business of the China trade. At the same time, they also made personal purchases, on a much smaller scale, of items for the private use of friends and family or for sale in their home ports.

The shopping list of Benjamin Shreve of Salem serves as a sample of what could have been the personal orders of a trader: one lady's parasol, six mother-of-pearl spoons, ten tin saucers for Mandarin cups, two 'teeth' brush cases with covers, two 'conscience' cups (material of the cup unknown), two tubs of sugar candy, and several jars of dried candy and preserves that his wife had requested.[2] Besides this personal list, he also bought silverware, tortoiseshell combs, lacquerware, silks, china, and nankeens for his wife and his investors.[3] What Shreve had been doing was what many other traders were doing, that is, besides the bulk purchases in China trade commodities, they spent days in and out of the shops at Canton placing small orders for locally produced arts and crafts and small volumes of tea, wine, and food for personal use. These items were just as John Francis Davis generalized, 'smaller articles not restricted to Hong merchants'.[4] Most of these items were export ware, but there were exceptions. Antique shops along Curiosity Street offered Chinese antiques that were not necessarily export ware. Antique vases were much more expensive than the contemporary ones (most export porcelain were described as 'modern') in these large, handsome museum-like shops.[5]

According to a mid-nineteenth-century narrative on shopping in Canton, a 'stranger in China may go from one store to another every day in the year . . . Men, none but men, he sees at every turn'.[6] Although the author was in fact noting the awkwardness of never meeting any women in the shops where they would normally be found in the West (foreign women were not allowed in the city), rather than describing shops packed with men, we could still catch a glimpse of the narrow streets packed with busy foreign shoppers. Figures 4.1a and 4.1b are enlarged details of maps with indications of the streets frequented by foreigners.

2. The quoted list was extracted from the Shreve papers in the Peabody Essex Museum. See Carl L. Crossman, *The Decorative Arts of the China Trade: Paintings, Furnishings and Exotic Curiosities* (Suffolk: Antique Collectors' Club, 1991), 21, 31, 33.
3. Crossman, *The Decorative Arts*, 21–33.
4. John Francis Davis, *The Chinese: A General Description of China and its Inhabitants*, 2 vols. (London: Charles Knight, 1840), Vol. 2, 10.
5. Osmond Tiffany Jr., *The Canton Chinese* or *The American Sojourn in the Celestial Empire* (Boston: James Munroe, 1849), 90.
6. Tiffany, *The Canton Chinese*, 59.

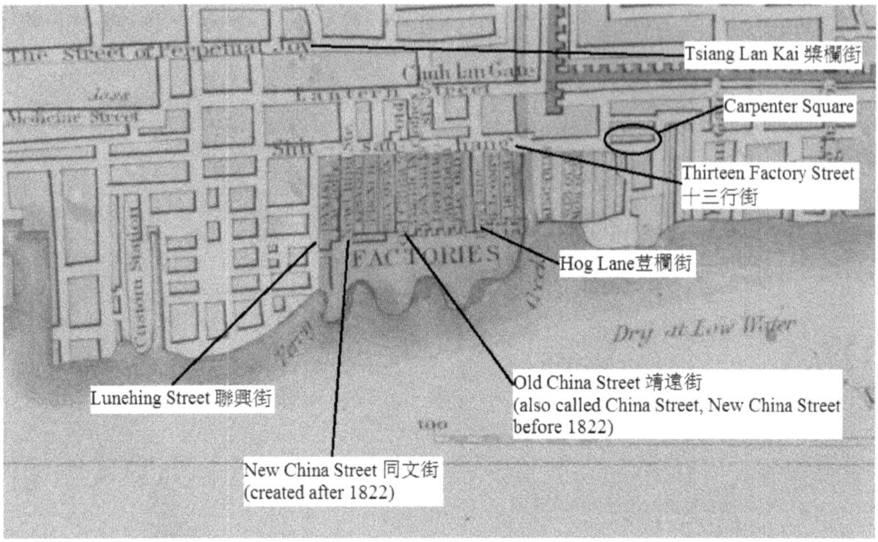

Figure 4.1a A Detail of a Map of Canton, Macao, and Hong Kong. Circa 1848. E. Belcher. Coloured Engraving. Hong Kong Museum of Art (AH1967.0015).

Shopping in Canton Was Disagreeable?

While this last image of foreign men in the hustle and bustle of shopping suggests the popularity of the activity, another account presents a contradicting scenario. John Francis Davis was particularly descriptive about the unsatisfactory conditions of shopping in China Street.[7]

> These [foreigners] are attracted to the several shops by inscriptions, in the European character, which sometimes promise more than they perform; as when the dauber of truculent likenesses calls himself a "handsome-face painter," &c. The shops, instead of being set out with the showy and sometimes expensive front of an English or

7. The English names of these streets can be very confusing. This China Street should be the Jingyuan Jie (靖遠街). From 1760 to 1822, there were only two shopping streets in the foreign quarter running north and south, perpendicular to the river. The first one, China Street (Jingyuan Jie 靖遠街), was built in 1760, and was sometimes referred to as New China Street, New Street, or Porcelain Street. The second one was Hog Lane (Doulan Jie 荳欄街). After the 1822 fire, a third street, Tongwen Jie (同文街) was created and was thus named New China Street. China Street then became Old China Street. In his book *The Chinese* (1840), Davis often recounted incidents from the 1810s when he was first in Canton, hence the China Street he commented on was probably Old China Street (Jingyuan Jie). See Figure 4.1a for the location of the streets discussed in this chapter. The common misbelief that there were always three shopping street in Canton: New China Street, China or Old China Street and Hog Lane has been debunked by recent research. See Chapter 9 in Paul A. Van Dyke and Maria Kar-wing Mok, *Images of the Canton Factories 1760–1822: Reading History in Art* (Hong Kong: Hong Kong University Press, 2015).

> French boutique, are closed in by gloomy black shutters, and very ill lit by a small skylight, or rather a hole in the roof. The inmates, instead of showing the civility and alacrity of shopkeepers in London or Paris, and anticipating the demands of their customers in the display of their goods, slowly, and sometimes sullenly, produce the articles from their cases and cupboards as they may be asked for; so that shopping at Canton is far from being an agreeable pastime.[8]

Next, he went on to describe Hog Lane, a well-known alley, where evil prevailed, or so it seems:

> nothing so narrow or so filthy exists in a European town. The hovels by which it is lined are occupied by abandoned Chinese, who supply the poor ignorant sailors with spirits, medicated to their taste with stimulating or stupifying drugs; and, when the wretched men have been reduced to a bestial state by these poisonous liquors, they are frequently set upon by their wily seducers, and robbed as well as beaten . . . the Chinese at length made their singularly unreasonable demand for payment, as, perhaps, a few *dollars* for what might be worth a few *pence*.[9]

To recapitulate Davis's observation, there were at least a few very prominent characteristics that made shopping in Canton 'far from being an agreeable pastime': boastful advertisements; unattractive displays; and unenthusiastic shopkeepers, even those who literally plundered and cheated their customers.

In fact, if Davis's portrayal were the only reference we had, we could easily believe that the shopping experience in Canton was indeed horrible. His accounts suggest that there was nothing more than a couple of dirty narrow streets lined with tiny gloomy shops run by nasty Chinese proprietors. As Wills has shown in his chapter, eyewitness accounts are very important for the details they contain. Without these individual views and opinions, we would have no idea what it was like to wander the streets of Canton.

In this study, I use Davis's comments as a starting point to examine the Canton shopkeepers in an attempt to determine to what extent, if any, his statements were true. Obviously, if it were as bad as Davis claimed, people would have simply stopped going there, and we know that did not happen. This outcome alone begs the question that if Davis's impression of the Canton shopkeepers was not representative of the majority of their customers, then what was? Eyewitness accounts often vary widely based upon each person's perspective. A negative encounter or a previously held prejudice can easily influence a person's overall outlook (such as Charles de Constant in Wills's chapter). It is only by cross-referencing and examining numerous eyewitness accounts that we can begin to weed out fact from fiction and come to some basic understanding of what the shopping experience in Canton actually meant to most of the people. First of all, Davis only talked about two streets. It is unclear whether he was only referring to what he witnessed in these two streets, when there were actually more shopping streets in the vicinity of the factories.

---

8. Davis, *The Chinese*, Vol. 2, 24.
9. Davis, *The Chinese*, Vol. 2, 24–25.

He mentioned other streets in other parts of the book.[10] But in reference to shopping, he only referred to China Street and Hog Lane, which does not present a complete picture.

During the eighteenth and nineteenth centuries, Canton was one of the greatest shopping centres in Asia, where foreign traders had access to a cluster of shops and streets within and beyond the foreign factories in the southwestern suburb of Canton.[11] Within the factory quarters, the shopping streets most frequented by foreigners after 1822 were Old China Street and New China Street.[12] A third street, Hog Lane, was indeed a place where sailors went for liquor and small souvenirs, with many shops being of substandard quality.[13]

There were other shops and more choices if one went beyond the factories. Even though officials forbade foreigners from wandering outside of the foreign quarter, they did so anyway.[14] In the 1830s and 1840s, they were often seen on Lunehing Street—a north–south avenue that was positioned to the west of the factories.[15] They also wandered to the north of the factory area on a street that ran perpendicular to the factories and parallel to Thirteen Factory Street. This avenue was known as 'Curiosity Street', as well as other names.[16] To the northeast of the factories, they visited a place known as Carpenter Square. It lay to the east of the Thirteen Factory Street beyond the Creek (Figure 4.1b). The shops were laid out in this area in the form of a parallelogram, which is probably why it was called a square.[17]

---

10. Davis, *The Chinese*, Vol. 2, 9. He described Carpenter Street, Curiosity Street and Apothecary Street and the business conducted therein.
11. For a comprehensive description of the location of the streets and what was sold on them, see Patrick Conner, *The Hongs of Canton* (London: English Art Books, 2009), 75–88.
12. For an in-depth discussion on the origins of the names of the streets and the confusion surrounding them, see Chapter 9 in Van Dyke and Mok, *Images of the Canton Factories*.
13. Tiffany, *The Canton Chinese*, 60; Melchior Yvan, *Inside Canton* (London: Henry Vizetelly, 1858), 41.
14. For issues concerning restrictions of access for foreigners in Canton, see Maria Mok, 'Some Restrictions on Westerners in Canton in the First Half of the 19th Century: A Study based on the Hong Kong Museum of Art Collection', *Arts of Asia* 41, no. 4 (2011): 102–15.
15. Similar to many names of people and places in China trade histories, multiple spellings were used for this street. It was also known as Leuenhing Keae, or Lunehing Kai, and Lianxing Jie 聯興街 in Chinese. It was a very busy street: 'As you pass along the street, you will see on your right and left, and sometimes almost blocking up the way, priests, necromancers, workers in iron, brass, wood, etc; apothecaries, victualers, changers of money, and retailers of almost an endless variety of commodities', *The Chinese Repository*, 4 (March 1836): 535. See also Figure 4.1a.
16. The exact location of the Curio Street, also called Physic Street (Tsiang Lan Kai 槳欄街), is noted in N. B. Dennys, Wm. Fred Mayers, & C. King, *The Treaty Ports of China and Japan: A Complete Guide to the Open Ports of those Countries, together with Peking, Yedo, Hongkong and Macao* (London: Trubner and Co, Hong Kong: A. Shortrede & Co, 1867), 150 and 183. It was where numerous shops sold ancient (and imitation) porcelain and bronzes. See Davis, *The Chinese*, Vol. 2, 9. The same street was referred to as Tseung-Laan-Kai in John Henry Gray, *Walks in the City of Canton* (Hong Kong: De Souza, 1875), 19 and 269. See Figure 4.1a.
17. Davis, *The Chinese*, Vol. 2, 9.

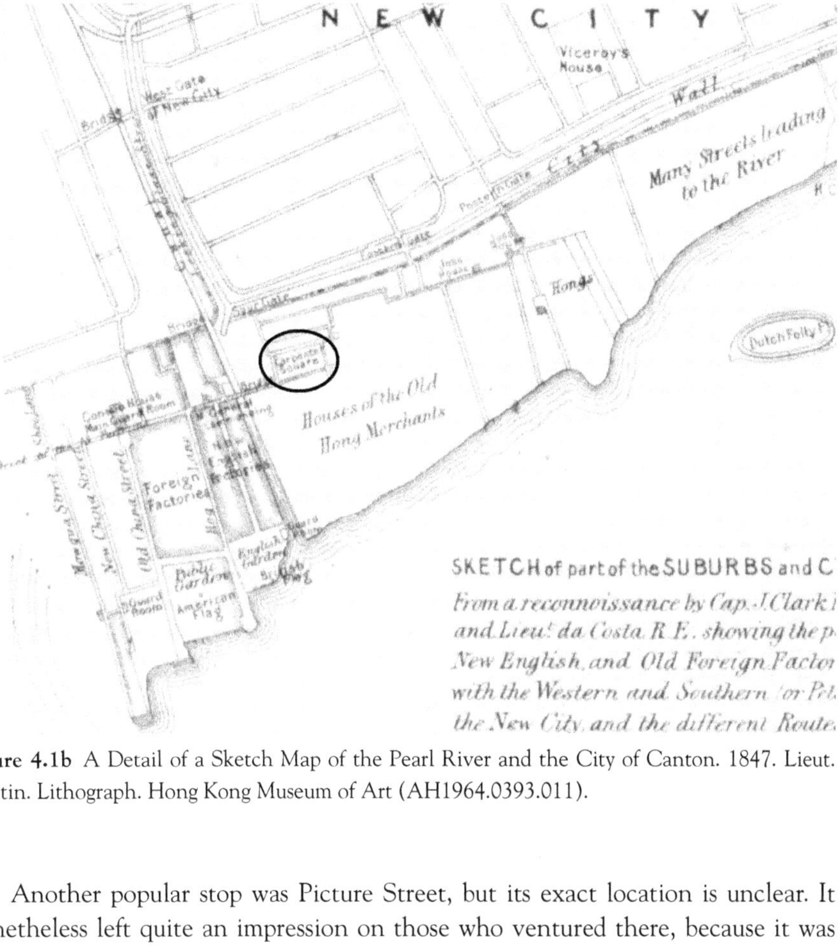

Figure 4.1b A Detail of a Sketch Map of the Pearl River and the City of Canton. 1847. Lieut. Martin. Lithograph. Hong Kong Museum of Art (AH1964.0393.011).

Another popular stop was Picture Street, but its exact location is unclear. It nonetheless left quite an impression on those who ventured there, because it was full of shops specializing in glass manufacturing, where glass paintings 'in extremely brilliant hues' were displayed for sale.[18] Foreign shoppers even ventured across the river to Honam Island. Honam was a popular shopping centre in the third quarter of the nineteenth century; its shopping streets were described as similar to those in the 'old' factories. Shops exclusively for Europeans were to be found in several streets. Unfortunately, the Chinese names of these streets and their location were not identified. Among them, Club Street was better known and was said to be close to the Red Fort. Nearby there were shops for cheap European goods and provisions.[19]

Most streets were grouped according to their specialty. This was a Chinese custom, where each branch of trade had its distinct and separate location. Charles Lockyer, who was in China in 1704, noted such a business pattern. While the

18. Tiffany, *The Canton Chinese*, 104. This may also be Looking-glass Street that Benjamin Ball visited in 1848, see Conner, *The Hongs of Canton*, 88n31.
19. See Dennys et al., *The Treaty Ports of China and Japan*, 181–82.

mercers had the whole street to themselves, they were not the only merchants who occupied an entire district. 'The Bamboo Cap-makers, Laquer-men, Smiths, and others, have some part or other in the Town . . . for their Trades'.[20] From the early eighteenth century to the nineteenth century, the local custom of allotting each trade a particular street was maintained. Bryant P. Tilden recorded in his 1818–1819 journal that he saw 'shoe makers in one street, and tailor etc etc. in another'.[21] Those who came later also remarked that it was customary to see on each side of a certain street, rows of shops in which commodities of one and the same kind were offered for sale. The shops of other streets would have items from another industry.[22] Davis also mentioned that 'several streets are commonly devoted to distinct trades . . . Curiosity-street (as the English call it) is devoted to the sale of antiques . . . Apothecary-street is full of druggists' shops'.[23] But he also remembered an exception: China Street contained shops which dealt in 'carved and lackered [*sic*] ware, silks, and other articles in common demand by strangers'.[24] As a different addition to local custom, the arrangement of gathering different trades on one street at the heart of the foreign quarter offered immediate convenience.

This part of Davis's recollection coincides with what other travellers remembered, such as James Wathen, who concurred that the streets within the factory quarters sold all types of items for convenience.[25] Unlike the avenues or districts that were restricted to one particular trade, the streets within the foreign quarter had shops of all kinds of goods for sale. On the two China Streets (New and Old), Osmond Tiffany from Baltimore recalled that a customer could find almost everything produced in China, and the variety was just 'too numerous to mention'. In his recollection, there were shops that sold porcelain, silverware, jewellery and ivory on these two streets.[26] Other shoppers also remembered the ivory shops on China Street where one could buy the best ivory.[27] A black and gilt lacquer folding fan in the Hong Kong Museum of Art collection came from Houqua's lacquerware shop at No. 15 New China Street,[28] which was next to Tinqua's famous painting studio at No. 16.[29] Another record indicates that further down the street at shop No. 17 was

20. Charles Lockyer, *Account of the Trade in India* (London: S. Crouch, 1711), 163.
21. Phillips Library, Peabody Essex Museum (PEM): Bryant P. Tilden Journal 1818–1819, typescript, p. 192.
22. Gray, *Walks in the City of Canton*, 20.
23. Davis, *The Chinese*, Vol. 2, 9.
24. Davis, *The Chinese*, Vol. 2, 24.
25. James Wathen, *Journal of a Voyage in 1811 & 1812 to Madras and China* (London: J. Nichols, Son, and Bentley, 1814), 192–93.
26. For colourful details of shops, see Tiffany, *The Canton Chinese*, 68–75.
27. Felix Renouard de Sainte-Croix, *Voyage Commercial et Politique aux Indes Orientales*, 3 vols. (Paris: Archives du Droit Français, 1810), Vol. 3, 191.
28. This fan (Accession no. C1991.0001) entered the Hong Kong Museum of Art's collection with a box that still carries a label with the name and address of the shop.
29. The address of Tingqua's studio is inscribed with the date of the 4th year of Xianfeng (1854) on the cover page of an album in the collection of the Hong Kong Museum of Art (Accession

a lacquerware man named Hipqua.[30] Clearly, these streets inside the factory quarter were not dedicated to a single commodity but were lined with different shops, offering a wide variety of merchandise. Traders, regardless of their nationality—for the Canton trade was open to all—were bound to find items that appealed to them.

Dark Gloomy Shops?

Davis opined that shops in Canton were no match for those in London or Paris, but other visitors' accounts disagree with that picture. A French visitor was so impressed with the shops and the animated streets that he thought he was strolling through Paris.[31] The charm of shops and shopping in Canton, its entertaining and colourful nature was vividly captured in a mid-nineteenth-century memoir:

> a European feels in the situation of a child, taken, for the first time in his life, into a large toy-shop containing what he considers a world of wonders. One object after another is taken up and examined and thought well worthy of bearing home, but is quickly eclipsed by the next thing which comes to hand. On the first visit to these shops, scarcely any purchase is made, because you feel a desire to possess the whole.[32]

This is not the only description of the 'toy-shop' fascination; there are others. The shopping alleys in the area of the factories and the streets along the periphery were lined with shops providing a staggering selection of goods and crafts made in China exclusively for the foreign clientele. One of the highlights of shopping in Canton was no doubt the stupefying experience of finding oneself in a treasure trove of ingeniously designed and finely executed products, nicely captured by the colourful portrayal of the wonderful display quoted earlier. The displays aimed to overwhelm, to create a sense of awe. To ensure an impressive effect, one strategy was to fill a relatively small space with a large number of items. Another tactic was to please the eye; for instance, vases of enormous size would be displayed to show the richness of their colour and to attract attention. Items that required specific skills were also showcased, which included porcelain pagodas, fountains, and waterfalls that were admired for their ingenuity in construction.[33] In fact, the intelligently designed displays were meant to entice customers into the shops, a practice that proved successful over time and accounts for almost all shops adopting a similar

no. AH1975.0001).

30. Hipqua's lacquer shop at No. 17 New China Street was noted by Crossman. Crossman, *The Decorative Arts*, 336. Another address given for Hipqua was the first shop on Club Street. Dennys et al., *The Treaty Ports of China and Japan*, 181–82. This shows that these shops might move to different locations.
31. P. C. Briand, *Les Jeunes Voyageurs en Asie, ou Description Raisonnée des Divers Pays compris dans cette Belle Partie du Monde* (Paris : Chez Hivert, 1829), 10.
32. C. Toogood Downing, *The Fan-qui in China in 1836–1837*, 3 vols. (London: Henry Colburn, 1838), Vol. 2, 49.
33. Downing, *The Fan-qui in China*, Vol. 2, 74–75.

approach. The effectiveness of the strategy was aptly recapped by a traveller: 'The Cantonese take great pains to make their goods strike the eye, and sell well'.[34]

The visual impact of the shop and the attractiveness of their display created lasting memories: 'The display of rich silks at the mercers, gave us equal pleasure and astonishment'.[35] In fact, paintings adopting a shop as its subject matter became a genre by itself in Chinese export painting. Figure 4.2, for example, clearly shows that the subject matter, and thus the selling point, is the magnificent display inside the shop. The British Museum has in its collection a series of drawings, possibly a repertoire of templates of this genre.[36] The emergence of these scenes as memorabilia confirms that the display of the shops was a phenomenal experience at Canton.

Attractive display might contribute to a fun visit but was certainly not the most essential part of shopping itself. No matter how sensational, or how carefully engineered, a shop display was only a decor if there was no one to conduct the sales. The master of the shop was the shopkeeper, and sometimes also the proprietor. What were these men like?

Half-Hearted Shopkeepers?

As mentioned earlier, shopping in Canton was not fun for Davis, partly because the shopkeepers seemed unenthusiastic. According to his report, some of them went so far as to drug, rob and/or overcharge their customers. One of the worst experiences William Hickey—a young EIC cadet—had during his stay was being tricked by a shopkeeper and made to pay double for some silk stockings.[37]

As far as eagerness was concerned, it could be true that some shopkeepers seemed disinterested. Tiffany vividly caricatured the bipolar behaviour of one of them. This shopkeeper did not bother to move or open any showcase for browsers. But when a customer showed intention to buy, he darted out 'like lightning', dived 'to the very darkest corners of his cases' and showed his goods 'with the greatest good humour ten thousand times'.[38]

The exuberant behaviour of this shopkeeper at the occasion of a possible deal—laughable as it may seem—contradicts the half-hearted image portrayed by Davis. In fact, Tiffany himself recalled another incident when the purser in Cumchong's (金昌) porcelain shop on Old China Street assiduously took down every piece of

34. Remark made by Olof Toreen who was in China in 1751, in John Reinhold Forster, trans., *A Voyage to China and the East Indies by Peter Osbeck*, 2 vols. (London: Printed for Benjamin White, 1771), Vol. 2, 244.
35. Wathen, *Journal of a Voyage*, 189.
36. I thank Paul Van Dyke and Susan E. Schopp for bringing this collection to my attention. There are at least 230 pieces of drawings, ink on paper, bound in 4 folders, in the British Museum collection.
37. Alfred Spencer, ed., *Memoirs of William Hickey (1749–1775)*, 4 vols. (New York: Alfred A. Knopf, 1921), Vol. 1, 226.
38. Tiffany, *The Canton Chinese*, 61–62.

Figure 4.2 A *Lacquer Shop, Guangzhou*. Nineteenth century. Guan Lianchang (active mid-nineteenth century). Gouache on paper. 57 × 45 cm. Hong Kong Museum of Art (AH1975.0002).

chinaware on the shelves for anyone who seemed interested.[39] The impressions that other foreign customers had of these shopkeepers were often characterized by pressing eagerness and enthusiasm. In his 1811–1812 journal, James Wathen remembered the shopkeepers as 'extremely attentive and obliging'.[40] Toogood Downing's 1836 memoir noted that the shopkeepers took the greatest pain to please, and were always eager to serve, even when the customer had no intention to purchase.[41] Dr. Melchior Yvan, surgeon to the French Embassy from 1844 to 1846, remembered that on both New and Old China Streets, 'as soon as a European heel resounds on the granite, every door exhibits a Chinaman with a naked head and a flat face, lighted up with an assumed smile, which is intended to tempt a customer to his shop.'[42]

Apart from drive and determination, the shopkeepers were also remembered as shrewd dealers, more or less honest, but certainly well qualified for their business. Some shopkeepers were of course equipped with common tricks, such as loose referrals to places of origin to help complete a sale. In order to finalize a purchase, these crafty salesmen would say that their goods came 'from Nanking, viz., Nanking silk, Nanking ink, Nanking fans, and even Nanking hams'.[43] Or in another case, 'Any thing rather out of the common way these shrewd shopkeepers will insist comes from Nanking . . . while any thing absolutely unique and scarce comes from Souchow, that being the Mecca of Chinese imagination.'[44]

Another known trick was exclusivity. Shopkeepers would not hesitate to claim that they were selling the exclusive item, with a good deal of dramatic flair, to the point where they would actually shut the street-door to 'prevent the neighbours spoiling the market', before they let their customer examine the 'treasure'.[45] Knowing the power of word-of-mouth and that customers were more likely to return if they got a good bargain, shopkeepers did what they could to make it an enjoyable experience. No one should 'lose face' in China, especially not a customer, so the shopkeeper would always complain that they did not make any profit.[46] Depictions of these practices give us a vivid image of these smart businessmen.

Outrageous Prices?

These tricks of the salesman were not exclusive to eighteenth- and nineteenth-century Canton. Shopkeepers of all times and periods and in all locations throughout the world adopt similar tactics to lure customers into their shops and win a sale. In fact, employing a few tricks is indeed good business so long as the customer is

39. Tiffany, *The Canton Chinese*, 69.
40. Wathen, *Journal of a Voyage*, 187.
41. Downing, *The Fan-qui in China*, Vol. 2, 53.
42. Yvan, *Inside Canton*, 51.
43. Olof Toreen in Forster, trans., *A Voyage to China and the East Indies*, Vol. 2, 244.
44. Tiffany, *The Canton Chinese*, 64.
45. Downing, *The Fan-qui in China*, Vol. 2, 63–64.
46. Tiffany, *The Canton Chinese*, 64.

satisfied. Davis's remarks seem a bit exaggerated and certainly do not represent the majority of Western patrons' opinions. While Davis accused Chinese shopkeepers of overcharging their customers, many other shoppers in Canton remarked on how reasonable the prices were, which would obviously have been necessary in order to carry on a competitive business.

When it came to shopping, most visitors turned into keen traders, and became highly sensitive to quality. Many records show customers constantly comparing the quality of different products and meticulously noting minute differences in order to make the best judgment of which one to buy. Their sensitivity to quality was shown by the fact that they were not just interested in local Chinese products when they simply wanted the best. Cotton fabrics from Madras and other cities in India, for example, were known for their durability and long-lasting colours.[47] Madras linen and handkerchiefs were supplied by English ships, and could be conveniently bought in Canton. When traders found goods of better quality, they would not restrict their purchases to Chinese products.

Just like any other goods, export art was closely examined by the scrutinizing customers. Chinese lacquerware, for example, was considered inferior by many foreigners to its Japanese counterpart.[48] Chinese ivory, on the other hand, was considered 'far superior to any to be found elsewhere'.[49] Porcelain, by the early nineteenth century, began to show a decline in popularity in the face of European competition. 'There was nothing to attract the particular notice of an Englishman in their porcelain—our own manufactories producing ware infinitely superior in elegance, taste, and materials.'[50] Silverware was still regarded as worth the price, owing to fine craftsmanship.[51] As for paintings, flowers and insects, or flower-and-bird genre paintings were thought of as *bien supérieures* (much better) than those in Europe.[52] Gold was considered far purer than what could be found in Europe.[53]

With a good idea of the type and the quality of goods in the market, foreign customers were also very sensitive to prices. Many of them made meticulous notations about the cost and quality of all sorts of products, even minor items meant for personal use.[54] What matters most in this discussion is not the actual prices

47. Forster, trans., *A Voyage to China and the East Indies*, Vol. 1, 242.
48. Sainte-Croix, *Voyage commercial et politique aux Indes Orientales*, Vol. 3, 193. Also in Charles Gutzlaff, *China Opened*, 2 vols. (London: Smith, Elder and Co., 1838), Vol. 2, 146, he commented 'Chinese lacquered ware is inferior to the Japanese'.
49. Wathen, *Journal of a Voyage*, 189.
50. Wathen, *Journal of a Voyage*, 188. Gutzlaff's also made similar comments, 'In regard to porcelain manufactures, the Chinese have been entirely outdone by foreigners. Foreigners buy it at present, merely as a matter of curiosity'. Gutzlaff, *China Opened*, Vol. 2, 146.
51. Sainte-Croix, *Voyage Commercial et Politique aux Indes Orientales*, 198.
52. Sainte-Croix, *Voyage Commercial et Politique aux Indes Orientales*, 199.
53. Tiffany, *The Canton Chinese*, 73.
54. On ivory fans, first class went for 20 piastres, second-class for 7 piastres, and third-class for 5 piastres. Sainte-Croix, *Voyage Commercial et Politique aux Indes Orientales*, 191.

themselves, but whether those figures represented 'value for money'. A comment on export paintings on pith paper certainly justified a satisfied customer: 'They cost, for the usual class of excellence, from one to two dollars a dozen; which is not high, when we consider their truth, the time spent upon them, and the variety of colours employed'.[55] Showing his utmost appreciation for the intricateness of an ivory ball, John Barrow, who visited China on the 1792–1794 Macartney mission, commented that 'A very small sum of money is the price of one of these difficult trifles . . . and other trinkets and trifles, are executed in a neater manner and for less money in China than in any other part of the world.'[56] Comparison between markets was also note-worthy; a set of ivory chess pieces which, in the nineteenth century, cost 'twenty or thirty dollars in the United States, may be obtained in China for eight or ten [dollars]'.[57] The Cantonese shops were aware that lower prices gave them a niche in the market. With workmanship of superior quality, Cantonese products were often found to be much cheaper than in foreign countries, which many satisfied customers attributed to the cheapness of labour in China.[58]

No other example would testify to such awareness better than that of Lamqua, who sold his paintings at a price significantly undercutting that of George Chinnery—the only European professional painter on the China Coast—by charging 80 per cent less.[59] A physical comparison (Figures 4.3a and 4.3b) not only shows that the two artists must have been serious rivals, but also testifies to Lamqua's work being worth every single (Spanish) dollar. Competitive pricing was crucial to business in view of the level of sensitivity of customers in examining and determining which item was the best value for their money. Being competitive was how the shopkeepers stayed in business, and not by overcharging and mistreating customers as Davis's comments suggest.

Boastful in Quality?

Price was important, which meant cheap labour was also important. But an overemphasis on these concerns might jeopardize quality, which was not good for business. Quality was often of utmost importance to foreign consumers. Davis mentioned that

55. Tiffany, *The Canton Chinese*, 84.
56. John Barrow, *Travels in China, Containing Descriptions, Observations, and Comparisons, Made and Collected in the Course of a Short Residence at the Imperial Palace of Yuen-min-yuen, and on a Subsequent Journey through the Country from Pekin to Canton* (Philadelphia: M'Laughlin, 1805), 206.
57. Tiffany, *The Canton Chinese*, 75.
58. Tiffany, *The Canton Chinese*, 73, 89.
59. The painting by Lamqua was about five times cheaper than one by Chinnery. Patrick Conner quoted the following entries in James Matheson's personal account dated 1840–1841: $34 and $60 to Lamqua, and $150 and $250 to Chinnery, and in March 1842: Lamqua $18.50, G. Chinnery $100. Patrick Conner, *The China Trade, 1600–1860* (Brighton: The Royal Pavilion, Art Gallery & Museums, 1986), 54.

Figure 4.3a *Self-Portrait.* Circa 1840. George Chinnery (1774–1852). Oil on canvas. 23.5 × 18.4 cm. Collection of the Peabody Essex Museum, Salem, Massachusetts. Gift of the Friends and Fellows of the Peabody Essex Museum, 1962 (M11510).

Figure 4.3b *Portrait of George Chinnery.* Mid-nineteenth century. Lamqua (active 1825–1860). Oil on canvas. 24.7 × 19 cm. Hong Kong Museum of Art (AH1991.0003).

the shopkeepers 'sometimes promise more than they perform', but other visitors reported otherwise. Very often, it was simply outstanding Chinese craftsmanship, or how it was presented, that impressed these visitors. Charles Gutzlaff was very complimentary to Cantonese craftsmen and their skills: 'When a foreigner for the first time arrives in Canton, he is struck with the ingenuity of the Chinese artisans [*sic*]. They possess considerable skill in working ivory, mother-o'-pearl, and tortoise-shell; in manufacturing trinkets, furniture, and silk piece-goods.'[60] These were the types of goods that were sold in the shops. They were popular not only because they were cheap, but because they were of excellent quality. Today, many such items are kept in the collections and displayed in museums around the world because they exemplify the high artistic and technical level of Chinese export art.

Quality was often seen not just in craftsmanship but in service as well. This sensitivity was mirrored in tailor-made products and services. Customers were often pampered by shopkeepers. The acclaimed success of *guangcai* ware in the export porcelain business testifies to the success of this strategy. By setting up workshops in Canton to take over the decorative processes of Jingdezhen, the porcelain dealers

60. Gutzlaff continued his lengthy discussion of the quality of each type of these goods. Gutzlaff, *China Opened*, 2: 142–47.

found the perfect means of catering to their customers' needs. Not only was porcelain painted to order, but customers even chose the patterns or combination of patterns on the spot, and in the workshops.[61] They added European designs as well such as ciphers and coats-of-arms. Barrow was referring to the special service of *guangcai* ware when he noted that 'Great quantities of porcelain are sent from the potteries to Canton; perfectly white, that the purchaser may have them painted in his own pattern'. [62]

Product by commission or special order was also offered in other businesses. In the Natural History Museum, London, is a collection of watercolours commissioned by English naturalist John Reeves. Reeves was appointed inspector of tea for the EIC in 1808, and was sent to Canton from 1812 to 1831, where he engaged a few Chinese artists to paint, under his supervision, over two thousand Chinese natural-history watercolours.[63] These paintings are realistic and naturally rendered and do not exhibit any of the gaudiness often seen in typical Chinese export botanical paintings. They are meant to be accurate pictorial documents of the botanical specimens Reeves collected.[64] They are examples of paintings by specific order. Artists were eager to cater to other special requests. Pehr Osbeck, for example, mentioned that the Europeans often brought glass to Canton in order to have it painted by Chinese artists with roses and flowers.[65] Almost any type of products could be ordered from the Canton shops.

Another type of special order that these Chinese export artists were so famous for was that of making copies or duplicates on demand. Carl Crossman, former curator of the Peabody Museum, remarked that oil paintings based on Western prints were very popular and were produced in large numbers. He discovered that certain examples in the Peabody collection are extremely faithful to their originals, so faithful that it is difficult to distinguish them from the originals. He further notes that some of them have passed for Western works.[66] The quality of the Cantonese copies was well known at the time. After George Washington sat for Gilbert Stuart for a portrait in 1795, numerous copies were made in Canton and brought back to America. Stuart was deeply troubled by the competition between his work and these excellent copies, to the point that he took legal action to prevent their sale in America.[67] This is mirrored by Barrow's comment, 'The coloured prints of Europe, that are carried out to Canton, are copied here with wonderful fidelity'.[68]

61. C. J. A. Jörg, *Porcelain and the Dutch China Trade* (The Hague: Martinus Nijhoff, 1982), 126.
62. Barrow, *Travels in China*, 218.
63. Conner, *The China Trade*, 68.
64. Images of the collection can be browsed at the Natural History Museum website at http://www.nhm.ac.uk (accessed 25 January 2017).
65. Forster, trans., *A Voyage to China and the East Indies*, Vol. 1, 233.
66. Crossman, *The Decorative Arts*, 162, 167, and 170.
67. Patrick Conner and Anthony Hardy, *Paintings of the China Trade: The Sze Yuan Tang Collection of Historic Paintings* (Hong Kong: Hong Kong Maritime Museum, 2013), plate 109, p. 124.
68. Barrow, *Travels in China*, 219.

To date, many extant examples testify to these copies.[69] Sometimes customers would bring their own work to Canton to be copied. Wathen, for example, requested that the artist Tanqua make copies of his own sketches, which were executed to his satisfaction.[70]

It was uncertain how many items were special ordered each year, but judging from Benjamin Shreve's list, some foreign customers were quite fussy. In one letter, the requester drew out the sizes and designs of four types of tortoiseshell combs which he hoped Shreve would acquire for him. Another request was also quite specific: 'The waiters of the oval form, extended like those at your house, the common ovals hold much less than yours', and a diagram accompanied this note.[71] Such minute attention was part of large company orders as well. Company officers would pass the specific details to the Hong merchants, who in turn had the items made. The individual traders often just went to a shop to place their orders, and found the keepers just as accommodating to their demands. Shoppers of both large and small quantities were all very well taken care of.

Many items have survived from the trade and testify to the great attention that Canton artisans paid to individual interests. One such typical feature was a crest or a cartouche pattern that provides ground for initials or monograms to be added. While the fan in Figure 4.4 might be made during the off-season months (February to June), the monograms would be added when the customers sent them the required initials to be inscribed on the items. The customers might even wait on site themselves for the items to be finished. This very common feature epitomizes the customer-oriented mentality that characterized Cantonese shops.

Still Far from an Agreeable Pastime?

Other marketing tactics testify to the fact that the Cantonese shopkeepers went to extraordinary measures in order to ensure that their customers had a truly enjoyable experience. They offered behind-the-scene tours. Many of these shops, except those selling antiques, were hybrids, and contained workshops; these shops combined sales with fabrication. To have products made in the shops seems to be a common Cantonese, if not Chinese, mode of business. Many examples in the above-mentioned British Museum collection of line drawings show actual manufacturing being done in the shops (Figure 4.5).

Osbeck visited a workshop on the second floor of a vault inside a shop where a famous 'face-maker' was at work, making figures for customers.[72] Wathen noted

69. There is a highly convincing reverse-glass painting of King George III now in a private collection in Hong Kong. The painting is by Chinese hands, based on a mezzotint engraving of the 1760s. See Conner and Hardy, *Paintings of the China Trade*, plate 110, p. 125.
70. Wathen, *Journal of a Voyage*, 188.
71. Crossman, *The Decorative Arts*, 24.
72. Forster, trans., *A Voyage to China and the East Indies*, Vol. 1, 220–21.

Figure 4.4 *Black and Gilt Lacquer Folding Fan Decorated with Floral Design.* Nineteenth century. 26 × 43.5 cm. Hong Kong Museum of Art (C1999.0012).

that on 'China Street, as well as all the others which we were permitted to see . . . The ground-floor of every house is a shop, and the upper stories work-shops and lodgings'.[73] The painting shop-studio of Lamqua best exemplified this combination of shop and workshop. Having both the salesroom and the work place together was a very effective marketing strategy; it offered a demonstration of the manufacturing process, which was a major customer attraction, together with the convenience of onsite purchasing after the customer enjoyed the demonstration. It is still a strategy used by many Chinese craftsmen in the present day.

Most of the shops in the factory area offered such a demonstration tour. Hickey recalled watching celebrated painters working upon glass.[74] On another occasion, he and his friend Pott went to watch a Chinese craftsman who made portrait figurines in clay at his shop near the factories.[75] Staunton witnessed the manufacture of chinaware and Chinese looking-glasses (probably mirrors).[76] Many other shops had their own workshops close by, very often at Honam, and frequently arranged

73. Wathen, *Journal of a Voyage*, 188.
74. Spencer, ed., *Memoirs of William Hickey*, 210.
75. Spencer, ed., *Memoirs of William Hickey*, 227.
76. Adam Matthew Digital: 'China: Trade, Politics & Culture, 1793–1980: Sources from the School of Oriental and African Studies and the British Library, London', Sir George Staunton, 'Journal of a Voyage to China', part 2, pp. 227–30.

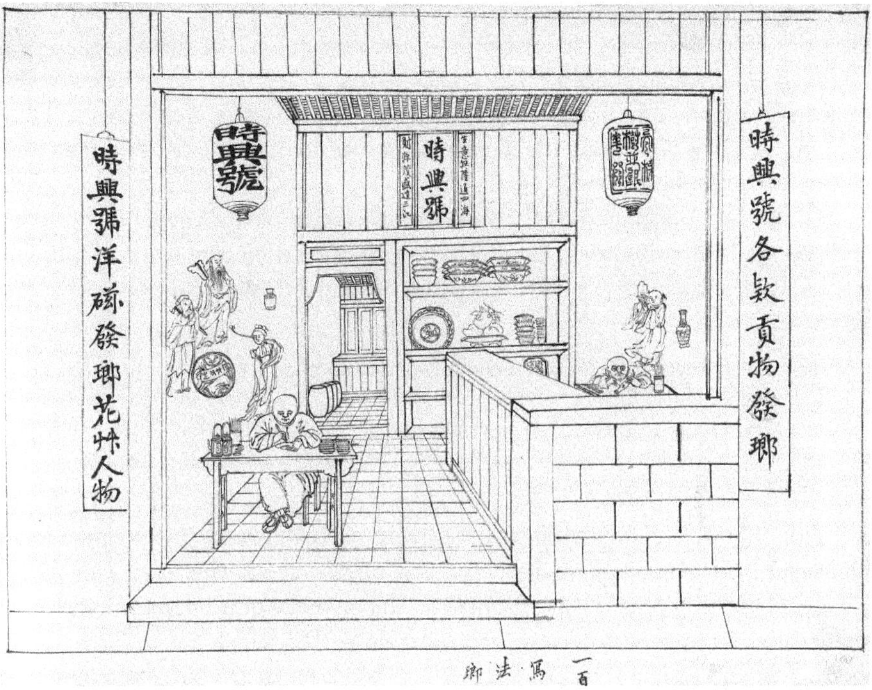

Figure 4.5 *Album. Occupation. Trades and Shops*. Circa 1801–1850. Painted on paper. (1877,0714,0.401-501) © The Trustees of the British Museum.

for customers to visit. Some of these workshops were offsite venues or warehouses. Tiffany was led by the owner of a lacquerware shop on China Street to visit his workshop in 'a different part of the suburbs up the river'.[77]

These behind-the-scene visits were usually an agreeable experience for the bored and stressed traders, which is why they were often recorded in diaries and memoirs. These tours and product demonstrations were more than simply entertainment; they were undoubtedly given in order to entice the customers to purchase something. After a tour through Hipqua's lacquerware factory where 'about forty persons' were at work, including young apprentices and old men, Tiffany was so impressed by their excellent craftsmanship, particularly appreciating the time taken—six entire weeks—to paint a lacquer fan, that he bought the item.[78] Thus the visit reinforced the 'value for money' factor, which was a notion well recognized by these foreign customers. For instance, when visiting the artist Sanhing, Wathen saw his pupils copying some English prints with a great deal of devotion and effort to the point that the visitor worried for them, 'Their progress was very slow; and unless

77. Tiffany, *The Canton Chinese*, 80.
78. Tiffany, *The Canton Chinese*, 80–82.

they had high prices for their copies, they would never make their fortune by their labour'.[79] From our earlier discussion of prices, we can see that these artists would not likely charge high prices for their copies, as that would discourage the customers from returning and others from coming. The painstaking efforts that were employed behind the scenes in making the items reconfirmed to the customer that they were getting value for their money.

Of all the workshop visits, Lamqua seems to have offered the most intriguing and popular behind-the-scene tours of export painting shop-cum-workshop. By the late 1830s, the popularity of his shop was unquestionable; the following is what one visitor recalled.

> Those who have been at Canton of late years, cannot fail to recollect the shop of Lamquoi [Lamqua] the painter. His house is the resort of all those who wish to pass away an hour in a pleasant and agreeable manner . . . a stranger has access to any part where he may choose to wander, and different branches of the business are transacted on each of the floors.[80]

Not only were customers allowed to freely wander about and look around, but craftsmen freely shared information and explanation about what they were doing. 'The Chinese are not at all discomposed by the presence of strangers . . . and show the greatest willingness to answer any question.'[81] This direct contact is a feature worth noting. Lamqua was certainly not only a master in art, but also a master in marketing. Visitors to his studio would often find him communicating directly and personally with his customers. 'The painter himself stands at his easel, generally incommoded by the numerous visitors . . . who cram in to watch his proceedings.'[82] He would converse with them in English.[83]

Apparently, a visit to Lamqua's studio-cum-shop was far more memorable than an ordinary shopping trip. No wonder his shop was a resort, as noted above, to those who wished 'to pass away an hour in a pleasant and agreeable manner'. It epitomized the strength of the Canton shops and the shopkeepers who ran them, defying adverse opinions such as those from Davis. No one has expressed appreciation for the Chinese merchants and shopkeepers better than John Phipps:

> The Chinese, considered as traders, are eminently active, persevering, and intelligent. They are, in fact, a highly commercial people; and the notion that was once very generally entertained, of their being peculiarly characterized by a contempt of commerce and of strangers, is as utterly unfounded as any notion can possibly be. Business is transacted at Canton with great dispatch; and there is no port in

79. Wathen, *Journal of a Voyage*, 188.
80. Downing, *The Fan-qui in China*, Vol. 2, 90–92.
81. Downing, *The Fan-qui in China*, Vol. 2, 95–96.
82. Downing, *The Fan-qui in China*, Vol. 2, 114.
83. Charles Lavollée, *Voyage en Chine* (Paris: Just Rouvier, 1853), 358–64. An English translation of this text can be found in an article entitled 'Art in China', *The Bulletin of the American Art-Union* 7 (October 1850): 118–19.

the world, where cargoes may be sold and bought, unloaded and loaded, with more business-like speed and activity.[84]

Conclusion

The foreign community in Canton was not easy to please. Most of the traders were very capable businessmen and tough negotiators, with specific and precise demands. Even in this environment, many of them seemed to have enjoyed the experience and held a high regard for the service and the products provided by the Canton shops. We have read about disappointments, highlighted somewhat by Davis's rather negative commentary, criticizing the use of boastful advertisements, unattractive displays, and the misconduct of shopkeepers. Other visitors, however, recounted the extraordinary shopping experience they had had at Canton. They are representative of the success of the shopkeepers in pleasing their customers. As a result, many other foreigners were attracted to Canton as well.

Convenience was a key factor in making the shopping experience a pleasant one. Not only were the shops located within the foreign factory compound, there were shopping streets in close vicinity where foreign customers came to visit on a daily basis. As soon as they passed the shops, the enticing displays drew them in, and ensured that they would at least have a look inside. The extraordinary display of high quality and fascinating items attracted many a visitor through the door. While they were being dazzled by the splendour of the items on the shelves, the next and most important factor—the shopkeeper—entered on stage, with all his mastery in manipulation and bargaining which many traders warned about in their memoirs. And those who had heard of shopkeepers who cheated customers might be relieved to find lots of top quality goods often supplemented with tailor-made service at reasonable prices, instead of dishonest shopkeepers.

Another activity that counters the notion that the shopping experience in Canton was a disagreeable one are the enjoyable onsite visits and behind-the-scene tours where the manufacturing process was explained and put on display. These bonus events often impressed and induced customers to buy after seeing the strenuous work behind the making of a product. The experience was indigenous in the sense that it tallied with the operation mode of these Cantonese shops; they were often a combination of a shop and a workshop, with retailing and manufacturing under one roof, or if not, the workshop would be close by. Judging from illustrative narratives by impressed customers, shopping must have been an agreeable and entertaining event, a colourful interval in a 'laborious, monotonous, and somewhat contemplative' sojourn.[85]

84. John Phipps, A *Practical Treatise on the China and Eastern Trade: comprising the Commerce of Great Britain and India, particularly Bengal and Singapore, with China and the Eastern Islands* (Calcutta: Baptist Mission Press, 1835), 134.

85. Melchoir Yvan summed up life in Canton with these words to describe the Western male

These examples, as well as the example of Charles de Constant in Wills's chapter, show clearly that when examining eyewitness accounts, it is important not to put too much trust into one source. Not only should we compare accounts from persons of the same nationality and background, but we should also compare accounts between ethnic groups. This factor is especially true with a place like Canton that was frequented by persons of many religious beliefs and diverse cultures. In this study, I have examined various eyewitness accounts from a variety of different Europeans and Americans. On the whole, they present a very positive view of their shopping experience in China, with a high regard for the Cantonese shopkeepers. Of course, there were negative experiences as well, but those were exceptions rather than the rule. While we cannot say that this picture represents other foreigners trading at Canton, such as Parsees, Muslims and Hindus, etc., the fact that all of them continued to go to Canton and trade there over many decades, suggests that their experiences were likewise positive. The shopkeepers' eagerness to please their customers, combined with the Qing government's consistent policy of guaranteeing all foreigners (except Japanese and Russians) equal access to the market, made Canton a very special place in world commerce.

community who according to him was either confined on the ship or in the small tract of land within the factories, while deprived of female companionship. Yvan, *Inside Canton*, 48.

5
The Private Eye in Old Canton
Questions and Agendas for Discussion

John E. Wills Jr.

From Columbus on, the testimony of an eyewitness has had special power in European-language accounts of places and peoples seen for the first time, especially when what was seen showed that the Greeks and the Romans had not known all that there was to know. Eyewitness texts were translated, added to, and reprinted in one European language after another. Of course, eyewitnesses did not always remember accurately, or found it more fun to tell bigger stories. By the late 1600s, some of the most reliable accounts of distant lands were being published by stay-at-home compilers with good connections, like the Amsterdam-based Olfert Dapper, who as far as I can tell never travelled farther from home than Utrecht.[1] But by that time another kind of eyewitness was becoming important, the artists or writers who had been there. Their work was brought to European readers by skilled, entrepreneurial print-makers like Jacob van Meurs, who was the main commercial mover of the publication of the Dapper books. Van Meurs was one of the originators of an entire genre of books, which is the subject of a large and ambitious new study by Benjamin Schmidt. Schmidt shows that these books were focused above all on pleasing and diverting the reader and viewer and thus on selling more volumes. They were often casual about mixing images of exotic scenes, people, animals and plants from different continents giving Europeans a sense of a world of diverting and unthreatening undifferentiated Other.[2] Images of the temples, processions and religious 'idols' showed Europeans a much more complicated world of the human spirit.[3]

Many of the documents we most value for the study of the Canton trade are the work of East India company committees and have little place for personal visions and experiences. Those records contain instructions from superiors, trade figures

1. John E. Wills Jr., 'Author, Publisher, Patron, World: A Case Study of Old Books and Global Consciousness', *Journal of Early Modern History* 13, no. 5 (2009): 375–433.
2. Benjamin Schmidt, *Inventing Exoticism: Geography, Globalism, and Europe's Early Modern World (Material Texts)* (Philadelphia: University of Pennsylvania Press, 2015).
3. Lynn Hunt, Margaret C. Jacob, and Wijnand Mijnhardt, *The Book That Changed Europe: Picart & Bernard's* Religious Ceremonies of the World (Cambridge, MA, and London: Belknap Press of Harvard University Press, 2010); and Lynn Hunt, Margaret C. Jacob, and Wijnand Mijnhardt, eds., *Bernard Picart and the First Global Vision of Religion* (Los Angeles: Getty Research Institute, 2010).

and reports, ledgers and balance sheets, and much more. They are indispensable and vital to our understanding of how the commerce worked, but they are also devoid of feeling. When reading such documents, we need to be alert for surprising bits of eyewitness testimony that might find their way into the records.

Private memoirs, on the other hand, are among the most descriptive documents we have of individual experiences. While subjective in nature, they nonetheless bring the discussion to life by revealing to us what the authors saw, felt, and heard at the time. We learn of personal preferences and prejudices, conflicts between foreigners and between foreigners and Chinese, lively descriptions of social gatherings, and details about the environment such as descriptions of plants and animals, the layout of the landscape, and cultural curiosities held by the writers of the different people they encounter. Most of this type of information is not contained in company records, and yet is vital to understanding their experiences. Thus, in addition to studying private traders for the sake of understanding the roles they played in the advancement and/or decline of commerce, their eyewitness accounts are essential to our knowledge of the people and environment in which they all lived.

In this chapter, I want to show the diversity of some European eyewitnesses of old Canton. Some of their accounts come to us as separate publications or as sources cited in one kind or another of modern study. Others open up aspects of interaction at Canton that we need to make part of our bigger picture of intercultural relations there, even when the immediate focus is on, for example, the trends in foreign loans to the Hong merchants. This chapter presents, in chronological order, a small number of eyewitnesses whose accounts shed light on British private traders and on European naturalists.

Robert Pitt was borne into a modest county gentry family in 1680. In 1698, his father, Thomas Pitt, was appointment to the British East India Company's (EIC) most important position in Asia, president at Fort St. George, Madras. Robert accompanied his father to Madras as a 'free merchant', not in the Company's employ.[4] Thomas served the Company with great loyalty and effectiveness in the face of challenges from a rival company and sieges by hostile Indian powers. Robert did not have his father's taste for the trading life, but he made three voyages to China, one to Amoy in 1699 and two to Canton in 1700 and 1701. The first voyage to Canton had him in charge of a Danish ship, which was freighted by 'the gentlemen of Madras'.[5] He wrote to his mother about this appointment in December 1700 saying that 'if it please God, [I] shall make no small advantage of it. On my return to Madras I intend going home by the first ship that sails thence for England'.[6]

4. Sir Cornelius Neale Dalton, *The Life of Thomas Pitt* (Cambridge: Cambridge University Press, 1915), 105–13.
5. Dalton, *The Life of Thomas Pitt*, 246–47. The Danish ship that was at Whampoa in 1700 was the *Prince Charles*. Captain Frederick Bloom, *Records of Fort St. George: Diary and Consultation Book of 1700* (Madras: Government Press, 1930), 44.
6. Dalton, *The Life of Thomas Pitt*, 247.

Robert, however, did not return home, but rather engaged in another voyage to Canton aboard the ship *Hampshire*. The *Hampshire* was actually an EIC ship that had arrived at Madras from England on 27 May 1701. After it was unloaded, several 'freemen of Madras' proposed hiring the vessel for a voyage to Canton, which the Company approved. Robert was then appointed supercargo.[7]

In Canton in the fall of 1701, Robert wrote to a friend that 'We live here very sociably together . . . we drink every night good claret; and by midnight after the shake of the elbow and several hearty curses, some people by degrees abate the commission on the gross', and to his mother that he was 'thanks to the assistance of my father, in a post of the most trust, credit, and profit of any private person in India'.[8] Robert then went back to England, never to return to India, with a comfortable fortune of £6,000.[9] For other participants in this trade, profits were said to be unsatisfactory, but this was partly because it was hard to obtain enough silver in the Indian ports.[10] This suggests a growing, attractive trade in which there was a great deal of competition, and in which insider access to capital like Robert Pitt's made a great deal of difference in profits.

Robert on his return voyage to England also was his father's confidential agent, carrying a huge uncut diamond, which Thomas discussed constantly but discreetly in his letters—the profits of the diamond trade depended on the Indian sellers not learning what diamonds were worth in Europe. In addition, Thomas may not have paid duty on his prize as he was legally required to do, because, as the story goes, Robert supposedly carried the diamond back to Europe in the heel of his left shoe.[11] When cut the Great Pitt Diamond weighed 'only' 140 carats. Thomas had paid £24,000 for it, and had owned it for about fifteen years when he sold it to the French court for £125,000.[12] One observer commented that with all his power and wealth he could have made a bigger capital gain investing in Indian Ocean trade for all those years.[13] Of course Pitt might also have lost everything in the wreck of one rich cargo.

Another subject that attracted the attention of eyewitnesses was that of plants and agriculture. *Pierre Poivre* belonged to a family that had been well-established merchants in Lyon for several generations. Being located at the centre of the French

7. Dalton, *The Life of Thomas Pitt*, 246–47; and *Records of Fort St. George. Diary and Consultation Book of 1701* (Madras: Government Press, 1930), 42–50.
8. Dalton, *The Life of Thomas Pitt*, 247.
9. Dalton, *The Life of Thomas Pitt*, 269–73, 388, and 405.
10. Ian Bruce Watson, *Foundation for Empire: English Private Trade in India 1659–1760* (New Delhi: Vikas, 1980), 92, 124, 151, and 306.
11. Henry Davison Love, *Vestiges of Old Madras 1640–1800*, 4 vols. (London, 1913; reprint, New Delhi: Mittal Publications, 1988), Vol. 2, 2–3.
12. Another source claims that Thomas sold the diamond for £135,000. Love, *Vestiges of Old Madras*, Vol. 2, 2. After the French purchased the diamond, it became known as the 'Regent' diamond and is presently part of the Louvre's collection in Paris.
13. Dalton, *The Life of Thomas Pitt*, 231–49, and 520.

silk industry, Pierre's Indian Ocean destiny was perhaps obvious. His Canton connections take up four or five pages of Louis Malleret's biography of 711 pages.[14] In his travels around the Indian Ocean he investigated the local systems of agriculture and gathering of forest products. His great claim to fame was his success in bringing the clove tree to Mauritius and Reunion. This was the first break in the Dutch monopoly in the provision of fine spices to Europe. Investigations of exotic agricultural products were a recurring theme in European contacts in both hemispheres; a special interest in tea is discussed in my next case, that of Pehr Osbeck. Eyewitness accounts such as these offer ample opportunities for a fresh approach to this fascinating combination of physiocratic and other kinds of Enlightenment thought and restless energy in a world that the great companies no longer could contain.

Poivre's first visit to Canton was in 1741–1742, when he was still a seminarian of the French Missions Étrangères. A charming young man, a great talker and an enthusiastic writer, he seems to have had a weakness for bad company, and was not at all well suited for the priesthood. He lost his seminarian status at some time during these years. Malleret cites a letter from him from Canton dated 3 December 1741,[15] which states that several missionaries have lodged at Canton from time to time in the house of 'a Syrian from Aleppo' (un Syrien d'Alep). Aleppo was a major centre for French trade in the eastern Mediterranean; it is possible that the missionaries' host spoke French, and fairly likely that he was a Maronite or Roman Catholic Christian. If he had been a Jew or an Armenian (or less probably, a Muslim), I think that would have been mentioned. Passing references to Muslim, Armenian, and other traders from South Asian ports turn up in company records as well as in private and personal ones; if we kept track of them and eventually put them together, I think we would find that they suggest very substantial volumes of trade in that channel.[16]

Poivre allied with an individual in the French factory whose name is transcribed as Friell, and who was an Irish nobleman. Poivre went on a short visit to the thriving port of Hôi An, in Cochin China (Vietnam), which was followed by a substantial commercial voyage there by Friell. The latter man returned with some profits and commercial information, which Poivre promptly put together with his own findings in a detailed 'Mémoire' of the products and trade possibilities of the central part of modern Vietnam. Pierre Poivre had found his calling; he compiled information

14. Louis Malleret, *Pierre Poivre* (Paris: École Française d'Extrême Orient, 1974).
15. Malleret, *Pierre Poivre*, 21.
16. See, for example, the passing references to Armenian traders, and the very good information on a 'Moor' (South Asian Muslim) ship from Surat—300 tons, 30 guns, 200 crew—in E. A. Voretzsch, ed., *François Froger. Relation du Premier Voyage des François à la Chine, Fait en 1698, 1699 et 1700 sur le Vaisseau "L'Amphitrite"* (Leipzig: Verlag de Asia Major, 1926), 90, 102–3, 112, 122, and 143.

in this way for every place he visited—Java, Manila, South India, Mauritius, even Martinique on his return to France.[17]

Poivre left Macao for India on 16 January 1745. He was back at Canton in 1750, and this time he was very much in the plant business. He took with him when he left Canton some mangosteen plants that he had acquired in passing by Java, several varieties of leechee from Guangdong, and 'some plants of the best tea which he had brought from the province of Fujian'. I have found no further trace of those tea shrubs, which were perhaps the first sign of the long European effort to produce tea outside the control of the Chinese.[18]

Like Poivre, *Pehr Osbeck* offers a number of glimpses into the botanical world. Osbeck was a chaplain for the Swedish East India Company.[19] He owed his appointment to the great Swedish scientist Linnaeus, with whom he had studied. Linnaeus continually urged Swedish voyagers to Asia to send him live plants of tea, mulberry leaves for silkworms, and other economically valuable plants, insisting that he could experiment with them until they could grow in Sweden. If successful, then the country would not have to pay hard currency to the English and the Dutch for their tea, silk, and so on. Only once did some live tea bushes reach him and flower, but they soon were killed by the harsh winter.[20] Osbeck, using the methods Linnaeus had taught him, worked on collecting specimens and trying to classify them throughout his voyage. His special interests led to pages on frogs, beans, yams, goldfish, insects, bamboo, and much more. No Chinese would give him full information on herbs and their uses.[21]

Osbeck was in the Canton delta area from 22 August 1751 to 4 January 1752. He enjoyed several excursions out in the country but never ventured within the walled city of Guangzhou. His observations include alert and detailed descriptions of the procedures at the customs barriers on the river, the watchful good order at the bankshalls at Whampoa, and one breakdown of that order when the British captain Congreve was robbed on French Island and went in pursuit with armed men. The Qing authorities quickly found four suspects and promised they would be punished. He comments in passing on the trade 'by the *Armenians*, and other *Asiatic* nations, besides the *Europeans*'.[22] His keen description of the shops and workshops in 'Porcelain Street' and of other specialized crafts ought to be read by anyone study-

17. Pierre Poivre, *Un manuscript inédit de . . . Les Mémoires d'un Voyageur, texte reconstitué et annoté par Louis Malleret* (Paris: École Française d'Extrême-Orient, 1968).
18. Malleret, *Pierre Poivre*, 190.
19. John Reinhold Forster, trans., *A Voyage to China and the East Indies, by Peter Osbeck: Together with a Voyage to Suratte, by Olof Toreen, and an Account of Chinese Husbandry, by Captain Charles Gustavus Eckeberg*, 2 vols. (London: Benjamin White, 1771). Osbeck's account of his stay in the Canton area is in Vol. 1, 177 to Vol. 2, 39.
20. Lisbet Koerner, *Linnaeus: Nature and Nation* (Cambridge, MA, and London: Harvard University Press, 1999), 50–52, 54, 115–18, 135–39, and 150.
21. Forster, *A Voyage to China*, Vol. 1, 224.
22. Forster, *A Voyage to China*, Vol. 1, 240.

ing a particular industry and trade.[23] Probably as part of Linnaeus's project, he had a living tea bush on board on his departure, but in the raucous departure celebration, its tub was kicked over and it was tossed overboard.[24]

Cooperation with colleagues in the natural sciences and the history of technology would be useful in sorting out Osbeck's varieties of tea, silks, porcelain, and even his insects and frogs. Interest in newly discovered plants and animals in distant parts of the world was an important part of the broad trend called 'natural history' in eighteenth- and nineteenth-century Europe and America. The shapes it took in relations with China are well laid out in Fa-ti Fan, *British Naturalists in Qing China: Science, Empire, and Cultural Encounter*.[25] Naturalists' interest in China had an aesthetic dimension as well, whether in finding new varieties of flowers and ornamentals to take home, or in buying Chinese flower paintings, or in going on an excursion to the area of wholesale gardens called Fa-ti (花地).

Commercial motives of the naturalists ranged from simply taking home seeds of a new variety and selling the resulting plants for a profit to major projects to transplant crops for which there was a massive market, to places where plantations and profits would be under European control. Devotees of natural history were interested in places, plants, and animals that they had not seen before, which made explorations of remote interior parts of China seem innocent and legitimate. Some of the most important promoters of the search for new plants from China never got near it; the most remarkable was Sir Joseph Banks, who sent collectors out in all directions for the Kew Gardens and the Chelsea Physic Garden, and in the 1780s obtained the appointment in succession of two brothers named Duncan as surgeons to the English factory at Canton and collectors for the London gardens.[26] At the end of our period, Robert Fortune appealed to both high capitalism and innocent adventure, writing vivid popular books about his adventurous inland travels, and contributing expert knowledge and tea plants smuggled out of China to the founding of the great Indian tea industry.[27]

23. Forster, *A Voyage to China*, Vol. 1, 219–37, 240, and 322–23. For the location of this 'Porcelain Street', where many of the Canton porcelain dealers were located before 1760, see Paul A. Van Dyke, *Merchants of Canton and Macao: Politics and Strategies in Eighteenth-Century Chinese Trade*, Vol. 1 (Hong Kong: Hong Kong University Press, 2011), Plate 02.02; and Paul A. Van Dyke and Maria Kar-wing Mok, *Images of the Canton Factories 1760–1822: Reading History in Art* (Hong Kong: Hong Kong University Press, 2015), 2, and Figure F27. It was an east–west street that was located a couple blocks north of the factory area.
24. Forster, *A Voyage to China*, Vol. 2, 38–39.
25. Fa-ti Fan, *British Naturalists in Qing China: Science, Empire, and Cultural Encounter* (Cambridge, MA, and London: Harvard University Press, 2004).
26. Fan, *British Naturalists*, 20. The best starting point in the extensive and fascinating literature on Banks is Patrick O'Brian, *Joseph Banks: A Life* (London: C. Harvill, 1987; Chicago: University of Chicago Press, 1987).
27. A full study of Fortune, including recent local history studies in the tea regions, would be a major contribution to Qing studies. For a brief and lively introduction see Sarah Rose, *For All the Tea in China: How England Stole the World's Favorite Drink and Changed History* (New York:

An occasional eyewitness's account was written years after the writer's period of residence in Canton, and may have been greatly embellished over time. Such is the case of *William Hickey*. While Hickey may have kept some notes on his voyages, he did not arrive home with them and as a result, wrote much of his diary from memory.[28] His vivid descriptions of places and people, his verbatim quotations of long and amusing conversations, make me suspect a great deal of telling and retelling of good stories that kept getting better. Nevertheless, there are rare and plausible gems, such as his account of the flower-boat trade; the memorable celebrations at Pankeequa's (also spelled Poankeequa, whose Chinese name was Pan Zhencheng 潘振承) country house; and a discussion of the tremendous sounds of the bands of the big ships playing across the Whampoa anchorage at every sunrise and sunset. Hickey does not seem to have been much interested in the plants and flowers so important to many others, but he gives us rare and convincing pictures of frank and informal interchange among Chinese and foreigners.

Charles de Constant. In the late 1800s, European fascination with the great civilizations of Asia as exotic others, in some respects superior to Europe, did not disappear entirely but was challenged by more jaundiced views. The eminent Jürgen Osterhammel has given us a remarkably creative and widely read account of the 'disenchantment of Asia' in European thought and practice in the eighteenth century that has much to offer our search for global and interactive trends around 1800.[29] An example of such disenchantment is illustrated by a remark made by the French-speaking Swiss eyewitness, Charles de Constant:

> Ah! Chinese! Chinese! How small you are! You are not aware that your minute exactitude has earned you the pompous name of *the People of Sages*! It is a Frenchman, the Abbé Raynal, who has given you that title, which no nation has deserved less than you. But he did not live for twelve years among you. He has not had perpetually before his eyes the spectacle of your infamies. He has been neither witness nor victim of your perfidies, your robberies. He has not seen the depravity of your morals, the sclerosis of your mandarins; he does not know the tyranny of your masters, the rigor and baseness of your servitude. Permit me then, with less eloquence but more truth, to change the eulogy into a critique, calling you *People of Laxity*, *People of Children*, *People of Thieves*, *People of Ignoramuses*, and what is even

Penguin, 2010). For a brief sample of what a master could make of Fortune's information see John K. Fairbank, *Trade and Diplomacy on the China Coast: The Opening of the Treaty Ports, 1842–1854*, 2 vols. (Cambridge MA: Harvard University Press, 1953), Vol. 1, 293–99.

28. Peter Quenell, ed., *Prodigal Rake: Memoirs of William Hickey* (New York: E. P. Dutton, 1962), 15–16 of Quenell's introduction. The account of Hickey's visit to Canton is on pp. 135–47. Quenell notes on pp. 17–18 that his text is shorter than the edition of 1913–1925 but includes some passages too frank for a prudish age. Maria Mok's chapter in this volume quotes a fine passage from Spencer's edition that is not contained in the Quenell edition.
29. Jürgen Osterhammel, *Die Entzauberung Asiens: Europa und die asiatische Reiche im 18. Jahrhundert* (München: C. H. Beck, 1998).

> more sad for you, *People of Slaves*; but do you have enough soul to feel the value of freedom?[30]

De Constant's roots were in the French-speaking areas around Geneva, bourgeois, Protestant, anti-Versailles, prejudiced against the pronouncements of Roman Catholic priests on the wonders of Chinese civilization. Charles knew well his famous cousin Benjamin Constant, lover of Madame de Staël and an active politician.[31] Francophone Switzerland produced more educated and ambitious men than it could support, and many younger sons took service in foreign armies or sought their fortunes abroad in other ways. Charles de Constant went to work in 1778 for the new Imperial Company based in Trieste, a particularly obvious and improvised project to tap the vast potential for smuggling tea into the United Kingdom and to fly a neutral flag in the midst of the global British-French war that began with French support of the American Revolution. He was only sixteen. The Imperial Company was sending a strange mix of inexperienced and unpromising people out to try to establish presence in various ports and learn on the job. The few fairly competent senior people were French, the ship was a renamed French ship, and it sailed from the French port of Lorient.

At Canton in 1779, de Constant made a promising connection with a Frenchman who had stayed behind after the end of the voyages of the old French Company. With time on his hands, de Constant wrote a lot about trade procedures and about his own views of China and the Chinese. Another ship flying the Austrian Imperial colours arrived in 1780 from Livorno, but it was really a private trade project of a couple of Scots, and produced neither work nor profit for de Constant. He gave up and left on an English ship in 1782, but when he reached London, he was informed that two Imperial ships were on their way to Canton and he should go right back, which he did, arriving in July 1783. But after the passage of Pitt's Commutation Act in 1784 the business of smuggling tea into Great Britain collapsed, and so did the Trieste (Imperial) Company. No more ships came, and he was back in England in 1786.

30. Charles-Samuel de Constant and Louis Dermigny, *Les Mémoires de Charles de Constant sur le Commerce de la Chine* (Paris: S.E.V.P.E.N., 1964), 396–97. Dermigny's introduction on pp. 13–17, has some intelligent summary on the shift from Jesuit idealizations of high culture to impressions derived from decades of massive and confusing commerce at Canton. On pp. 21–132, Dermigny has pulled together an excellent short biography of Constant, with apt long quotations from his letters and diaries. The rest of the volume prints a wide range of his commercial records and analyses. A more recent study finds many more manuscript sources and uses them in a lively biographical sketch: Marie-Sybille de Vienne, *La Chine au Déclin des Lumières: L'Expérience de Charles de Constant, Négociant des Loges de Canton* (Paris: Honoré Champion Éditeur, 2004).
31. For excellent introductions to the enormous amounts of writing by and about Benjamin Constant see Helena Rosenblatt, ed., *The Cambridge Companion to Constant* (Cambridge and New York: Cambridge University Press, 2009).

Despite being able to claim experience of China, his efforts to find a position related to the flourishing trade met with little success. But eventually he made contact with the people who were really working to revive French trade with China. He spent hours answering their questions, and wrote long memoirs on commodities, prices, procedures, and so on. De Constant was placed in charge of a new effort, and sailed in January 1789, remaining in Canton until the end of 1792. He was in Canton as the depredations of the Heshen clique (和珅, 1786–1792) neared their peak, when the Canton officials were expected to send a steady stream of clocks and other luxuries and about a million *liang* of silver a year to the Court. The governor-general of the two Guangs, Sun Shiyi 孫士毅, had also just overreached himself in a very expensive botched invasion of Vietnam.[32]

Two passages from de Constant's journal for December 1789 are as fine pieces of eyewitness reporting on the outrages of these times as I have read:

> December 1. Today I sold coral worth 50,000 écus. It caused a great deal of trouble and annoyance. The mandarins, avid for whatever they see of value, wanted it, not to buy but to steal; it was the poor security merchant for the ship who was obliged to pay for it. They sent to me one of their people whose impertinence made me angry. I asked the security merchant, who is this person? He said 'He is the valet of the *Tsomptou* [*zongdu* 總督]'. 'But why is he so insolent?' 'Alas, sir,' replied the merchant, 'when the mandarin's dog leaves his house and comes to us, he is also a mandarin'.
>
> December 5. Today there came to our factory a favorite of the *Tsomptou*, viceroy or more god of this country. I had a really beautiful gold hunting-mount watch which had cost me 25 louis; he saw it and immediately wanted to take it, which did not cost him anything more than to say to the security merchant 'You will pay this foreign devil for this watch.' I had no desire to sell it but I saw it go; the security merchant had no desire to buy it but had to pay for it. When I complain to some Chinese about this kind of theft, they say 'What is it to you? You got paid.' These villains put a price on something only by the silver it will bring. I could have demanded a big sum from the security merchant for my watch, but God shield me from profiting from the vexations of the mandarins to vex others in turn! They soon will take everything from us down to our shirts, and they think everything is permitted because we get paid. It is true that they must think us well motivated, since despite their injustices we continue to come here for the money.[33]

The sale of the cargo of the ship that brought Constant and the purchase of exports seem to have gone fairly smoothly. Constant stayed in Canton until December 1792. He was making some money, especially by loans to the Hong merchants; this is a theme in the history of the Canton Trade that is taken up in other chapters in this volume and awaits full study. But the new revolutionary government threw open French trade to any investors and shippers, and declared that it would

32. John E. Wills Jr., 'Functional, Not Fossilized: Qing Tribute Relations with Đại Việt (Vietnam) and Siam (Thailand), 1700–1820', *T'oung Pao* 98 (2012): 439–78. See pp. 471–72.
33. Constant and Dermigny, *Les Mémoires de Charles de Constant*, 74–75; and de Vienne, *La Chine au déclin des Lumières*, 264–65.

not be necessary to keep permanent agents in Canton, a decision which de Constant protested vehemently.

De Constant took passage home on the Italian ship *Etrusco* in early January 1793; the vessel was taken by the English, who were now at war with revolutionary France, and all of Constant's goods were confiscated. He never published his writings on Canton; we owe our access to his remarkable experiences to the modern publications of Louis Dermigny and Marie-Sybille de Vienne. They contain a lot of commercial detail and some rather frank passages about the individual Hong merchants, especially Pan Khequa, who 'hides beneath a seductive exterior the hardest soul that has ever inhabited a human body'.[34]

In conclusion, the five individuals briefly introduced above provide glimpses of the Canton trade that are generally not found in more official records. They had in common the fact that all of them were welcomed at Canton so long as they were in some way connected to the trade. Three of these men visited Canton more than once, and all five of them came to China without any prior permission or arrangement. As long as they arrived on a merchant ship, no questions were asked.

The five men represent a diversity of backgrounds: two hard-living young Englishmen, two plant-collectors, one a Lutheran chaplain and the other a failed priest, and a French-Swiss of good family encountering the worst times in Canton. Their observations contribute to the larger picture of the trade, and they remind us of the variety of visions that make up the human condition, whether at home or far away. Finding additional eyewitness reports could considerably enrich our understanding of the trade. The continuity from botanizing as a hobby to the great efforts to get tea plants to India and Fortune's final success, for example, links eighteenth century 'natural history' to the new nineteenth-century phases of plantation agriculture in ways that could be of world-historical importance. So could more mentions of merchants of Middle Eastern and Indian origin doing business at Canton, especially if we could find some figures on their trade.

34. Constant and Dermigny, *Les Mémoires de Charles de Constant*, 411. The Pan Khequa mentioned here would be either the same man as the Pankeequa (d. 1788) mentioned above, or his son and successor, who was also called Pan Khequa.

6

Nathan Dunn (1782–1844) as Anti-Opium China Trader and Sino-Western Cultural Intermediary

Jonathan Goldstein

Introduction

Nathan Dunn's story has been told and retold many times making it challenging to come up with something new to say about his life. The American social historian John Haddad has written one of the most recent and extensive accounts of Dunn's influence on American thought and ideology.[1] My study is not an attempt to duplicate what Haddad and other scholars have done. Although some repetition is perhaps unavoidable, my objective is rather to use Dunn's example to understand better the wide range of experiences of private traders in China. His story is perhaps one of the best that we have that shows how difficult it is to generalize the private traders and their roles in the advancement and/or decline of the commerce. As is pointed out in the preface, there were hundreds of these men who were active in Canton in the eighteenth and early nineteenth century. We need many more of their stories before we can begin to understand them as a group.[2]

As several other chapters in this volume show, individuals like Dunn who became wealthy could lose their fortunes as quickly as they gained them. As an anti-opium advocate and as a mediator between Chinese and Western cultures, Dunn brings out an entirely different side of the private trade experience. Dunn stayed

1. John Haddad, *Romance of China: Excursions to China in U.S. Culture, 1776–1876* (New York: Columbia University Press, 2008), Chapter 4 'China in Miniature. Nathan Dunn's Chinese Museum', 86–128. See also John Haddad, *America's First Adventure in China* (Philadelphia: Temple University Press, 2013), 120–22.
2. Earlier versions of this chapter were presented as lectures at Sun Yat-sen University, Guangzhou, China, at a 15 November 2013 conference on 'Private Merchants of the China Trade 1700 to 1842' and at Sichuan International Studies University, Chongqing, China, on 22 November 2013. Those versions serve as the basis for chapters in books tentatively entitled 'Empathizers East: Idealists Who Left America for East Asia' and 'Diminishing Conflict, Fostering Reconciliation: Essays in Honor of Hilary Conroy'. The research, writing, and editing of this chapter was conducted during the author's Plumer Visiting Fellowship at St. Anne's College, Oxford University, in 2013–2014. The author would like to thank St. Anne's colleagues Robert Chard, Jonathan Katz, Anne Mullen, Derek Penslar, Cathryn Setz, and the entire college library staff for their collegiality and unwavering academic and research support.

more than a decade in China. He had great freedom in purchasing whatever he wanted, without restrictions, so long as the goods were legal items of trade. Even non-traditional items such as life-sized figures of Chinese persons and a wide variety of common artefacts from all over China were ordered by Dunn without any questions being asked. As long as he conducted some trade, he was welcomed to stay in Canton and/or Macao.

Perhaps the most important aspects of Dunn's career are that he went broke twice in his life, once before going to China, and once afterwards. And yet despite his need for money to pay creditors, Dunn refused to trade in opium, and still managed to earn a substantial fortune while in China. His most important role, however, was perhaps his unwavering devotion to preserving and spreading knowledge and understanding about Chinese society and culture in the West. Despite his limited resources, Dunn managed to put together the largest and most comprehensive collection of artefacts on China known at the time. Even the large East India companies with their huge budgets and influence and which traded in Canton for a hundred or more years did not come as close to spreading knowledge about China to their respective populations as Dunn accomplished within a few years, and all at his own expense. Europeans collected and ordered paintings and albums depicting Chinese architecture, landscapes, and a wide variety of daily activities, many of which are now held in museums throughout Europe. These items, however, were originally purchased for private use and enjoyment and were never intended to become tools to educate the general public, like what Dunn had in mind. These factors make him an extraordinary example of an individual private trader who was not in the business only for the money.

Dunn's commercial activity will be described first, then his critique of the opium trade, and finally his role as an early Sino-Western cultural intermediary.[3]

Dunn's Early Life and Business Career

Nathan Dunn Jr. (hereafter Nathan Dunn) was born on 11 November 1782, in Piles Grove Township, Salem County, New Jersey. He was the fifth child of Quaker farmers Nathan Dunn Sr. and Rhoda Silvers. Nathan Sr. died shortly after Nathan Jr.'s birth. In 1788, Rhoda Dunn married Thomas Osborn. Nathan's siblings from his mother's first marriage included an older sister, Deborah Dunn (m. Caleb Pancoast). Nathan

3. Dunn was among the earliest Americans to appreciate and publicize the positive aspects of Chinese culture, along with fellow Philadelphian Quaker Robert Waln Jr. See Haddad, *Romance*; Haddad, *America's*; Jonathan Goldstein, 'Philadelphia's Old China Trade and Early American Images of China', *Pennsylvania Legacies* 12, no. 1 (May 2012): 6–11; Aaron Caplan, 'Nathan Dunn's Chinese Museum' (unpub. research paper, History, University of Pennsylvania, 23 April 1986, courtesy of the author); and Haverford College Library, Haverford, Pennsylvania, Quaker Collection (henceforth HC): Ian Shinn, 'Encounters of a New Kind: Nathan Dunn's Chinese Collection and the Construction of Race in Nineteenth-Century America', unpub. BA honors thesis, American Studies, Amherst College, 2006.

Dunn seems to have been especially close to Deborah and her daughter Hannah C. Dixey, stipulating in his will that they inherit a large share of his estate. His half-siblings from his mother's second marriage included Phoebe Osborn (d. 1848) and Rhoda Osborn (circa 1794–1881, m. Restore S. Lamb, d. circa 1867?). Rhoda and Restore were distinguished ministers of the Hicksite branch of the Quakers. Phoebe and Rhoda ultimately resided in the 'Chinese Cottage', which Nathan built in Mt. Holly, New Jersey, after returning from China and prior to moving to Europe for his last years (Figure 6.1). Nathan's devout Quaker faith, into which he was inducted in 1802, dictated the parameters of his personal life and commercial activity, even though he was formally excluded from the movement early in his career.[4]

In 1802, Dunn moved to Philadelphia and transferred from the Salem Monthly Meeting of Friends to that of Philadelphia. He apprenticed to William Fowell, a merchant at 58 North Front Street. Thereafter Philadelphia directories list him as engaged in business on his own account or with a series of partners.[5] Although there are few records of his early business activity, it is clear that by 1816 he had fallen deeply into debt. Several of his creditors were Friends. He was called before the Philadelphia Meeting and charged with favouring some creditors over others. Dunn denied the charge, would not express regret, and was 'disowned' (excommunicated), on 28 November 1816, for being 'unable to meet his engagements'. As in similar cases, the Meeting offered Dunn the possibility of readmission if he 'morally reformed' by paying off his financial obligations. Bankrupt at the age of thirty-four, Dunn began investigating ways of restoring financial solvency.[6]

He engineered his fiscal rescue through innovative approaches to trade. Unlike Great Britain and other European countries, the United States did not have a state-sponsored Asiatic trading company. Rather, there were many American solo-practitioners, family firms, and other small partnerships. It was widely known that if a person showed up on the China coast with a ship and merchandise to trade that they would be allowed to go upriver to Canton, without any prior license or written agreement. It did not matter how large the ship was or what country it came

4. HC: 'Last Will and Testament of Nathan Dunn, Late of the City of Philadelphia, Deceased, March 7, 1840', with codicils dated 1841.07.13, 1841.11.13, 1844.10.24, 1844.10.26, 1844.10.29, and 1844.11.02 and with appendix entitled 'Agreement between Nathan Dunn and William B. Langdon, July 13, 1841'; Leah Blackman, *History of Little Egg Harbor Township, Burlington County, N.J., from its First Settlement to the Present Time* (Camden, NJ: Proceedings . . . of the Surveyors' Association of West New Jersey, 1880), 281–85; Robert C. Smith, 'Friend Dunn', *Haverford College Publication Horizons* 67, no. 6 (Summer 1969): 8–13; Historical Society of Pennsylvania (HSP): Nelson B. Gaskill, 'Nathan Dunn' scrapbook; and Arthur W. Hummel, 'Nathan Dunn', *Quaker History* 59 (1970): 34–39.
5. HSP: Nelson B. Gaskill, 'Nathan Dunn' scrapbook, 'List of Philadelphia directories, 1802–42'.
6. HSP: Nelson B. Gaskill, 'Nathan Dunn' scrapbook, Testimony against Nathan Dunn, 28 November to 5 December 1816, Minutes of the Philadelphia Monthly Meeting of Friends, Philadelphia directory listings; Jean Gordon Lee, *Philadelphians and the China Trade, 1784–1844* (Philadelphia: Philadelphia Museum of Art, 1984), 14; HC: Ian Shinn, 'Encounters', 156; Hummel, 'Nathan Dunn', 34–38; and Haddad, *Romance*, 88.

from (as long they were not from Russia or Japan). Without this assurance, many Americans would not have risked sailing halfway around the world to engage in the China trade.

By 1818 Dunn was almost surely aware of the China trade activities of Robert Morris, a financier of both the American Revolution and America's first lucrative China trading voyage—the *Empress of China* in 1784. Dunn would have been aware of the activities of Philadelphia-based China trader Stephen Girard, one of the earliest American millionaires, and of Philadelphia's Waln family. That Quaker dynasty, which included Robert Waln Sr. and Jr. and Jesse Waln, pioneered American opium shipments from Smyrna in the Ottoman Empire to China.[7]

In evaluating schemes for restoring personal solvency, Dunn realized that, despite the prospect of success, the China trade was always a risky business. A trader might die suddenly from ague, colic, or other ailments, not to mention as a casualty of piracy and war. He might be the victim of debts which were uncollectable in remote commercial environments such as is mentioned in Jessica Hanser's chapter. And Dunn in particular faced difficulties as a result of his determination to seek wealth in a 'moral' manner (not violating Quaker ethics), which he saw as including compliance with the laws of foreign countries. Commercially challenged now for the second time, Dunn entered the China trade with a determination to profit without dealing in what he saw as its most nefarious contraband commodity, opium.[8]

Nevertheless, the business strategies of his less ethical fellow traders suggested schemes which Dunn could modify on his road to recovery. His first obstacle was the lack of start-up capital for a vessel and outbound cargo. His solution, once again, was to form a partnership. As Haddad has shown, in 1818 Dunn turned to his friend and creditor John Field, who had previously traded at Canton. Dunn wrote that 'I proposed this voyage to him, and though he at the time had no intention to make another voyage to China, he finally acquiesced on the condition that all profits help

7. The American opium trade from Smyrna began with the 1805 voyage of the *Sylph*, James S. Wilcox, supercargo, carrying thirty-three chests of the drug. Charles C. Steele, *American Trade in Opium to China in the Nineteenth Century* (Chicago: University of Chicago Libraries, 1938), 440. On Americans who had already made fortunes in the China trade by the time of Dunn's entry, see Jonathan Goldstein, *Stephen Girard's Trade with China 1787–1824: The Norms versus the Profits of Trade* (Portland, ME: MerwinAsia Publishers, 2011). Hao Yen-p'ing reports that 'Chinese and American tea merchants generally made money . . . the net profit of the *Empress of China* was 25 percent of the original investment . . . The net profits of the *Betsy* in 1797–98 came to $53,118'. Hao Yen-p'ing, 'Chinese Teas to America—A Synopsis'. In *America's China Trade in Historical Perspective*, ed. Ernest R. May and John K. Fairbank (Cambridge, MA: Harvard University Committee on American-East Asian Relations, 1986), 11–32, 29. According to diplomatic historian John Curtis Perry, a fortunate American shipowner might make a 400 to 500 per cent profit on a single round-trip voyage to China, and 'even the lowly seaman might be given the opportunity to carry cargo on his own account'. John Curtis Perry, *Americans and the Opening of the Pacific* (Westport, CT: Praeger, 1994), 41–42.
8. HC: Ian Shinn, 'Encounters', 156.

liquidate a debt owed him'. That year Dunn embarked for Canton as supercargo, or chief commercial officer, aboard a vessel optimistically named *Hope*.[9]

Except for a brief westward return in 1821–1822, Dunn would remain in Canton for twelve years. He traded there until January 1831 under the name of Nathan Dunn & Company. His primary objective was to ship tea and porcelain back to America. He also transported nankeens, the tough cotton fabric manufactured at the central Chinese city of Nanjing. Before New England mills began mass-production of cotton cloth, this durable yellow fabric was cheap material for men's trousers as well as children's play clothes.[10]

Americans also coveted finer Chinese textiles. Silk was manufactured near Canton. It arrived at the foreign factories in May, a period of low business activity. Most traders timed their voyages to coincide with the start of the autumn tea season. They set sail long before new silks appeared. Thus, in the silk market, advantage accrued to companies with permanent resident agents. Dunn, who remained in the Canton/Macao region year-round, was able to outmanoeuvre his competitors and procure many varieties of this fabric at reasonable prices.[11]

Dunn also shrewdly observed that the British East India Company had developed a Chinese market for English cloth. Many of Dunn's competitors, obsessed with the smuggling of Indian and Levantine opium, overlooked British textiles as an inbound cargo. Haddad points out that Dunn found 'an opening for the introduction of different kinds of British goods'. By procuring other types of goods that were 'better calculated for the Chinese wants', he could secure a fair profit.[12]

Dunn located English manufacturers willing to supply goods for the Chinese taste. That task complete, he set into motion an innovative triangular shipping scheme. On the first leg of the triangle, he shipped American goods to England. Then, he invested the proceeds from the sale of those goods in English manufactures. On the second leg, he shipped the British goods to Canton, where he exchanged

---

9. Haddad, *Romance*, 89; and Hummel, 'Nathan Dunn', 34–38.
10. *Poulson's American Daily Advertiser*, 1820.01.03 and 1820.02.16. The American journalist Horace Greeley recalled that 'in my early boyhood, Chinese cotton fabrics known as Nankins [*sic*] were extensively worn even by the poor in New England'. Horace Greeley, *Essays Designed to Elucidate the Science of Political Economy* (Boston: Fields Osgood, 1870), 45.
11. Carl Crossman, *The China Trade: Export Paintings, Furniture, Silver and Other Objects* (Princeton: Pyne Press, 1972); 'Silk samples from Eshing given by Pickering Dodge of Salem to Benjamin Shreve in 1819 as a Buying Guide', 240; Enoch Wines, *A Peep at China in Mr. Dunn's Chinese Collection* (Philadelphia: Printed for Nathan Dunn, 1839), 10–11, reprinted in *Sermons Collected by the American Sunday School Union* 3: 27 (n.d.) and in *The Chinese Repository* 8 (March 1840): 583. See also *The Chinese Repository* 12 (November 1843): 561–82; Haddad, *America's*, 120–21; Haddad, *Romance*, 86, and 90–110.
12. Haddad, *Romance*, 90–91. See also John Haddad, 'China of the American Imagination: The Influence of Trade on US Portrayals of China, 1820 to 1850', in *Narratives of Free Trade: The Commercial Cultures of Early US-China Relations*, ed. Kendall Johnson (Hong Kong: Hong Kong University Press, 2012), 57–82, 65; and Henry Simpson, *Lives of Eminent Philadelphians* (Philadelphia: William Brotherhead, 1859), 209.

them for Chinese tea, porcelain, silk, and nankeens. Those products were then shipped to America, via the Cape of Good Hope, which completed the third leg of the triangle.

In this way, Dunn successfully engaged in the China trade without selling opium. With the single interruption of his aforementioned trip to Liverpool in November 1821 to oversee the British end of this scheme, he resided in China for twelve years. During that residence, he benefitted from close ties with the Chinese merchant Tingqua. During the disastrous Canton fire of November 1822, Tingqua dispatched about eighty workers and a small flotilla of boats to douse the flames of Dunn's warehouse. Tingqua's men retrieved some $150,000 worth of Dunn's goods and removed them to the safety of ships offshore. Although contemporaneous paintings of the fire show Chinese efforts to rescue the merchandise of other traders, many Chinese and foreign merchants incurred substantial losses. An impoverished Chinese who walked away from Dunn's flaming warehouse with several bags of silver later returned them. That act of generosity impressed Dunn. Indeed, the Canton fire may have been the epiphany in the formation of Dunn's attitude toward the Chinese. He wrote that the return of the funds 'says something for the poor people of China'.[13]

Dunn maintained a positive view of the Chinese up to the time he left Canton for Philadelphia on 3 January 1831. Nathan Dunn & Company thereafter was managed by his partners Jabez Jenkins and Joseph Archer. Dunn arrived in Philadelphia on 21 November 1831 as one of the city's wealthiest citizens. Fellow Philadelphian China trader John Latimer estimated Dunn's worth at $200,000, a substantial sum in those days.[14]

---

13. Library Company of Philadelphia (LCP): Am 1835 Dunn 2603.Q.14, 'Jones vs. Dunn'. Commonwealth of Pennsylvania. Supreme Court. July term, 1835, No. 52. Isaac C. Jones, Richard Oakford, and Samuel T. Jones, who survived Samuel Archer, to the use of I. C. Jones, Oakford. Vs. Nathan Dunn. This file includes Letters: I. C. Jones, Oakford & Co. and Samuel Archer to N. Dunn, 1832.02.02, N. Dunn to I. C. Jones, Oakford & Co. and Samuel Archer, 1832.03.07, I. C. Jones, Oakford & Co. and Samuel Archer to Nathan Dunn, 1832.03.12, N. Dunn to I. C. Jones, Oakford & Co. and Samuel Archer, 1833.12.21, I. C. Jones, Oakford & Co. and Samuel Archer to N. Dunn, 1834.03.05, and N. Dunn to Samuel Archer and I. C. Jones, Oakford & Co. 1835.01.31. 'The Fire at Canton, 1822, by the Master of the Fire of 1822', is reproduced in Crossman, *The China Trade*, 50. According to Crossman, the 'master' painted a set of three small oil paintings of the fire on canvas and yet another on brass. The painting reproduced on p. 50 shows a massive rescue effort, with goods being salvaged from a large number of buildings. See also Carl L. Crossman, *The Decorative Arts of the China Trade* (Woodbridge, Suffolk, UK: Antique Collectors Club, 1997), 427; Patrick Conner, *The Hongs of Canton* (London: English Art Books, 2009), 89–110; Joan Thill, 'A Delawarean in the Celestial Empire' (MA thesis, University of Delaware, 1973), 40; Haddad, *Romance*, 87, 120; and Paul A. Van Dyke and Maria Kar-wing Mok, *Images of the Canton Factories 1760–1822* (Hong Kong: Hong Kong University Press, 2015).
14. Mystic Seaport Museum, G. W. Blunt White Library (BW): Misc. Vol. 552, Nathan Dunn Letter copybook 1829–1830, Nathan Dunn to John Sergeant, Esq., 1838.10.26. On 30 June 1833, Dunn relinquished his liability in Nathan Dunn & Co. and announced that his former

One of Dunn's first acts upon returning was to pay off his creditors. He invited them to a banquet at his house at Ninth and Spruce Streets, where he placed under each plate a check for the amount of debt plus interest in full. He thereby regained his good name. As a by-product of his restored social status, he became host of a Friday evening 'collection of gentlemen of all professions who enjoy each other's converse'.[15]

Dunn also went on to become a member and benefactor of other regional causes and charitable and educational institutions, notably Philadelphia's Academy of Natural Sciences.[16] Upon his death, the *Philadelphia Ledger* characterized Dunn's social conscience as 'sensible that the public good could be promoted by a liberal dispensation of his ample means'.[17] Other examples of his beneficence included his participation as a director of the Philadelphia House of Refuge, his support of the Apprentices' Library Company of Philadelphia, the Indigent Widows' and Single Women's Society of Philadelphia, the Mercantile Library Company, the Pennsylvania Academy of the Fine Arts, the Philadelphia Athenaeum, and societies for prison reform and African colonization, a priority for Abolitionists in general and Philadelphia Quakers in particular. He gave the Pennsylvania Institute for Instruction of the Blind volumes of raised print books. In 1840, as a successful bachelor without significant family expenses, he donated $20,575 to struggling Haverford College in suburban Philadelphia, sustaining that Quaker institution then on the verge of bankruptcy. Dunn was one of five directors, and one time president and a major stockholder, of Laurel Hill Cemetery, where he was buried on 6 August 1845.[18]

---

associates in Canton, Jenkins and Archer, would continue the firm. *The Canton Register*, 1833.07.15; Newark, University of Delaware Library (UDL): John R. Latimer Papers, Latimer Letterbook, John Richardson Latimer to James Latimer, 1831.08.02; and Downs, *Golden Ghetto*, 85. On 3 August 1832, Matthew Ralston of Philadelphia wrote John Latimer in Canton that Dunn 'has been paying off all his debts, both principal and interest, and has established an excellent name'. Library of Congress: Latimer Papers.

15. Dunn referred to his soirees as 'weekly socials for the season'. LCP: Letters: Nathan Dunn to Jas. Rush, 1837.12.22, 1839.01.28, 1839.12.30, and 1840.04.10; Massachusetts Historical Society (MHS): Shattuck Collection, George C, Shattuck Jr., Philadelphia, to G. C. Shattuck, M.D., Boston, 21 December 1831; James Silk Buckingham, *The Eastern and Western States of America*, 3 vols. (London: Fisher, 1842), Vol. 1, 468; and Robert C. Smith, 'Friend Dunn', *Haverford College Publication Horizons* 67, no. 6 (Summer 1969): 8–13. Philadelphia literati P. S. du Ponceau, N. Chapman, and I. K. Kane hosted an honorific 'Dinner to Nathan Dunn, Esquire . . . at the Mansion House Hotel, (Head's)' on 20 May 1840. LCP: McAllister Collection.
16. In 1836 Dunn was also elected to the American Philosophical Society (see below). Marine Historical Association, Mystic, Connecticut, on microfilm at American Philosophical Society Library, Philadelphia (APS): letters Nathan Dunn, Philadelphia, to Alex. Bache, 1836.01.28.
17. *Public Ledger* (Philadelphia), 1844.10.24, Dunn obituary.
18. After succumbing to an attack of 'bilious fever', which may have been malaria, Dunn died on 19 September 1844 in Vevey, Switzerland. HC: Commonwealth of Pennsylvania, House of Representatives. 'No. 40. RE-PRINT SENATE NO. 2, READ December 20, 1836, AN ACT

Dunn's will, dated 7 March 1840, distributed an estate of more than $200,000 to relatives, friends, and institutions. Because of codicils, the amounts actually dispensed are difficult to determine. He specified bequests of $40,000 to his half-sisters, Phoebe and Rhoda Osborn, and the use in trust of his Mt. Holly home as their place of residence. In 1882, after their deaths, the property was sold for $10,600, which was transferred 'to purchase books and in forming a useful library to be opened in some appropriate and well situated institution in or near Mt. Holly'. That institution, the Burlington County Lyceum of History and Natural Sciences, is today's Mount Holly Public Library. It contains an important collection of books on Asia, some of which Dunn may have purchased in London on his return from China. As of 2017, some support of the Mt. Holly Library still derived from Dunn's bequest.[19]

The Opium Trading Debate

Throughout his China trading career Dunn was outspoken in his condemnation of opium trading, whether it be conducted directly or indirectly, by Chinese, Americans, or other foreigners. According to Philadelphia minister Enoch Wines, Dunn considered the trade to be 'contrary to the laws of the [Chinese] Empire' and was never interested 'to the amount of a dollar' in the 'illicit commerce'.[20]

Dunn's anti-opium stance brought him into the ongoing debate over the drug within the Anglo-American trading community, and he was also much opposed to slavery and the slave trade. When the opium arrived, it was passed from foreign

to incorporate the Laurel Hill Cemetery'; HSP: letters George Brown, Laurel Hill Cemetery, to Nelson Gaskill, 19, 24, and 25 July 1944, Nelson B. Gaskill, 'Nathan Dunn' scrapbook, 'Last Will and Testament of Nathan Dunn, Late of the City of Philadelphia, Deceased, March 7, 1840', pp. 4–7; Haverford Alumni Association, *A History of Haverford College for the First Sixty Years of Its Existence* (Philadelphia: Porter and Coates, 1892), 123, 143–44, and 200; Smith, 'Friend Dunn', 10 and 12; HC: Ian Shinn, 'Encounters', 157; Hummel, 'Nathan Dunn', p. 39; Haddad, *America's*, 120–21; Haddad, *Romance*, 102–5, and 112. Eulogies for Dunn appeared in *The New-Jersey Mirror and Burlington County Advertiser* (Mt. Holly) on 31 October and 12, 14 and 21 November 1844. Dunn's philanthropic activity dated back to his days in Canton, when he donated $200 to a Christian group for the printing of scripture lessons in Chinese. Eliza A. Morrison and Samuel Kidd, *Memoirs of Life and Labours of Robert Morrison Compiled by his Widow*, 2 vols. (London: Longman, Orme, 1839).

19. HC: 'Last Will and Testament of Nathan Dunn, Late of the City of Philadelphia, Deceased, March 7, 1840'; *Friends' Weekly Intelligencer*, 1844.10.25, p. 245 and 1844.11.23, p. 277; Charles Coleman Sellers, *Mr. Peale's Museum* (New York: Norton, 1980), 273; HC: Ian Shinn, 'Encounters', 157; Hummel, 'Nathan Dunn', 39; Haddad, *America's*, 120–21; and Haddad, *Romance*, 102–5, and 112.
20. Wines, *A Peep at China*, 10–11; William Hinshaw, *Encyclopedia of Quaker Genealogy* (Ann Arbor, MI: Edwards Bros., 1936–1963), Vol. 2, 27–67; Hummel, 'Nathan Dunn', p. 35; Elma Loines, ed., *The China Trade Post-Bag of the Seth Low Family of Salem and New York* (Manchester, ME: Falmouth Publishing House, 1953), 7 and 298; Downs, *Golden Ghetto*, 365–66; Ann White, 'The Hong Merchants of Canton' (PhD diss., University of Pennsylvania, 1968), 128–49; and Jonathan Goldstein, *Philadelphia and the China Trade, 1682–1846* (University Park, PA: Pennsylvania State University Press, 1978), 50, 58, 66, and 68.

to Chinese hands offshore. But it was in Canton, and not aboard ships, where the operations centre of the trade was located, where deals were finalized, where English-language circulars listed prices, and where Western merchants spent the hard cash for a return cargo. Chinese authorities had every right, even in terms of Western law, to confiscate such ill-gotten wealth. Dunn saw the economic and social ruination of China as the logical consequence of the opium trade. Writing from London in 1843, where the opium debate raged as fiercely as in America, Dunn summarized his objections:

> Missionaries are going out [to China] in great numbers. When I am enquired of I give my opinion that they had better stop the opium trade first . . . Opium and the Bible cannot enter China together. When I left in 1831 the annual amount of opium smuggled into China was 15 [to] 17,000 chests of 133 lbs each . . . Now it reaches to 35 to 40,000 chests and . . . is paid for [in] silver . . . draining that country of all [its] pressious mettles [*sic*] . . . It is thought that the Government will put a stop to it ere long . . . but if they should not, in ten, or fifteen years more, China will be a poor country.[21]

Dunn and a few others highly criticized their fellow merchants. They asserted that half of the latter men's annual income derived from the opium trade. The dealers, for their part, were unapologetic in defending their entrepreneurship. An 1829 letter from American opium dealer John Latimer to his kinsman Henry Latimer may be considered the 'smoking gun' of this dishonourable profession:

> You are aware that the trade in opium is illegal. The system is perfect. A dealer pays the money down and at the same time receives the order to go to the ship for it. We never see it at all. Foreign merchants reside here constantly who are known to have no other business than opium and are never mentioned.[22]

Perhaps the most outspoken abstainer was New Yorker D. W. C. Olyphant, who characterized the opium trade as 'an evil of the deepest dye'. He was sarcastically nicknamed 'Holy Joe'. In a classic defence of a dishonourable profession, Bostonian John Murray Forbes, of Russell and Co., wrote of Olyphant: 'Protect me from the all the hallowing influence of holy Joe—his ships are commanded by J-C [Jesus Christ]—officered by Angels and manned by Saints— . . . Happy thrice happy is the ship even consigned to them'.[23] Another blunt defender of the trade was Benjamin

21. HC: Letters Nathan Dunn, London, to niece Hannah C. Dixey, New Hatborough, 1843.03.03.
22. University of Delaware: Latimer Papers, John Latimer to Henry Latimer, 1829.04.23; and Goldstein, *Philadelphia and the China Trade*, 48–52.
23. Harvard Business School, Boston, MA, Baker Library: Heard Papers, Interoffice memo, John Murray Forbes, Macao, to Augustine Heard, Canton, 28 August 1832; Downs, *Golden Ghetto*, 207. A member of Olyphant & Co. lamented that 'our nation is involved in dishonor and perhaps losses here for the sake of a few chests of opium, a mere trifle in all'. APS: letters Charles King to Talbot, Olyphant & Co., ca. 1837–38, Charles Talbot Papers, property of Miss Frances Talbot; Goldstein, *Philadelphia and the China Trade*, 50, 58, 66, 68; Jonathan Goldstein, review of Kendall Johnson, *Narratives of Free Trade: The Commercial Cultures of Early US-China Relations*, in *Journal of Chinese Studies* 56 (January 2013): 356; and Jonathan

Chew Wilcocks, pioneer of American drug shipment from the Ottoman Empire and simultaneously American consul in Canton. In 1829 Wilcocks offered John Wittall the captaincy of the ship *New Jersey* on a China opium run, but Wittall refused. Wilcocks retorted that

> I almost wished I had not heard his objections to going into our employ, which have lessened him in my opinion. I hope I have due and proper respect for the prejudices of my fellow man, but when a Captain stipulates for the particular articles which he will take on my ship, why let him go you know where for a cargo. I have done with him forever.[24]

The American Sinologist John K. Fairbank concluded in his book *China Watch* in 1987 that 'the opium trade from India to China was the longest-continued systematic international crime of modern time'.[25] Dunn, for his part, went beyond legal considerations and condemned the opium trade as immoral. 'Opium is a poison', he wrote, 'destructive alike of the health and morals of those who use it habitually'. The trade 'is nothing less than making merchandise of the bodies and souls of men'. Philadelphia's *Public Ledger* noted that 'while many merchants of equal standing degraded their calling and sunk their morality by entering into the opium trade, Mr. Dunn, with the conscientiousness becoming a Philadelphia Quaker, kept his hands pure from the taint of the murderous drug'.[26] Fellow China trade colleagues William Wood and Peter Dobell reinforced the moral argument, characterizing the commerce as 'pernicious'. They refrained from the trade as did many British abstainers.[27]

Goldstein, review of James Fichter, *So Great a Profitt*, in *International Journal of Maritime History* 23, no. 1 (June 2011): 367–68.

24. WLC: Latimer Papers, letter Benjamin Wilcocks to John Latimer, 1829.04.26.
25. John K. Fairbank, *China Watch* (Cambridge, MA, and London, England: Harvard University Press, 1987), 13. In yet another contemporaneous account confirming Latimer's observations, Philadelphian China trader John Gibson wrote in 1807 that 'opium, although strictly prohibited by law, is so constantly introduced that there is no difficulty . . . getting it from on board at any time. The Whampoa mandarins have a fixed price per picul and come aboard themselves to see it weighed.' Cornell University, Kroch Library: MSS HF.G44, John Gibson, 'Observations on the Manner of Trading at Canton', dated 1807.11.13.
26. *Public Ledger* (Philadelphia), 1844.10.24, Dunn obituary.
27. William Wood, *Sketches of China With Illustrations From Original Drawings* (Philadelphia: Carey and Lea, 1830), 206–7; Peter Dobell, 'Travels in Kamchatka and Siberia', *American Quarterly Review* 9 (March–June 1831): 52–81, see 53; Arthur W. Hummel and Nan P. Hodges, eds., *Lights and Shadows of a Macao Life: The Journal of Harriett Low, Travelling Spinster*, 2 vols. (Redmond, WA: History Bank, 2002), passim. The other employees of Nathan Dunn & Co. who refused to join in the opium trade were Jabez Jenkins and Joseph Archer. After the onset of the Opium War in 1839, Wetmore & Company, and specifically its employees Samuel Rawle and James Legee, refused to partake in the opium trade, but at that point their motivation was almost surely the economic hardship of dealing in the drug rather than a moral stance. HSP: Joseph Archer Letterbooks, Joseph Archer to George Carter, 1834.02.03; BW: Misc. Vol. 552, Nathan Dunn Letter copybook, 1829–1830, Nathan Dunn to Joseph Archer, 1830.02.02; William Hunter, *Bits of Old China* (London: Kegan Paul, Trench, 1885), 166; James Wetmore, *The Wetmore Family of America* (Albany: Munsell and Rowland, 1861), 358;

In December 1841, ex–United States President John Quincy Adams and John Worth Edmonds joined the debate, basing their condemnation on both legal and moral issues. Their public lectures were published and widely discussed.[28]According to one contemporary source, Dunn's opposition to the trade reached as far as Beijing, where the Daoguang emperor took note. If true, the monarch must have regarded Dunn as an anomaly, as most of the intelligence he received pegged foreign merchants as the root of the problems. If the emperor had indeed made such an observation, it would have been well founded.[29]

John Latimer and John Murray Forbes were otherwise upright citizens, which makes one wonder how they could rationalize the opium trade. Latimer, for example, was President of the Society of the Cincinnati and the person who took charge of Benjamin Chew Wilcocks' illegitimate daughter when the latter man abandoned the child in China. He was also an outspoken advocate of business ethics in other areas.

A partial answer lies in the realization that very few Americans in nineteenth-century America, except those cited here, saw the trade as inappropriate. This was the era of De Quincey's *Opium-Eater* and a time when Samuel Taylor Coleridge and many other Westerners practically lived on laudanum.[30] The persons who denounced the trafficking were ahead of their times, crying out in an eighteenth- and nineteenth-century wilderness of unbridled entrepreneurship. The opium trade was, in many respects, a product of its time, along with privateering; the purchase and sale of indentured servants; and 'sweatshop labour' in coal mines, textile mills, and aboard ships. Some considered the sale of laudanum to be less cruel than these other activities. When Philadelphia social reformer Mathew Carey criticized his city's opium traders, he did so not for their actions abroad but rather for their abuse of workers on Pennsylvania canal projects and within the cities. Peter Dobell emphasized in his condemnation that Chinese collaborators and compradors also profited handsomely from the opium trade.[31]

The Chinese Repository 5 (January 1837): 413–15; 7 (April 1839): 636; and 8 (June 1839): 76; Downs, *Golden Ghetto*, 217.

28. John Quincy Adams, 'Lecture on the War with China, delivered before the Massachusetts Historical Society, December 1841', *The Chinese Repository* 11 (May 1842): 274–89. See pp. 281 and 288. John W. Edmonds, *Origins and Progress of the War Between England and China: A Lecture Delivered Before the Newburgh Lyceum, December 11, 1841* (New York: Narine & Co.,1841).
29. Wines, *A Peep at China*, 10–11; and Haddad, *America's*, 121.
30. De Quincey, *Confessions of an English Opium-Eater* (London: Taylor and Hersey, 1823).
31. Mathew Carey, 'Essays on the Public Charities of Philadelphia', in *Miscellaneous Essays* (Philadelphia: Carey & Hurt, 1830), 153–203, 173; Letter: John Latimer to Joseph Lesley, June 23, 1847, Latimer Papers, University of Delaware; Carol Ranshaw, 'Calendar of the University of Delaware Collection of the John Latimer China Trade Papers' (MA thesis, School of Library Science, Drexel Institute of Technology, 1953), 23; and Dobell, 'Travels in Kamchatka and Siberia', 53.

In the end, the opium traders prevailed. The drug was legalized in China after the Opium War. By 1906, the taxes collected from the trade became one of Imperial China's major sources of revenue.[32]

Dunn's Role as a Sino-American Cultural Intermediary

Besides his anti-opium campaign, Dunn was also a dedicated educator of Chinese culture. In the late 1820s, he was preoccupied with creating a collection of Chinese artefacts. There were attempts made to collect and display things about China, but nothing on the scale of what Dunn had in mind. In 1797, for example, the first American museum, that of Charles Wilson Peale in Philadelphia, displayed a Chinese shoe and two life-sized Chinese figurines. Daniel Bowen's Columbian Museum in Boston contained statuettes of 'Two Chinese Mandarines'.[33] The East India Marine Society, of Salem, Massachusetts, relied on sea captains to randomly acquire artefacts representative of the cultures of East, South, and Southeast Asia and Oceania, as well as that of the North Shore of Boston.

Of all these, Salem's 'cabinet of curiosities' was the most expansive by attempting to represent the ethnography of much of the world. To this day, its successor institution, the Peabody Essex Museum, includes Chinese objects within a much broader context of world maritime history and ethnography. Later in the nineteenth century, the Peabody systematized its acquiring and collecting under the guidance of Professor Edward Sylvester Morse, which was long after Dunn. The British East India Company, for its part, tried and failed to obtain a Chinese collection of its own, despite the vast resources at its disposal. Simultaneously the Dutch East India Company was only able to assemble in The Hague a random assortment of Asian artefacts which, in the final analysis, was far smaller than Dunn's. Writing in 1842, British historian James S. Buckingham concluded that Dunn, by contrast, concentrated on China and was able to create 'the most beautiful and perfect [exhibit] of its kind that perhaps, exists in the world'.[34]

32. John M. Carroll, 'The Other "Inner Opium War": British Traders' Debates about Opium in the Canton Period'. Unpublished paper presented at *Association for Asian Studies* (March 2014), passim.
33. Charles Sellers, *Mr. Peale's Museum* (New York: Norton, 1980), 34 and 92; and Mabel Stivers, 'Wax Figures in Old Museums', *Old Time New England* 17 (July 1926): 44.
34. Buckingham, *The Eastern and Western States of America*, Vol. 2, 42; *Public Ledger* (Philadelphia), 1844.10.24, Dunn obituary; Walter Muir Whitehill, *The East India Marine Society and the Peabody Museum of Salem: A Sesquicentennial History* (Salem, MA: Peabody Museum of Salem, 1949), 37–38; Goldstein, 'Philadelphia's Old China Trade and Early American Images of China', 6–11; Jonathan Goldstein, 'Cantonese Artefacts, Chinoiserie and the Formation of an Early American Image of the Chinese', in *The Chinese American Experience: Papers from the Second National Conference on Chinese American Studies (1980)*, ed. Genny Lim, 255–56 (San Francisco: The Chinese Historical Society of America and The Chinese Culture Foundation of San Francisco, 1984); Hummel, 'Nathan Dunn', p. 39; Haddad, *America's*, 120–21; Haddad, *Romance*, 102–5 and 112.

Librarian of Congress Arthur Hummel evaluated Dunn's museological effort as the first systematic collection of Chinese objects in the United States or the United Kingdom. Unlike earlier attempts, Dunn was very focussed.[35] Haddad suggests that Dunn was motivated by an 'ideology of Enlightenment science' which sought to understand China 'comprehensively and categorically'.[36] After his return from China, Dunn was nominated to membership in Benjamin Franklin's American Philosophical Society. His Enlightenment-infused sponsors affirmed that 'none of our citizens have shown a warmer desire to promote useful knowledge than this Gentleman'.[37]

As one of the few Philadelphia merchant/intellectuals who had resided in China for an extensive period of time, Dunn defined his mission as the creation of an all-encompassing exhibition that would portray 'China in miniature'.[38] He did not offer any startlingly new interpretation of China or the Chinese; using museums as his medium, his message was rather simple, one generating an idea that Chinese civilization had great merit and deserved attention.

His systematic method of collecting artefacts, however, was original and innovative. He forged friendships with Chinese officials who appreciated his opposition to opium and genuine empathy for China and its culture. His Chinese assistants, along with a few Hong merchants, helped him obtain objects from all over the country. Philadelphia China trader William Wood, who shared Dunn's condemnation of opium, trained Chinese agents to locate and retrieve specimens from nature such as plants, animals, fish, fowl, and insects.[39]

A 'Memoranda for Mr. Dunn', dated 18 March 1829 and presumably compiled in Canton, lists some of the specific artefacts Dunn sought to acquire. His enormous collection included Chinese agricultural instruments; watercolour drawings; costumed life-sized figurines; intricate ivory carvings; specimens of cotton goods, silk, grass cloth, and embroidery; paintings, porcelains, and other household furniture; and what Dunn described as a 'thousand and one' other things that were part of everyday life in the Eastern Empire. His wish list included 'a specimen of opium', which was used as an educational aid rather than as an example of a trade commodity.[40]

In 1838, Dunn erected his 'Chinese Museum' at Ninth and George (now Sansom) streets, on the site of what today is the Benjamin Franklin Hotel. It filled a

35. Hummel, 'Nathan Dunn', p. 38.
36. Haddad, *Romance*, 87–88.
37. APS: letters Joseph Hopkinson et. al. to President American Philosophical Society, 1834.03.07, Peter S. Du Ponceau et. al. to Isaac Lea et. al. 1835.11.18, Nathan Dunn, Philadelphia, to Alex. Bache, 1836.01.28.
38. Nathan Dunn and William B. Langdon, *"Ten Thousand Things Chinese": A Descriptive Catalogue of the Chinese Collection in Philadelphia* (Philadelphia: Printed for the Proprietor, 1839), 3.
39. Caplan, 'Nathan Dunn's Chinese Museum', passim; Shinn, p. 156; Smith, 'Friend Dunn', 12.
40. HC: 'Memoranda for Mr. Dunn', 1829.03.18, p. 8.

163 × 70 ft. hall. Just before Christmas that year, he gave a dinner party to celebrate the opening. There was Chinese food and drink and Chinese guides to explain, in broken English, the exhibition of a replicated 'street in Canton'. Chinese artisans had modelled fifty life-size clay figurines, from different social and economic classes ranging from mandarins to coolies. They were displayed in eleven cases with dioramas which were meticulously correct, e.g., a shop with attendants. The statuettes wore authentic Chinese clothing and were situated amidst Chinese furniture and trinkets.[41]

We have only fragmentary evidence of how Dunn's collection was received in the United States and the United Kingdom. From a commercial and statistical point of view, more than 100,000 visitors paid to see Dunn's 'Chinese Collection in Philadelphia'. His *Descriptive Catalogue* sold 50,000 copies within the first few months it was open. Although these numbers may seem large, the earnings were not enough to keep the museum going. By 1841, it was clear that his museum would not be able to sustain itself in Philadelphia so he made the bold move to relocate it to London. For the second time in his life, regaining solvency became his major objective. Philadelphia's *Public Ledger* lamented the city's loss and England's gain of 'America's most splendid scientific distinction'.[42]

In 1843, Dunn's exhibit guidebook went into an eighteenth edition. The very fact that this many printings were necessary is an indication of the museum's popularity. Although popular it was still struggling with sustainability. According to inconclusive reports, part of the exhibit was supposedly destroyed by a fire when en route to a third venue in Edinburgh.[43] Some of the items eventually ended up in P. T. Barnum's museum of curiosities. Fortunately, Dunn had the collection insured for $60,000, which enabled him to retire in Vevey, Switzerland. He died there on 19 September 1844 at age 62. His body was returned to Philadelphia for burial at Laurel Hill, where an imposing monument still stands astride the Schuylkill River.[44]

41. HSP: Albert Newsam Collection, 'The Chinese Collection in the Lower Saloon of the New Building at Ninth & George Street . . .' Coloured printed advertisement in Chinese and English, engraved by J. & W. Watt (?), n.p. (probably Philadelphia), n.d. (approx. December 1838), and Agreement, Hon. Joseph Barnes and the Philadelphia Museum Company, 1836.01.29; *Poulson's American Daily Advertiser*, 1838.12.24; *Public Ledger* (Philadelphia), 1839.01.05; APS: Deed, Joseph Barnes Esq. + Wife to Nathan Dunn Esq., 1836.04.16; Smith, 'Friend Dunn', 11.
42. *Public Ledger* (Philadelphia), 1844.10.24, Dunn obituary; APS: letters William Vaughan, London, to John Vaughan, Philadelphia, 6 August and 29 September 1841; *The Times* (London), 1842.06.23, 'Mr. Dunn's Chinese Collection' and 'Chinese Collection' (advertisement); *The Times*, 1843.11.13, 'The Chinese Collection'; *The Times*, 17 and 26 October 1844; Casper Souder, *History of Chestnut Street* (Philadelphia: Sunday Dispatch, 1858), 148–49.
43. *The Times*, 1849.11.17, reported that 'the Chinese Collection was seriously damaged' while en route to Edinburgh and that the loss was estimated at 1,500 to 2,000 pounds. On 2 May 1851, *The Times* reported that the collection was back in London.
44. APS: letters William Vaughan, London, et. al. to (brother) John Vaughan, Philadelphia, 6 August and 29 September 1841; William B. Langdon, *A Descriptive Catalogue of the Chinese*

Up to his dying day Dunn remained dedicated to his educational pursuits. When he made the decision to relocate to London, China was engaged in a losing war with Britain over the shipment of opium. Aside from commercial concerns, the move to London was also an effort to raise concern and empathy for China. From Dunn's point of view, his exhibit was representing and paying respect to his old friends in China. Although well intended, as historians we might rightfully ask if Dunn's educational efforts made any difference.

The level of engagement with participants and the extent to which they may have been influenced by the exhibit is difficult to quantify. Although there were many positive comments and reviews, the level of actual influence and engagement probably ranged from the serious to the frivolous. It is clear that in both Philadelphia and the United Kingdom, Dunn's museum represented a significant effort to give a positive representation of China. The very fact that people recognized this to be the case, and that there were so many people interested in seeing it, are indications in themselves that the museum had rather substantial effects on the local population. Philadelphia's *Public Ledger* stressed in its obituary of Dunn that, unlike British and French pillaging of Asian artefacts, 'the treasures of Eastern art and curiosity which Dunn brought to Philadelphia were procured at a just price'.[45] Yale scientist Benjamin Silliman stressed that Dunn's displays 'afforded us barbarians new ideas on the subject of Chinese manufactures'. Europeans, by contrast, 'have never succeeded in transporting a respectable collection of Chinese curiosities . . . Dunn had learned to respect the ingenuity and intelligence of the Chinese with whom he was in contact'.[46] Perhaps overly optimistically, Silliman expressed the hope that the museum would counteract negative images of eighteenth-century China conveyed to the American public by missionaries with self-serving agendas. Silliman's upbeat appraisal was widely circulated, appearing in the January 1839 edition of the *American Journal of Science and Arts*, in Washington's *Niles' National Register* the following month, and in book form in Philadelphia in 1841.[47]

Collection Now Being Exhibited at St. George's Place, Hyde Park Corner, London (London: Printed for the Proprietor, First English Edition 1842, Eighteenth English printing 1843); *Friends' Weekly Intelligencer*, 1844.10.25, p. 245 and 1844.11.23, p. 277; HC: Ian Shinn, 'Encounters', 157; Hummel, 'Nathan Dunn', 38; Haddad, *Romance*, 87–88; Smith, 'Friend Dunn', 12; Goldstein, *Philadelphia and the China Trade*, 7.

45. *Public Ledger* (Philadelphia), 1844.10.24, Dunn obituary.
46. Silliman added 'if an architect desires to examine his science in China, he will find models of ancient and majestic bridges [and] the Great Wall; the artist, paintings admirably colored; the mercer, rich silks; the porcelain manufacturer, the grand origins of his art.' Benjamin Silliman, *Mr. Dunn's Chinese Collection in Philadelphia* (Philadelphia: Brown, Bickering, and Guilbert, 1841), 2–25.
47. Silliman advised that 'the design of the exhibit is to present a faithful delineation of the mode of life of a wonderful people'. [Benjamin Silliman], 'Chinese Museum', *Niles' National Register* 55 (16 February 1839): 5, and 25; [Benjamin Silliman], 'N. Dunn's Chinese Collection, at Philadelphia', *American Journal of Science and Arts* 35 (January 1839): 391–400; Silliman, *Mr. Dunn's Chinese Collection in Philadelphia*, 2–25; *Public Ledger* (Philadelphia), 1838.12.28 and

Other contemporaries posted similar reviews. Minister E. C. Wines, in an account published in Philadelphia in 1839 and in Canton the following year, asserted that

> a better idea may be obtained of the characteristic intelligence and national customs of the Chinese from Mr. Dunn's collection than by an actual visit to the small portions of the suburbs of Canton, which is all that foreigners are permitted to see . . . Dunn, in the collection he has made and now offers to public examination, has done more than any other man to rectify prevalent errors and disseminate true information concerning a nation everyway worthy to be studied by the philosopher who delights in the curious, the economist who searches into the principles of national prosperity and stability, and the Christian who desires the universal spread of the Gospel.[48]

British historian James Buckingham included an entire chapter on Dunn's museum in his American travelogue and expressed the hope that, after its transfer to London, it would 'induce some of our statesmen to turn their attention to this suggestion [friendship] and act upon it in practice'. According to Buckingham, the museum aided

> the breakdown of prejudices and apathies, the increase of new information, and the correction of old errors [and] the substituting in their stead kindly feelings and sympathies . . . adding new links to the chain of union and friendship, interest and pleasure between countries now ignorant of and despising each other; and the possible initiation of such collections . . . in all the capitals of the world.[49]

China trader Brantz Mayer of Baltimore called Dunn's effort 'a panoramic pageant of Oriental life' so 'eerily accurate' that 'we almost expect to hear them speak and see them move'.[50] When Queen Victoria and Prince Albert visited Dunn's 'Chinese World in Miniature' on 18 June 1842, at St. George's Place in London, they intended only a brief stay but remained for an entire Saturday afternoon.[51] Early twentieth century American-East Asian historian William Griffis reminisced that, as a result of visiting Dunn's 'great Chinese museum' in Philadelphia as a child, 'I longed to know more of what the Chinese thought and felt, than of what they made, ate, bought, or sold.'[52] The fullest expression of that early fascination was his entire career in the academic discipline of East Asian Studies.

1844.10.24. On the negative image of China conveyed by missionaries, see also Raymond Dawson, *The Chinese Chameleon* (London: Oxford University Press, 1967) and Stuart Creighton Miller, *The Unwelcome Immigrant* (Berkeley: University of California Press, 1969).

48. Wines, *A Peep at China*, vi–viii, and 13–14.
49. Buckingham, *The Eastern and Western States of America*, Vol. 2, 72–73.
50. Brantz Mayer, 'A Nation in a Nutshell', *Baltimore Literary Monument* 2 (1839): 274; Brantz Mayer, 'China and the Chinese', *Southern Quarterly Review* (July 1847): 6–7, and 29; Brantz Mayer, *A Nation in a Nutshell* (Philadelphia: Brown, Bicking, and Guilbert, 1841); Wines, *A Peep at China*, 10.
51. *The Morning Post* (London), 1842.06.21, and *The Morning Herald* (London), 1842.06.23, both quoted in *The Chinese Repository* 12 (November 1843), 562.
52. William Griffis, *China's Story in Myth, Legend, Art, and Annals* (London: Constable, 1911),

Figure 6.1 Nathan Dunn's 'Chinese Cottage', Mount Holly, New Jersey, 1832, designed by John Notman. Drawing from A. J. Downing, *A Treatise on the Theory and Practice of Landscape Gardening*. New York and London: Wiley and Putnam, 1841, p. 345.

Thus, in multiple ways, the commercial success of one early American China trader translated into the communication of a positive image of China and to sympathetic and open-minded early Americans and British.

Dunn's 'Chinese Cottage'

Dunn also personally immersed himself in the material culture of the civilization that he so admired. Upon his return to Philadelphia in 1832, he commissioned the local architect John Notman to build a country house 'in the Chinese style' in Mt. Holly, New Jersey.[53] The lot was planted with imported Asian trees and shrubs. The stable had two towers representing Chinese pagodas. The main house, according to contemporaries, was 'a combination of the Chinese and English cottage style'.[54]

vii–viii; Buckingham, *The Eastern and Western States of America*, Vol. 2: 71; HC: Ian Shinn, 'Encounters', 156.

53. Henry C. Shinn, *History of Mount Holly* (Mt. Holly, NJ: privately printed, 1957), 155 and 157; HC: 'Last Will and Testament of Nathan Dunn, Late of the City of Philadelphia, Deceased, March 7, 1840'. In constructing a monumental mansion upon returning from China Dunn may have been inspired by other British and American China traders, including his long-time friend John P. Cushing (1787–1862), of Watertown, Mass. Hummel, 'Nathan Dunn', 37.
54. John Barber and Henry Howe, *Historical Collections of the State of New Jersey* (Newark:

A Chinese-style roof adorned the entrance, and pointed arches, pendants, and two bulbous pinnacles accompanied the porch colonnades.

The nineteenth-century American architectural critic A. J. Downing praised Dunn's innovative effort in creating in America a cottage with an 'oriental air'. Downing featured a drawing of the cottage in his 1841 architectural treatise. According to Downing, Chinese architectural motifs produced a delightful result 'adapted to the American climate' and enlivened and enriched early American life.[55]

The cottage may have also had a Chinese interior. A probate listing of 1844 mentions '2 Green China Stools in the verandah'.[56] Dunn also kept a large collection of books about China and East Asia in the house. The oldest book may be a history of China by a Portuguese explorer published in London in 1655. The entire collection has been preserved in the Mount Holly Library. Dunn's edifice still stands on Bartram Street today, albeit much remodelled.[57]

Conclusion

Dunn's experience as a private China trader indicates that neither the Quakers nor the Americans were in any sense cohesive trading networks. Both communities were composed of individuals with distinct ethical and commercial agendas. Dunn pioneered innovative trading strategies while championing a mercantile code that was unusual for his day.

Intellectually, Dunn's scholarly and educational activity paralleled that of Philadelphian Robert Waln, the first formal American historian of China. Both of these China traders were of Quaker origin and saw their missions as the presentation of a positive view of the Celestial Kingdom. Unlike Waln, who was a published scholar and not a museologist, Dunn seems to have had even greater success in

---

Benjamin Olds, 1857), 113. Dunn's cottage was characterized in 1964 as 'probably New Jersey's most famous example of an "exotic" style'. Alan Gowans, *Architecture in New Jersey* (Princeton: Van Nostrand, 1964), 67.

55. A. J. Downing, *A Treatise on the Theory and Practice of Landscape Gardening* (New York: Wiley and Putnam, 1841), 345; Shinn, 155; Clay Lancaster, 'The Chinese Influence in American Architecture and Landscaping', in *Nineteenth Annual Washington Antiques Show 1974* (catalogue), 92; HC: 'Last Will and Testament of Nathan Dunn, Late of the City of Philadelphia, Deceased, March 7, 1840'; *Dictionary of Quaker Biography*, passim; Blackman, *History of Little Egg Harbor Township*, passim; Hummel, 'Nathan Dunn', 37; Goldstein, *Philadelphia and the China Trade*, 70 and 74–76.
56. HSP: Nelson B. Gaskill, 'Nathan Dunn' scrapbook, 'A true and perfect Inventory of . . . the "Cottage" in Mount Holly' 1844.11.21.
57. Dunn's 'Cottage' was occupied by his half-sisters Phoebe and Rhoda until 1882, after their death. As of 1957 the edifice was the nucleus of Mt. Holly Regional Catholic School. APS: letters Nathan Dunn to Samuel Morton, 1839.02.19; HSP: Nelson B. Gaskill, 'Nathan Dunn' scrapbook, Sarah? to Nelson Gaskill, 1944.08.24; HC: 'Last Will and Testament of Nathan Dunn, Late of the City of Philadelphia, Deceased, March 7, 1840'; Mary B. Hendry, 'Historical Sketch of the Mount Holly Library', brochure dated 1935.09.19; HC: Ian Shinn, 'Encounters', 157; Robert C. Smith, 'Friend Dunn', 10.

popularizing his ideas. He seems to have found his life's purpose in these activities. Unlike virtually all of his contemporaries, other than Robert Waln Jr., his aim was not to trade and get wealthy purely for the sake of personal aggrandizement. Rather, it was to become a self-educated, self-proclaimed advocate for China in America and later in the United Kingdom.[58]

Dunn's career could be summarized as that of a cultural philanthropist who was in search of personal and intellectual gratification. Dunn was determined to get rich in a respectable way, without trading in opium, and then use that wealth to pursue his higher calling. Without the wealth, he could not carry out his mission.

The fact that Dunn was able to put together such an enormous collection of artefacts is also testimony to how open the trade actually was. As an individual businessman, he was allowed to come and go as needed to carry out his trade; he was allowed to stay in China (Canton or Macao) as long as he wanted, so long as he was there to trade; and he was permitted to order and purchase anything he desired (as long as it was legal), without restrictions and without prior approval from officials. Most of the items he ordered for his museum were not common articles of trade. He undoubtedly paid export duties on those items, but even that is testimony to the flexibility of the Canton system. As long as the items were not contraband, no questions were asked.

Dunn was arguably the pioneer of Sinological museology and ethnology in both America and Europe. Because of the earnestness and thoroughness of his quest, he elevated both sciences beyond the level of randomly collecting 'cabinets of curiosities'. Several 'Chinese Museums' appeared in America and England shortly after Dunn's. None were as focussed and all-encompassing or as positively inclined.[59]

---

58. Waln was the author of *China; Comprehending a View of the Origins, Antiquity, History . . . &c of that Empire to which is Added a Commercial Appendix* (Philadelphia: Published by the author, 1825); and an 1821 series of articles in Philadelphia's *National Gazette*. See Jonathan Goldstein, 'Philadelphia's Old China Trade', *Pennsylvania Legacies*, 6–11; and Jonathan Goldstein, 'A Philadelphian Author Turns to China: Robert Waln Jr., as America's First Sinologist', *The American Asian Review* 21, no. 3 (Fall 2003): 187–203. Alternate versions of this Goldstein article on Waln article have appeared in *Asian Culture Quarterly* 27, no. 1 (Spring 1999): 1–13; *Sino-American Relations* 27, no. 4 (Winter 2001): 82–101; *The Virginia Review of Asian Studies* 4 (Fall 2002): 9–19; and *Mains'l Haul: A Journal of Pacific Maritime History* 39, no. 2 (Spring 2003): 20–28.

59. Museums established in the decade after Dunn's include that of John R. Peters, a member of Caleb Cushing's 1844 diplomatic mission to Beijing. Peters founded his institution in Philadelphia in 1847. Another was erected at Fairfield in London's East End, with Chinese scenes 'faithfully reproduced'. The Chinese yacht *Keying* featured a 'cabinet of curiosities' when it docked in the River Thames in July 1848. That collection, like Dunn's, was visited by Queen Victoria. Impresario P. T. Barnum opened 'China House' in Knightsbridge, London, in 1851, simultaneous with the Crystal Palace exhibition. He exhibited artefacts purchased from Dunn's collection. Like many of Barnum's displays, this exhibition of 'things Chinese' bordered on the voyeuristic. Finally, a gallery at Hyde Park Corner, London, which once housed Dunn's museum, came to be called 'The Pagoda' because of its conspicuous East Asian façade. In 1854 it featured a broadly focused 'Oriental and Turkish' museum. Stephen Davies,

American intellectual historian Harold Isaacs has noted that an 'Age of Contempt' for China and things Chinese began in America in approximately 1840, just as Dunn's museum was en route to England.[60] Dunn's (and Robert Waln Jr.'s) positive views toward China were superseded in the late nineteenth century by those of politically powerful Sinophobes and advocates of Chinese exclusion, individuals with little or no awareness of American or British scholarship and/or museology. Late nineteenth-century American Sinophobia was in large measure a product of labour-management tensions in the American West, a topic beyond the scope of this chapter. Instead, we have focussed on one eccentric contributor to early Sino-American relations whose life mission seems to have been the creation of a respectful relationship between the United States and China. His example does indeed show that one man could make a difference. If we took Dunn out of the historical equation—as if he never existed—we would have a very different story to tell about Sino-Western interactions.

A Note on Source Material

Creating a commercial and cultural profile of Nathan Dunn requires scrutiny of evidence that can best be described as fragmentary. Standard published archives of the China trade, such as *The Canton Register* and *The Chinese Repository*, mention Dunn. There is no comprehensive Dunn archive comparable to the Stephen Girard papers in Philadelphia. Company correspondence, personal papers, court records, and letter books are scattered among repositories all along the American East coast.

East Sails West: The Voyage of the Keying, 1846–1855 (Hong Kong: Hong Kong University Press, 2014); Caplan, 'Nathan Dunn's Chinese Museum', 122–28.

60. Harold Isaacs, *Scratches on Our Minds: American Images of China and India* (New York: John Day, 1958).

7

The Life and Loves of Michael Grubb

A Swedish Trader in Eighteenth-Century Canton and Macao

Lisa Hellman

In 1750, the young Michael Grubb arrived in Canton for the first time on the Swedish East India Company (SOIC) ship *Adolph Friedrich*. With him as our guide, we are able to get a glimpse of an interesting time in the Canton trade—a period when the trade was going through transitions and Canton was a vibrant, multinational environment. This study presents a view from one individual trader who worked for the SOIC; in doing so I hope to show not some particular importance of the Swedish participation, but rather the complex makeup of the groups that traded in eighteenth-century Canton. While Grubb was indeed a 'company man', he remained behind in China at his own expense[1] and had a lot of private transactions and relationships that help to expose the entangled and complicated nature of his personal life.

Certain individuals in Canton and Macao helped to tie the disparate groups together to make the trade work. Such people, while not unique or remarkable in themselves, are worth studying for the role they played in moving commerce forward. Moreover, by focussing on a single person, we are able to examine his social life, and thereby come to some understanding of the importance of these relationships for foreign traders in China. Certainly, networks and contacts influenced the trade, but perhaps friendships and romantic relationships could be important as well. Thus, the questions we might ask are, what can the life of Michael Grubb tell us of the Swedish East India Company? How might his example contribute to our knowledge of the private trade in China? Finally, what social relations are discernible and how did they shape his life in Canton and Macao?

The Early Years of Michael Grubb

Michael Grubb was born on 6 July 1728 in Stockholm. The family can be traced back to the seventeenth century, and were involved in trade long before his birth. Michael Grubb's male cousin became a trader and his five female cousins all married

1. National Archives, The Hague (NAH): VOC 4388, *dagregister*, 1762.01.05, p. 68r and Canton 223, report dated 1762.12.31, p. 191.

businessmen and ironworks owners. Two of these men were part of the SOIC: the director of the board Niklas Sahlgren and the supercargo Vollrath Tham. From the beginning we can thus see the close ties between the early international industries of Sweden, the ironworks, the Stockholm and Gothenburg trade families, and the Company. This family connection was pivotal for Grubb's career.

Michael Grubb's sister Catharina Elisabeth married a Finnish ironworks proprietor, Johan Jacob Kijk. For this reason, Michael began his studies at the age of 16 at Åbo Academy, where he eventually defended his thesis in 1748, having just turned twenty. His dissertation, a description of the ironworks of Finland, was dedicated to his father. He voiced his gratitude in time; within a year, his father had passed away, leaving the young Grubb to make a living for himself. In 1749, he travelled to Gothenburg, where he enrolled in the Swedish East India Company.[2] To venture out with a company ship was a natural choice for a young man in Grubb's position: that of having little capital, but excellent contacts. Not everyone could get a place in the company so quickly and easily.

The Swedish East India Company

The Swedish East India Company, established in 1731, was small and never had colonial ambitions. It was modelled after other chartered companies, and was an international enterprise, where in particular Scotsmen acted as driving forces behind its formation and as supercargoes and officers during the first charter (1731–1745). By the time that Grubb was taken on, however, the officers and supercargoes were predominantly Swedish.

The company tried to establish itself in Bengal, but had to abandon this enterprise after having met with hard resistance from other European companies. Instead, it focused its trade on Canton, where they were welcomed and where other European companies had no control over who came or went. In total, the Company sent out 132 ships over 74 years. The main commodity was tea, but it also imported porcelain, silk, and other goods.

There is not a great amount of earlier research on the SOIC, especially not regarding its activities in Canton.[3] This is partly because its economic records were incinerated, probably to hide traces of smuggling. What remain are correspondences, journals, and travel writings—records that work quite well for studying the everyday life of the Swedish traders.

2. August Nachmanson and David Hannerberg, *Garphyttan: Ett gammalt bruks historia* (Stockholm: Bonnier, 1945), 257–61.
3. Tore Frängsmyr, *Ostindiska Kompaniet: Människorna, äventyret och den ekonomiska Drömmen* (Höganäs: Bokförlaget Bra Böker, 1976; reprint, Höganäs: Wiken, 1990); Sven Kjellberg, *Svenska Ostindiska Compagnierna 1731–1813: Kryddor, Te, Porslin, Siden* (Malmö: Allhems Förlag, 1974); and Christian Koninckx, *The First and Second Charters of the Swedish East India Company (1731–1766): A Contribution to the Maritime, Economic and Social History of North-western Europe in Its Relations with the Far East* (Belgium: Van Gemmert Publishing Co., 1980).

A new charter had been established for the Company in May 1746. The same board of directors that had led the first charter were entrusted with the second. But some things changed. The new generation of supercargoes were, like Grubb, born in Sweden, many of them part of an up-and-coming group of tradesmen in Stockholm. Grubb was consequently typical in terms of family connections, nationality, as well as city of birth. The new charter sent out twenty-six ships, and Michael Grubb sailed to Canton on one of the first, the *Adolph Friedrich.*

The Company was certainly the place to be for a young man who wanted to make his fortune. Grubb kept returning to Company service, and gradually moved up through the ranks. In 1758 he finally made third supercargo on the ship *Prins Carl.*[4] From around this time he seems to have established a trading firm in Canton.

Grubb and Grill

Grubb was joined in Canton by another Swede, Jean Abraham Grill (1736–1792). The two men were probably friends, both coming from international mercantile families based in Stockholm. Just like Grubb, Grill had close ties to the Sahlgren and Tham families, who were influential in the Swedish East India Company.

Jean Abraham Grill had the misfortune of sailing to China with the only ship that was shipwrecked during the second charter—the *Fredric Adolph*, which sank near the coast of China in 1761. The crew and much of the cargo were saved and brought to Canton where Grill met Grubb, and decided to stay on. They were the first Swedish traders staying for any length of time, and their relationship to the company was ambiguous. While they lived in the Swedish factory, during the months they were in Canton, they did not receive a salary; they mediated in company purchases in Canton, while continuously carrying on an extensive private trade.[5]

Grubb took Grill into his confidence, and they soon did most of their business together. Despite assurances by Grubb and Grill to the board of directors that they only had the company's best interest at heart, it is questionable how much the investors back in Sweden benefited from their good fortune.[6] The partnership

4. Kjellberg, *Svenska Ostindiska Compagnierna*, 69–73, 142–76, and 203. As Kjellberg shows on p. 206, the captain of the *Prins Carl* in 1758 was Baltazar Grubb. As one of that ship's supercargos, Michael Grubb would have certainly been in close contact with the captain. But whether the two Grubbs had any close family ties or relationship outside of the Company, is unclear.
5. Leos Müller, '"Merchants" and "Gentlemen" in Early-Modern Sweden: The World of Jean Abraham Grill, 1736–1792', in *The Self-Perception of Early Modern Capitalists*, ed. Margaret C. Jacob and Catherine Secretan (New York: Palgrave Macmillan, 2008), 125–46, 134.
6. For an example, see The Nordic Museum Archive, Godegårdsarkivet (henceforth NM: GG), Received letters dated 1765.12.05. In Canton, Michael Grubb and the merchant Poankeequa were accused of secretly conducting some trade without reporting it to the regulatory body known as the Cohong. According to the accusations, they cheated the Cohong out of 45,000 taels worth of duties, which Poankeequa and Grubb were suspected of splitting between them. This connivance had supposedly taken place in 1762, but it was not revealed until April 1764.

between these men was of immense importance for their futures, demonstrating the pivotal role of social relations to understand how this trade was organized, and the difference it could make for the individuals involved. While Grubb remains the focus, he cannot be understood without his association to Grill.

International Go-Betweens

Grubb kept his close ties with the SOIC. The Company was comparatively small, and made up roughly 7 per cent of the total value of the Canton export trade during the time Grubb was in Canton.[7] The expedition that arrived in 1760 relied on him from the moment the supercargoes disembarked. They were straight away 'persuaded by Mr Michael Grubb to dine at his place until the factory was in order'. When the supercargos and captain heard that *Fredric Adolph* had run aground, they convinced Grubb to see what could be done about salvaging the ship, and to borrow money in Macao 'since Mr Michael Grubb was well-known in this place'. A few weeks later the captain summarized how 'Mr. M. Grubb has been of great help, in Macao as well as here'.[8] He was the first and self-evident company contact.[9] A few years later, in 1763, he signed a request to three Hong merchants 'on behalf of the Swedish company'.[10]

From this time forward, Grill and Grubb recur in the sources, most often together and involved in some manner of international transaction.[11] They constantly moved between different places and groups. The Dutch wrote in May 1763 that '[t] he Swede Grubb, who is here on his own account . . . left for Macao five weeks ago (as we already guessed) to take out money from the Portuguese merchants'.[12] Grubb's trade was rarely an exchange between just two parties. When the Dutch bid against him in 1763 they noted: 'It is said that Grubb has received a large part of this money from the most prominent merchants at Macao, and they probably also have a share

---

By that time, Grubb had already left China and was on his way back to Sweden so he was not questioned about the affair. Paul A. Van Dyke, *Merchants of Canton and Macao: Success and Failure in Eighteenth-Century Chinese Trade*, Vol. 2 (Hong Kong: Hong Kong University Press, 2016), 66; and Cynthia Viallé and Paul A. Van Dyke, *The Canton-Macao Dagregisters*, 1764 (Macau: Macau Cultural Institute, 2009) (henceforth CMD 1764), 59–68.

7. Paul A. Van Dyke, *The Canton Trade: Life and Enterprise on the China Coast, 1700–1845* (Hong Kong: Hong Kong University Press, 2005), 147.
8. The National Library of Sweden (NLS): Manuscript Collection (MC), Carl Rappe, 'Dagbok För Skeppet Rycksens Ständer På Resa till Surat Och Canton 1760–1762', pp. 18–23. Translated from Swedish.
9. NLS: MC, Fredric Christian Sternleuw, 'Utkast till En Beskrifning Om Mina Sjö-resor Upsat Af Mig Sjelf Frid. Crist. Sternlöw På Fogelvik År 1794', note 1 and Rappe, 'Dagbok', 21–27.
10. Paul A. Van Dyke and Cynthia Viallé, *The Canton-Macao Dagregisters*, 1763 (Macau: Macau Cultural Institute, 2008) (henceforth CMD 1763), 25 and 68.
11. Paul A. Van Dyke and Cynthia Viallé, *The Canton-Macao Dagregisters*, 1762 (Macau: Macau Cultural Institute, 2006) (henceforth CMD 1762), 6.
12. CMD 1763, 59.

in this.'[13] His transactions involved people from Canton and Macao, Protestant, and Catholic, and from different groups such as the Armenians, English, or Dutch. Grubb imported European commodities on ships bound for China, participated in the intra-Asian junk trade with Southeast Asia, the Philippines, and Japan, and was an intermediary in trade with the supercargoes who were in Sweden.[14] The Dutch seem to have kept a closer eye on Grubb than on any of the other free merchants.[15]

Both Grubb and Grill were particularly active in the profitable credit market. Most commonly they offered bottomry loans to the junk traders and/or loans to Chinese merchants.[16] They channelled credit between financiers (Portuguese, British, Armenian, and others) in Macao and Chinese merchants in Canton.[17] Furthermore, the opium trade had started to pick up, and Grubb and Grill were in the thick of it.[18] The SOIC never allowed trade in opium, but Grill and Grubb made a neat profit of it nevertheless. In fact, their brokerage was very lucrative in general. Already in 1761, it was said of Grubb in Sweden that: 'Young Grubb has made a great fortune in a short time by venturing considerable cargoes in Jonks [junks] to Manilla & Japan.'[19]

In 1764, the Swedish company established a permanent capital fund in Canton, with which the supercargoes purchased cheap goods in the off-season. The fund was supposed to borrow money from the local market to circumvent the dependency on the precarious transports of Spanish silver. That required participation in local trade, the creation of proper commercial contacts, networks and credit links, all of which Grill and Grubb had established.[20]

Explanations for Their Success

What made it possible for Grill and Grubb to become so successful? Part of the reason might be the timing. The Seven Years' War raged from 1757–1763, and while Sweden did participate, the war did not affect its merchant fleet as strongly as it did the English and French companies. In fact, the depleted supply in silver from the English and French ships benefited the SOIC's price negotiations in Canton.[21]

13. CMD 1763, 68.
14. Kjellberg, *Svenska Ostindiska Compagnierna*, 111.
15. CMD 1762, 8, 117; and CMD 1763, 42, 88, 107, and 127.
16. NM: GG, Sent letters dated 1763.10.03, 1763.11.07, 1763.11.23, 1766.11.21, 1767.03.14, and 1768.01.25; see also Müller, '"Merchants" and "Gentlemen"', 134–37.
17. Müller, '"Merchants" and "Gentlemen"', 135.
18. NM: GG, Received letters dated 1765.01.22, 1765.01.29, and 1767.05.01; see also Van Dyke, *The Canton Trade*, 123.
19. Kjellberg, *Svenska Ostindiska Compagnierna*, 111. The quote is from Müller, '"Merchants" and "Gentlemen"', 135.
20. Leos Müller, 'The Swedish East India Company-Strategies and Functions of an Interloper', in *Small Is Beautiful? Interlopers and Smaller Trading Nations in the Pre-industrial Period*, ed. Jan De Vries and Philipp Robinson Rössner (Stuttgart: Steiner, 2011), 83–101, 98.
21. Van Dyke, *The Canton Trade*, 158.

Another part of the explanation lay in differing company regulations. The Swedes were allowed to participate in country trade as long as it did not infringe on the monopoly trade of the SOIC, and during the six years that Grubb spent in Canton, the company failed to draw a clear line between the company's business and its associates' private trade. These factors, combined with the Qing's policy of welcoming all traders, large and small—companies and individuals alike—made it possible for Grill and Grubb to stay on in China. Thus, the Swedish supercargoes had relatively great freedom to conduct private trade, which smoothed the way for them to act as go-betweens. Regardless, there was considerable tension between private and company interests, which Grubb and Grill's successful enterprises did nothing to ease. On the contrary, their involvement in the trade probably spurred the company board to clarify their rules. From 1764, the employees and associates were forbidden to establish any affairs, whether in their own name or in that of friends, in competition with the SOIC's charter.[22]

Moreover, it is possible that a Masonic lodge helped to establish and keep up the networks these traders needed so badly. Grubb was initiated as a freemason in the Gothenburg lodge *Salomon à trois Serrures* in 1757 just before his long stay in China. The same went for Grill, who was initiated in 1760. The overlap between the men who were officers in the SOIC and those initiated in this lodge was very large.[23] Grubb took part in lodge meetings on board the *Prins Carl*, both on the way to and in Canton. This lodge was named St. Elisabeth and is commonly credited with having introduced freemasonry to China. The lodge thereafter met in the Swedish factory. The membership list from 1766 shows Swedish, English, Dutch, French, Danish, and Scottish names, and includes some of the top officers of the respective East India companies.[24] While those companies were in fierce competition with each other in Canton and in Europe, which made them very protective of their commercial secrets, the officers of those enterprises might share other private trade information through the Masonic lodge meetings.

While there was an English lodge, Amity, it did not receive its warrant until 1767, and there are no records of its activities in Canton.[25] The role that the St. Elisabeth Lodge played in the trade is still ambiguous, but in a world so dependent on personal trust and contacts and lacking public gathering places, it was probably a very valuable hub. Of course, the grandmaster, Grubb, would have benefited greatly

22. Müller, '"Merchants" and "Gentlemen"', 134; and Müller, 'The Swedish East India Company-Strategies and Functions of an Interloper', 98.
23. Andreas Önnerfors, *Mystiskt brödraskap-mäktigt nätverk: Studier i det svenska 1700-talsfrimureriet* (Lund: Lunds Universitet, 2006), 199.
24. NM: GG, 'Frimureri i Kanton och Macao, Logen St Elisabeth', Accounts 1766.
25. Christopher Haffner, 'Eastern Masonic Frontiers Before the Union', in *Transactions of Quatuor Coronati Lodge No 2076*, 104; and John Lane, *Lane's Masonic Records*, Amity Lodge no. 225 https://www.hrionline.ac.uk/lane/index.php (accessed 11 January 2017).

from being the nucleus of this network. When Grubb left Canton, Grill took over the leadership of the lodge.[26]

Another part of the explanation might be Grubb's extensive social network. Grubb had dinner at several different companies.[27] In the Dutch *dagregister* of 1762 it is noted that 'At midday [September 17], while Schartow and I were having a meal at the Swedish free merchant Grubb's', they received news of the arrival of two Swedish ships.[28] The European traders in Canton regularly exchanged courtesy meals during the time they were in residence.

All these spheres were exclusively male. But if we want to understand how social relations affected the traders' lives and, in turn, the trade itself, the role of women must be taken into account.

Women in Canton and Macao

It is well known that European women were banned from Canton. In fact, they were banned time and time again, which normally signals that a ban was violated.[29] Indeed, there are a number of references to European women going upriver and staying with their husbands in Canton and/or aboard the ships at Whampoa.[30] But more significant for the social relations were the lives the traders led in Macao, and the women they met there.

At this time, foreigners were forbidden to stay in Canton when the trade season had ended. According to Captain Carl Gustav Ekeberg, 'Finally in 1759 and 1760

26. According to Roy Murray, the St. Elisabeth Lodge in Canton did not receive its warrant until 1786. D. Roy Murray, 'Freemasonry in China', in *United Masters Lodge No. 167*, Auckland, New Zealand (June 1989). Available online at http://euclidlodge158.com/documents/FreemasonryinChina.pdf (accessed 12 January 2017). Gould, on the other hand, states that the St. Elisabeth Lodge did not receive its warrant until 1788. Robert Freke Gould, *The History of Freemasonry* (1882), 339. In his book on Freemasonry published in 1783, George Smith points to Bengal being the first lodge established in Asia in 1740, which was followed by many others including China. Unfortunately, he does not give names or dates. George Smith, *The Use and Abuse of Free-Masonry* (London: Printed for the author and sold by G. Kearsley, 1783), 227. This present study shows that the Swedish St. Elisabeth Lodge was already in operation in Canton before the British Amity Lodge was established in 1767. NM: GG, 'Frimureri i Kanton och Macao, Logen St Elisabeth', Accounts 1766.
27. CMD 1762, 10.
28. CMD 1762, 12.
29. Roderich Ptak, 'Macau: Trade and Society, Circa 1740–1760', in *Maritime China in Transition 1750–1850*, ed. Wang Gungwu and Ng Chin-Keong (Wiesbaden: Harrassowitz Verlag, 2004), 197–204; and Fu Lo-shu, *A Documentary Chronicle of Sino-Western Relations (1644–1820)* (Tucson: University of Arizona Press, 1966), 22 and 189.
30. Paul A. Van Dyke, 'Port Canton and the Pearl River Delta, 1690–1845' (PhD diss., Department of History, University of Southern California, 2002), 134–35; Pehr Osbeck, *Dagbok Öfver En Ostindisk Resa Åren 1750, 1751, 1752* (Stockholm: 1757; reprint, Redviva Publishing House, 1969), 169; Olof Torén, *En Ostindisk Resa* (Stockholm: Tiden, 1961), 98; and Carl Gustav Ekeberg, *Capitaine Carl Gustav Ekebergs Ostindiska Resa Åren 1770 Och 1771* (Stockholm: Henr. Fougt, 1773. Facsimile reprint, Stockholm: Rediviva, 1970), 78.

this little benefit was abolished.'[31] The regulation that foreigners had to spend the off-season in Macao was starting to be enforced, but was not routine until 1765.[32] Thus, for almost half the year the traders lived in Macao—a place where there were more women than men. Macao had Chinese, Portuguese, Armenian, Macanese, and other permanent female residents. These women were sometimes involved in the trade.

Foreigners were not permitted to own property in Macao. In the early eighteenth century, non-Portuguese were not supposed to rent houses there either, but practice did not always follow policy.[33] Many references show foreigners renting accommodation in the city despite it being against Macao law.[34] The attitude towards this rule, as with so many rules during this time, oscillated between enforcement and relaxation. And if the Chinese government in Guangzhou ordered foreign traders to remove to Macao, then the Portuguese administration had little choice but to accept them. The Swedish supercargo Anders Ljungstedt noted that some Swedes settled in Macao in 1762, which might refer to Grubb and Grill.[35] Still, I have not found any employees in the SOIC during the second charter who married in China. This is not surprising. Marriage was of utmost importance to the Company's employees, and was connected to certain future ambitions. The outspoken goal was to earn enough money as quickly as possible in order to make their way home, marry and settle down.[36] To marry in Macao would not be conducive to their personal goals.

From this point of view, there was no economic need for relationships with local women. When Grubb made a brief stop at Cape Horn on his way back to Sweden, he wrote: 'I admit that I have been somewhat smitten here, but that is not strange; seven years of absence from the fairer sex must have some consequences.'[37] But rational need or not, how complete had this absence really been?

Isabel Jackson

One woman in particular recurs in the correspondence of Grubb and Grill: Isabel Jackson. We know nothing of her identity or nationality, but her poor Portuguese indicates that she was either not a native speaker or was poorly educated. She did,

31. Ekeberg, *Ekebergs Ostindiska Resa*, 78. Translated from Swedish.
32. Van Dyke, *The Canton Trade*, 14.
33. George Bryan Souza, *The Survival of Empire: Portuguese Trade and Society in China and the South China Sea, 1630–1754* (Cambridge: Cambridge University Press, 1986), 212; and Van Dyke, *The Canton Trade*, 13.
34. For some examples, see Van Dyke, *The Canton Trade*, 13.
35. Anders Ljungstedt, *An Historical Sketch of the Portuguese Settlements in China* (Boston: James Munroe and Co., 1836; reprint, Hong Kong: Viking Hong Kong Publications, 1992), 30.
36. Müller, '"Merchants" and "Gentlemen"', 137; and Leos Müller, 'Mellan Kanton och Göteborg: Jean Abraham Grill, en superkargörs karriär', in *Historiska Etyder*, ed. Janne Backlund (Uppsala: Historiska institutionen, Univ., 1997), 149–61.
37. NM: GG, Received letters dated 1764.05.05. Translated from Swedish.

however, know enough to carry on a business correspondence. Isabel Jackson and, through her, a Mrs. May were involved in the Canton credit trade. They entrusted Grill with silver to lend, probably to Chinese, for an excellent rate: 'In the year of 66 you won 20 per cent.' Just like other traders, Isabel Jackson did business with several partners simultaneously, to minimize risk and maximize profit. She wrote: 'My Lord I apologize but at this moment I do not have the silver to deliver to your brother because I delivered [it] to someone who could give me a higher profit than the present one.'[38] The women of Macao took part in the private trade via Swedes as well.

Isabel Jackson constitutes an interesting example of the tension between different behavioural norms for a man like Grubb, some of which were conflicting. In Europe there had emerged an ideal 'man of business' who was supposed to be the linchpin of the rational being, and eulogies over tradesmen in Sweden stressed probity, reason, and temperance as crucial characteristics.[39] It is almost as if Grubb read Grill the rules when he told him in 1763: 'My dear brother, should we be businessmen, then let us act like businessmen, careful, resolved, deliberate and exact.'[40] What complicated matters was that a man was not supposed to be cold or unfeeling, in particular not towards women.[41] Ideally, a man doing business during the 1760s should at the same time be cool and rational, and fiery and emotional. Grubb was caught in between these norms.

The connection to Isabel Jackson went beyond business: Michael Grubb began to visit her at home. Before long, he brought Grill with him. In the end of summer 1763 the relationship between these three came to a head. Grubb had just left Macao for Canton, to conduct some business, while Grill stayed behind. In his absence, Grill went to see Isabel at home, and they kissed. Isabel told Grubb, who on the 13th of August wrote an angry letter to Grill: 'The kiss you received my brother, I imagine, was not the only one, and once you have called a few more times I suppose you will be just as used to them as I am. I do wonder that they were given in my absence, since she assured me that she did not want to give you any.' The letter ends with a rhetoric flourish: 'Greet my I[sabel]. a million times, and assure her that I only with difficulty can endure her absence. I long for her with a mournful heart . . . Reassure her that I eternally honour her and that she never leaves my thoughts.'[42]

38. NM: GG, Received letters dated 1768.08.18, 1768.11.15, and 1768.11.26. The quote is from the letter dated 1768.12.09. Translated from Portuguese.
39. Richard Grassby, *The Business Community of Seventeenth-Century England* (Cambridge: Cambridge University Press, 1995), 11; and Stefan Lundblad, *Hedersam handelsman eller verksam företagare: Den ekonomiska kulturens omvandling och de ledande ekonomiska aktörerna i Gävle 1765–1869* (Uppsala: Acta Universitatis Upsaliensis, 2007), 209.
40. NM: GG, Received letters dated 1763.11.13. Translated from Swedish.
41. Colin Mackerras, *Western Images of China* (Oxford: Oxford University Press, 1989), 56.
42. NM: GG, Received letters, 'Privata affärer med Mikael Grubb', 1763.08.13. Translated from Swedish.

These greetings re-established the connection between Grubb and Isabel, showed Grill how close they were, and how refined a man Grubb was.

In the next letter a few days later, Grubb questioned Grill's behaviour 'towards the person you know I prize highly'. He was particularly concerned with how little precaution Grill took to keep his visits a secret, and admonished him: 'I have never let Appu [a Chinese comprador] know that I this year have had an acquaintance there, since she is M.'[43] This need for secrecy might have been because the 'M.' stood for 'Married'.

That gives us another clue to the identity of Isabel. There are several references to a Captain Jackson being active in Macao from at least 1760, but it is not always clear whether they are referring to the same person. Isabel's husband was probably the Englishman named Robert Jackson, who in 1761 requested to reside in Macao for a few months. Within a year he was twice reported for illegal trade and avoidance of customs fees, and in October 1763, an order was issued to expel a man called 'Robert Jackasson', who had married in Macao. Jackson dragged out the expulsion, and by 1764 he had mollified the governor, and was naturalized by a special grant of the viceroy.[44]

The exact time of Isabel's marriage to Robert Jackson is unclear. The reference noted above to Isabel being married is dated 15 August 1763.[45] In a letter dated 24 December 1763 the Dutch also mentioned that Robert Jackson 'married at Macao', which presumably happened in the current year.[46] Earlier references to Captain Jackson in the Dutch records from 1761, 1762, and early 1763, mention that he had been residing in Macao for a long time, but with no mention of him being married. The Dutch were keeping close track of Jackson partially because he sailed his ship from Macao to Batavia each year.[47] These references suggest that Jackson may have married Isabel sometime shortly before mid-August 1763, and that it may have been a ploy to avoid being expelled from the city. If this is true, then Grubb's earlier relationship with Isabel would have taken place when she was still single.

Regardless of her marital status, Grubb seems to have argued a special claim on Isabel. He admonished Grill: 'I am stunned by your great liberty with her. In my presence you have never dared ask her for a single kiss, but I had barely turned my back on Macao before you forcibly take many from her.' His reputation was now shattered and he was no longer unaffected: 'I have often told you my brother that I have felt, and feel, for her the same friendship as had she been my wife.' Up-and-coming

43. NM: GG, Sent letters, 'Privata affärer med Mikael Grubb', 1763.08.15. Translated from Swedish.
44. Macao Archives: Leal Senado 1760–1770, Robert Jackson.
45. NM: GG, Sent letters, 'Privata affärer med Mikael Grubb', 1763.08.15. Translated from Swedish.
46. 'Robbert Jackson is op Macao getrouwt'. NAH: Canton 224, 1763.12.24, p. 224.
47. NAH: VOC 4386, *dagregister*, 1761.01.03, p. 154, VOC 4390, report dated 1762.12.29, p. 130, and Canton 223, report dated 1763.01.25, p. 192. I thank Paul Van Dyke for these references to captain Jackson in the Dutch records.

Swedish traders did not see the women of Macao as suitable prospects, but when Grubb argued that he revered Isabel as a wife he changed how Grill might treat her. Grubb was categorical in his criticism: 'One should not go so far with a woman one claims to hold in high regard, because such a bold beginning seldom stops therewith, although I suppose it did not go further since I in this trust her more than you.' To say that Grubb trusted Isabel more than Grill must have been a hard blow; trust was a crucial part of the friendship these traders tried to establish with each other. Grubb continued to say that after treating a woman like that, the man will soon consider her to be more 'depraved than honourable, and then one can never say that appreciation had ever been a motive, for a true appreciation makes one refrain from all bold liberties against her will'. He was quite clear: Grill's actions showed the impurity and baseness of his feelings. In the margin, he scribbled: 'You could from this letter soon think me to be jealous, but do not think so. Your visiting her, which can hurt her, has moved me, and your violent liberty against a person I love and that in my absence, has made me forget the friendship I felt for you.'[48] Grubb argued that he was not emotional. Rather, he was putting a stop to lewd behaviour.

Grill wrote a long letter in reply on the night between the 17th and 18th of August, saying that not even the news of his father's death had moved him more strongly than this, and that 'bitter tears give me no comfort'. He claimed innocence, which he would prove as soon as he arrived in Canton. Grill desperately asked for Grubb's 'complete and honest forgiveness, and his former friendship completely restored, or I am for all my days an unhappy man, and who knows how long those days can last after such a blow'. This sounds far from a sensible businessman. It was a matter of friendship, where the discourse on politeness was activated.[49] Grill was during his years in France known to be a man of fashion and sociability.[50] In contrast to Grubb, who tried to argue that he was not emotional or jealous, Grill used these emotions to demonstrate a bond between them. He makes the argument into a matter of proving himself as a friend.

Grill defended himself by quoting a letter Isabel sent on the 10th of August where she invited him to her house that night, to 'comfort her in her great sadness', after Grubb has left. So, claimed Grill, he saw no harm in going—he held Isabel responsible for the visit. But when Grill returned to the topic of the kiss, he yet again used politeness to get his message across: 'I start to shiver, sweat and cry, and words fail me,' he writes. He was sure Grubb would not begrudge him the kiss, he said,

48. NM: GG, Received letters, 'Privata affärer med Mikael Grubb', 1763.08.15. Translated from Swedish.
49. NM: GG, Received letters, 'Privata affärer med Mikael Grubb', 1763.08.17–18. Translated from Swedish. For more on politeness in Swedish correspondence, see Valborg Lindgärde and Elisabeth Mansén, *Ljuva möten och ömma samtal: om kärlek och vänskap på 1700-talet* (Stockholm: Bokförlaget Atlantis, 1999).
50. Philip Carter, *Men and the Emergence of Polite Society: Britain 1660–1800* (Harlow: Longman, 2001), 34–42.

as it only showed how he cared for Isabel. He then argued 'it can never be called violence when one removes a hand, which the woman holds loosely between you, as if to hide her blush, when she lets herself be kissed'.[51] Grill made the visit about the questionable virtue of Isabel, who invited him and his kisses.

After the two men met in Canton after the incident, it all seems to have calmed down. The next letter between Grill and Grubb only treats business matters.[52] In a later letter, Grubb said that he was reassured about their friendship through a letter 'from the person it concerned, which has completely brought me out of my former impression'.[53] This whole time Isabel's husband Robert Jackson worked as a free trader, which included dealings with both Grubb and Grill.[54] Later in September Grubb wrote to Grill, and mentioned Jackson, which gives us another clue about Isabel's life and Grubb's relationship to her: 'His wife is carrying her cross daily with him, which has completely changed my view of him; I wish he had died. He is also jealous since no one has seen her, not even me . . . She has gotten a Beast for man.'[55]

This letter exchange demonstrates the conflict between the two sides of the ideal businessman: the rational and profit-oriented, on one side, and the sociable and polite on the other.[56] The conflict around Isabel brought both sets of ideas to the surface. Isabel's virtue should be protected, but Grubb argued for his right to visit her. And her husband, 'the beast', stands out as a contrast—as a domineering and evil man. Ultimately, these letters show that some Swedish traders already established close personal connections to local women in the 1760s. Since the private and business parts of their lives cannot be separated, this aspect has to be taken into consideration. Who Isabel Jackson did or did not kiss threatened the Swedish company's most profitable partnership.

Annica de Queros and Pascual da Silva

The correspondence of Grubb and Grill reveals other local relations that affected the company; for example, the connection to Annica de Queros. She was a resident of Macao, probably a part of the Macanese minority. She first appears in Grill's personal correspondences in 1769.[57] Grill returned to Sweden as first supercargo aboard the ship *Cron Prins Gustaf*, which left China at the end of December 1768.[58]

51. NM: GG, Received letters, 'Privata affärer med Mikael Grubb', 1763.08.17–18. Translated from Swedish.
52. NM: GG, Received letters dated 1763.09.13. Translated from Swedish.
53. NM: GG, Received letters dated 1763.09.07. Translated from Swedish.
54. Kåre Lauring, 'Kinahandelen – et spørsmål om finansiering'. In *Søfart, Politik, Identitet: Tilegnet Ole Feldbæk*, eds. Ole Feldbæk and Hans Jeppesen (København: Falcon, 1996), 215–26, 219.
55. NM: GG, Received letters dated 1763.09.10. Translated from Swedish.
56. Grassby, *The Business Community of Seventeenth-Century England*, 178.
57. NM: GG, Received letters from Annica de Queraz.
58. Kjellberg, *Svenska Ostindiska Compagnierna*, 203.

In 1770, Grill assured Grubb that Annica was well.[59] Grill took some responsibility for her, and several times transferred her money.[60] Before returning home, Grill arranged to provide 72 piastres a year for her and her—their—son.[61]

This was the start of years of correspondence in which the Swedish company employees in China tried to convince Grill to increase this sum, which already in 1778 was too small to subside on. Their son, Juan Francisco Xavier, garnered much interest from these traders: 'He seems to be a nimble and kind boy; it would be of great benefit to get him away from there—I shall ask to get him to sea.'[62] A year later, the son was unfortunately still not at sea, and Annica was 'in so poor circumstances that she can impossibly live without such an aid and immediate payment'.[63]

In 1784 the traders still appealed to Grill on behalf of Annica and her son: 'It is certain that if he [Juan] stays in Macao, he will be lost in all regards.' They told Grill that '[s]ix piaster per month is these days in Macao such a meagre allowance that she, even with good housekeeping, often is in need'.[64] Grill told them off, arguing that 'I doubt that anyone else would have cared this well for his Macao girl and her child'.[65] Still, in December 1785 the Swedes in Macao insisted that they could not refuse helping this boy 'who in Macao is generally considered being part of the Swedish house, of which also his appearance bears witness, and it is held against us that he has not been sufficiently taken care of'.[66] There is no trace of Annica de Queros or her son after this year, a silence that tells us that Grill probably washed his hands of them.

While the Canton trade grew, the economy of Macao was struggling. Poverty was widespread: men of some wealth moved to other ports, leaving behind wives, concubines, and female servants.[67] The sources do not tell us much about this woman and her boy. Nor do we know exactly why the employees of the SOIC took such an interest in them, but how Annica and her son were treated seems to have mattered to the Company's local respectability, and affected its standing. Relations with locals were nothing that could be shrugged off.

While he was in Macao, Grubb took great interest in the young Pascual da Silva.[68] In September 1763 he sent a greeting to Grill from Pascual. But something is

---

59. NM: GG, Received letters dated 1770.01.21.
60. In July 1769, for example, Grill made a payment to 'Aa de Queiro' for 49 piastres. NM: GG, 'Privata affärer med bröderna Hahr, W. och Jacob. Kalkyl och räkningar parterna emellan 1767–1772'.
61. NSL: MC Bref och handlingar rörande Eric von Stockenström, IS 46, Diverse Mindre Räkningar and Conto Couranter Hållne Uti Canton Åren 1780–1787, 21.
62. NM: GG, Received letters dated 1778.12.19. Translated from Swedish.
63. NM: GG, Received letters dated 1779.01.22. Translated from Swedish.
64. NM: GG, Received letters dated 1784.01.08. Translated from Swedish.
65. NSL: MC Bref och handlingar rörande Eric von Stockenström, IS 46, Letter to Eric Stockenström in Canton from Jean Abraham Grill 1784.01.02.
66. NM: GG, Received letters dated 1785.12.01. Translated from Swedish.
67. Souza, *The Survival of Empire*, 212.
68. NM: GG, Received letters dated 1763.09.11.

amiss with Pascual: 'He is now just as before, his state no better, but varying, one day good another bad.' Consistently, this young man was called 'poor Pascual'. The best clues as to why come in two letters, one of them from September 1763: 'Again Sr Pascual da Silva sends his greetings; at this moment I heard, not without emotion, of his sorrowful life; Tigers and sheep cannot be herded together, let alone breed . . . I pity those whose daily meal is the chalice of sorrows. Poor Pascual.'[69] Another clue is in a postscript saying 'The honest Pascual sends his greetings, his life now as before lamentable . . . Thereto, the father is a judge!'[70]

There are two possible explanations here. One is that he is a young Macanese man who has somehow fallen in love with a Chinese girl, and been ostracized from the non-Chinese community in Macao. It could explain the comments of 'tigers and sheep', and such things did happen, albeit rarely. Another clue comes from the words 'let alone breed'. Pascual could be one of the children left behind by foreign traders every year. They were left to fend for themselves, if they survived at all. Grubb sent greetings to Pascual both in and on the way home from China.[71] What we can conclude for Annica de Queros, Juan Francisco Xavier, and 'poor Pascual' is that the employees of the Company were from this time onwards involved in the life of the inhabitants of Macao, for good or for bad.

Grubb Leaving Macao

We find Grubb in transition: between trade systems, between behavioural discourses for businessmen, and between short- and long-term relations in Macao.

In the beginning of 1764, only a few months after his argument with Grill, Grubb embarked on the *Riksens Ständer* back to Sweden.[72] In his farewell letter to Grill he wrote, 'Thank you for the great friendship you also have shown me regarding the person I love in Macao . . . help her with whatever matter she engages you with, I ask this of you with a bleeding heart and wet eyes.'[73] When Grill left Macao a few years later, we find a final message from Isabel: 'here I include a letter to Mr Grubb and I sincerely ask you to deliver it in his hands and I would like you to deliver it making sure it won't be read by anyone.'[74]

We know little of what happened to Isabel after that. In a letter to Grill from China there is a note from 1772: 'Old Macao Jackson dead here in Canton a month ago.'[75] This could be the same man who according to the Portuguese records in Macao died in 1772. Isabel remarried to another trader, called Antonio de Campos.[76]

69. NM: GG, Received letters dated 1763.09.13. Translated from Swedish.
70. NM: GG, Received letters dated 1763.09.16. Translated from Swedish.
71. NM: GG, Received letters dated 1763.09.29, 1763.10.02, 1764.01.19, and 1764.05.05.
72. Nachmanson and Hannerberg, *Garphyttan*, 261.
73. NM: GG, Received letters dated 1764.01.19. Translated from Swedish.
74. NM: GG, Received letters dated 1768.11.26. Translated from Portuguese.
75. NM: GG, Received letters dated 1772.12.12. Translated from Swedish.
76. Macao Archives: Carl Smith Collection, Antonio de Campos.

At first Grubb often included a letter or a greeting to Pascual in his correspondence.[77] In February 1764 Grubb wrote to Grill: 'I own in China two dear friends, that I never can forget: you my prized friend and brother and the dear Pascual.'[78] As he leaves Grubb says that he 'surely will come next year'.[79] But he later takes this back, and in January 1766 he sends a short greeting: 'tell Pascual that I will not come to China again.'[80] Grubb never did return, and no other trader took any interest in Pascual. Eventually, Grubb stopped writing, too. Not all of the intercultural contacts in Macao ended well for the locals.

Homecoming

Back in Sweden, Grubb followed the norm for company traders: he married and bought land. As mentioned, Grubb's sister married an ironworks proprietor, and in 1765 Grubb married this man's daughter from an earlier marriage. Consequently, Grubb's father-in-law was also his brother-in-law.[81] Grubb wrote to tell Grill of this wedding with a woman 'to whom I have been secretly engaged ever since 1757'.[82] Grubb was apparently not free to kiss Isabel, either.

In 1766, the third charter for the Swedish East India Company began, and Grubb took his place on the board of directors. In 1767 he was elected to the Academy of Science, thus exemplifying the golden age for cooperation between the company and the Academy of Science. He even had a flower named in his honour, the Grubbia.[83] In 1768 he was knighted by the name of Grubbens, and his future looked bright.

Grubb bought part of the iron works Garphyttan, even though it was in economic difficulty. The shareholders trusted the riches of this East India traveller to put things right.[84] Through Grill, Grubb kept his hands in the Canton trade for a few more years.[85] Grill was happy to stay, and thanked Grubb in particular for this opportunity. But in the same letter he admitted that a large bill of exchange that he had received from Grubb would be impossible to cash.[86]

77. NM: GG, Received letters dated 1764.02.10, 1764.02.12, 1765.01.22, 1764.05.05, 1766.12.10, and 1767.01.07.
78. NM: GG, brev, Letter 1764.02.10. Translated from Swedish.
79. NM: GG, brev, Letter 1764.05.22. Translated from Swedish.
80. NM: GG, brev, Letter 1766.01.14. Translated from Swedish.
81. Nachmanson and Hannerberg, *Garphyttan*, 257.
82. NM: GG, Received letters dated 1766.01.14. Translated from Swedish.
83. Sten Lindroth, *Kungl. Svenska Vetenskapsakademiens Historia 1739–1818* (Stockholm: Kungl. Vetenskapsakademien, 1967), 2, Tiden 1783–1818; and Kjellberg, *Svenska Ostindiska Companierna*, 148.
84. Nachmanson and Hannerberg, *Garphyttan*, 262.
85. NM: GG, Sent letters dated 1767.11.21, 1767.11.22, 1768.11.09, and 1768.12.20.
86. NM: GG, Sent letters dated 1765.12.05, 1766.01.26, and 1766.02.14.

Soon, Grubb had squandered his fortune in high-risk business ventures.[87] In 1769, after just three years at Garphyttan, he had to file for bankruptcy. The same year he quit the board of directors of the company. By the end of 1773 Abraham Grill (his friend Jean Abraham Grill's uncle) impounded the iron works as security for the large loans Grubb had been granted. As an effect, Grubb filed for a second bankruptcy. Accomplishments in the Canton trade did not always translate to prosperity in Sweden.

When Jean Abraham Grill came home he invested wisely, and fared much better. He was elected to the Swedish Academy of Science in 1773 and in his inaugural speech he talked of the invaluable help and contacts Grubb had provided for him in Canton. These words might have had a sour taste for Grubb.[88] To add insult to injury, the Swedish Academy of Science eventually reviewed its membership registry, and Grubb was excluded, together with others who were found to be 'useless'.[89]

Grubb moved back to Finland, where his wife died in 1786. He remarried, but economic problems forced him back to Stockholm where he borrowed money from Grill. When Grill had passed away, his widow demanded repayment, forcing Grubb to declare bankruptcy a third time. During this time, he talked bitterly about Grill. In Grubb's eyes, Grill arrived in Canton without a penny to his name, and Grubb took him under his wings. According to Grubb, Grill's father had said that Grubb 'had done more for his son than he could have done himself'. Unfortunately, the Grill family did not agree. Michael Grubb spent his remaining years in poverty and died the 10th of July in 1808. Towards the end of his life, Grubb stated in a letter that 'my six years in Canton on my own behalf, that was the happy time of my life'.[90]

By this time the activity of the Swedish East India Company had waned. The expeditions of the fourth charter never became profitable, and the fifth charter never sent out any ships. When the ship *Gustaf III* returned to Sweden in November 1805, it marked the end of the company's expeditions. In 1813, just five years after the passing of Grubb, the company was dissolved.

Conclusion

Michael Grubb lived between groups and norms and in the midst of historical change. Even though he was a 'company man', he also had a private side, which connects with all the other traders discussed in this book. Grubb's life can therefore tell us a great deal about the trade in general and also the Swedish East India Company's activities in the 1760s. He arrived before the golden age of the Company as a whole (which was the end of the 1770s), but experienced the time when the largest private

87. Müller, '"Merchants" and "Gentlemen"', 139.
88. Johan Abraham Grill, *Inträdes-tal, Om Orsakerna, Hvarföre Chinas Natural-historia Är Så Litet Bekant; Hållet För Kongl. Vetenskaps Academien* (Stockholm, 1773).
89. Lindroth, *Kungl. Svenska Vetenskapsakademiens Historia 1739–1818*, 63.
90. Nachmanson and Hannerberg, *Garphyttan*, 261–66.

fortunes were made.[91] Furthermore, he exemplifies several changes in the company: its domination by Swedish traders, the strong connections to Stockholm trade families, the relationship to the ironworks industries, and the close ties between the Company and the Royal Academy of Science.

His story also contributes to our knowledge of the trading environment in Canton, again being in the middle of a transition. Grubb arrived before the Swedish company had completely established the strict division between company and private trade, but when most trade restrictions were already in place. He was an opium trader before opium dominated the trade, and constantly worked as a go-between for different trade groups. Men like Grubb and Grill were the reasons the trade worked; they demonstrate multinational involvement, and how it was intertwined with social relations. But they were only able to remain in China on their own private accounts and fill in holes in global financial structures because of the Qing government's open-door policy of welcoming everyone.

Finally, Grubb serves as an example for how social relationships could shape the Canton trade, and be shaped by it. Grubb moved between different social strata in Sweden, and between different behavioural norms for men of business. He had more permanent social relationships in Macao as well. The traders depended on contacts and networks from the very beginning to get a position on a ship, in the everyday trade practices, and when trying to keep in touch with the trade once they had returned home. Finally, Grubb and Grill show the expectations of the homecoming and life in Sweden for a China trader, and how arduous it could be—no matter how successful his past.

Michael Grubb has left some traces to this day. One street in central Stockholm where he lived is still named 'Grubbensgata', the street of Grubb.[92] And his flower, the Grubbia? It is now known as the Sillyberry.

91. Müller, 'The Swedish East India Company-Strategies and Functions of an Interloper', 99.
92. Hans Harlén, *Stockholm Från A till Ö, Innerstaden* (Älvsjö: Brännkyrka hembygdsförening, 1998).

8

'Money, Credit, and Strong Friends'

Warren Delano II and the Importance of Social Networking in the Old China Trade[1]

Thomas H. Cox

Friendly Advice

On Sunday, 11 March 1838, Warren Delano II, writing from the factory district of Canton, China, scribbled a concerned letter to his younger brother Franklin Hughes Delano half a world away in New York. Franklin had recently lost his position with the transatlantic shipping firm of Grinnell, Minturn and Company. Drawing from his own experiences as an agent for Russell and Company, the largest American merchant house in China, Warren counseled that 'Money, credit and strong friends are a requisite for a young man to commence a commercial business any where with a chance of success—and though you may have some of each, I fear you have not enough.'

Seeking to entice Franklin to Canton, Warren extolled the reputable insurance companies, British banks willing to extend credit, and trustworthy ship captains eager to conduct business with enterprising Americans willing to do business in China. As such, Warren provided his brother with not merely sound business advice but unparalleled access to his network of personal contacts—to the very web of human relationships that made trade in Canton possible. By expressing hope that Franklin had 'decided on getting up a voyage and are already on your way to China, in preference to trying to do commission business in New York', Warren implied

1. Early drafts of this chapter were presented at the Association of Asian Studies Annual Meeting in San Diego, California (2013), Private Merchants in the China Trade Conference at Sun Yat-sen University, Guangzhou, China (2013), Naval History Symposium, Annapolis Maryland (2015), Chinese Academy of Social Sciences, Beijing, China (2015), Histories of Capitalism 2.0 Conference, Cornell University (2016), and American Historical Association Annual Meeting, Denver, Colorado (2017). The author wishes to thank Benjamin Armstrong, Terry Bilhartz, Ty Cashion, Judith Cox, Jeremiah Dancy, Jonathan Goldstein, Ronda Harris, Jeff Littlejohn, Ronnie Littlejohn, David Mayes, Bernadette Pruitt, Stephen Rapp, Christopher Renfrow, Susan E. Schopp, Paul Van Dyke, Rachel Van Tamar, Dong Wang, Jack Wills, and Gregory Witkowski for their assistance with this chapter. Special thanks go to Brian Domitrovic for the extensive support provided by the SHSU history department. Frederic D. Grant, a descendant of Warren Delano and a leading old China trade scholar, provided unstinting advice and assistance at every turn of this project.

that Canton offered better business opportunities than America's largest commercial port.[2]

Scholars have long recognized the unique mix of free trade policies and personal relations that underwrote Canton's dynamic growth in the early 1800s. H. B. Morse asserted that both Chinese and American merchants 'had a reputation for commercial honour and integrity such as has not been surpassed in any part of the world or at any time in its history; trading operations were entirely on parole, with never a written contract: and there was much help and sympathy from one to the other.' Jacques Downs likewise observed in his seminal work *The Golden Ghetto*, 'commercial bonds in the China trade were heavily dependent first on kinship, then on friendship, and only thirdly on reference and reputation'. More recently, John R. Haddad has argued that China traders practiced 'meritocratic nepotism', giving hiring preferences to family or friends but retaining them only if they proved reliable.[3]

To be certain, Qing officials tried to control trade in Canton, delegating all international commerce to ten or twelve licensed Hong merchant houses and restricting foreigners to a small area in the west suburb of the city. Precisely because of such constraints, however, Hong merchants and Western traders forged bonds of trust to carry out complex financial transactions. Warren Delano's career reveals that such connections helped facilitate both legitimate trade and illicit smuggling. During his 1834–1843 sojourn in Canton Delano learned that cultivating a reputation as a community organizer and diplomat generated good relations amongst Chinese merchants who took seriously Confucian concepts such as familial relations, friendship, and social responsibility. In the short run, such good relations advanced Delano's financial interests in both the legal tea and illegal opium trades.

Only the rise of formal diplomatic ties between the United States and China which marked the end of the Canton system could dissuade Delano from smuggling. Returning to America in 1843, Delano married and returned to China a year later with his sister Deborah and new bride, Catherine Lyman Delano. Settling into a spacious mansion in Macau, Delano once again pursued tea and opium profits, but now as a respectable family man on par with leading British, French, Portuguese and Parsee merchants. Although forced by financial bad luck and personal tragedy to return to the United States two years later, Delano's early career in China reveals the changes American merchants faced in Canton during the turbulent 1830s and

2. New Bedford Whaling Museum Research Library and Archives (NBWMRLA): Delano Family Papers (DFP), Warren Delano to Franklin Hughes Delano, 1838.03.11.
3. Hosea Ballou Morse, *The International Relations of the Chinese Empire: The Period of Conflict, 1834–1860* (New York: Paragon Book Gallery, 1910), 85; Jacques M. Downs, *The Golden Ghetto: The American Commercial Community at Canton and the Shaping of American China Policy, 1784–1844* (Bethlehem, PA: Lehigh University Press, 1997), 233; John R. Haddad, *America's First Adventure in China: Trade, Treaties, Opium, and Salvation* (Philadelphia: Temple University Press, 2013), 36.

1840s. He had been lured to Canton by a commercial culture that had unofficially tolerated opium smuggling, but changing Chinese and American attitudes towards the opium trade during the First Opium War forced Delano to both transform the ways in which he did business and relocate his enterprises to Macao in the early 1840s.

Entering the China Trade

On 22 May 1833, at the age of 24, Warren Delano departed for China on the aptly named freighter *Commerce*. After stops in South America and a rough passage around Cape Horn, he arrived off the Cantonese coast in July 1834. As per Chinese trade regulations, the vessel docked at Whampoa and Delano then journeyed upriver to the 'factory district' of Canton, arriving on 24 April.[4] He settled into a cramped back room on the third floor of the Swedish Hong, a warehouse rented by Russell and Company.[5] Created in 1824 by the merger of two rival firms, Russell and Company represented a large corporation controlled by the wealthy Forbes, Sturgis, and Russell clans of Boston. Beset by quarrels and mismanagement, the senior partners hired Delano and other formally educated clerks to institute reforms.[6] Steeped in New England merchant culture that celebrated delayed gratification and profit maximization, Delano often paced the halls outside of his room 'backward & forwards, there & on the story below, calculating and hoping for the future, sometimes for hours'.[7]

Delano's regular duties included inspecting tea purchases, evaluating company employees, and making recommendations to purchase larger, better-insured ships to keep pace with competing New York forms. Revealing both his entrepreneurial outlook and a growing desire to cultivate personal connections, Delano mused:

> I think there will be a chance for making money one of these days on the Coast of China. Had I the friends and a suitable vessel I should not hesitate now to take such a voyage off along the East Coast. One of these days I shall try to gain friends relative to the trade to South America & across to China which may be useful but I cannot now.[8]

Building Relationships

Delano soon learned that his job required many informal responsibilities such as bookkeeping, unloading and loading of cargo, procuring supplies from Chinese

4. Downs, *The Golden Ghetto*, 21–39.
5. NBWMRLA: DFP, Warren Delano to Joseph Delano, 1834.04.24.
6. He Sibing, 'Russell and Company, 1818–1891: America's Trade and Diplomacy in Nineteenth-Century China' (PhD diss., Miami University, 1997), 64–72.
7. New York, Hyde Park, Franklin Delano Roosevelt Presidential Library (FDRPL): Delano Family Papers (DFP); Russell Sturgis to Warren Delano, 1851.04.04.
8. NBWMRLA: DFP, Warren Delano to Joseph Delano, 1837.07.28.

merchants, and representing Russell and Company at the Canton Chamber of Commerce. Created in 1834 by British merchants, the Chamber gradually evolved into a truly international organization. It protected the interests of the foreign community in Canton and settled commercial disputes. The Chamber thus afforded Delano a unique opportunity to stay abreast of local news and interact with the leaders of rival firms.[9]

Given the small size of the Western community in Canton and their confinement to the factory district, social activities were an important part of expatriate life. Delano kept up an active social life of dances, dinners, sing-a-longs, games of whist or poker, and Pearl River cruises. In one instance, he and John Murray Forbes, a senior Russell and Company partner, took a day trip to Lappa Island off the coast of Macao. Far away from the din and bustle of the factory district, they 'gathered wild flowers and some running evergreen fern and heather for Mrs. Sturgis [the wife of another Russell and Company partner], and had some good runs over the hilltops, and drank out of a leaf from a pure stream of clear water, and laid down in the sun for a couple of hours'.[10]

In 1837, Delano served as a steward of the course in the Canton Regatta, an annual boat race held by foreign merchants and sailors that drew large crowds. Delano's boat, a six-oared gig named *The Not So Green* manned by a joint American and Chinese crew, defeated a British boat in a tough race. Although seemingly trivial social events, nature excursions and boat races allowed Delano opportunities to build personal relations with the co-workers and patrons he needed to advance his career.[11]

Relations with the Chinese Hong merchants were another important part of Delano's job. He dealt directly with Wu Bingjian (伍秉鑑), who was more commonly known as Houqua. A long-time partner of the British East India Company, Houqua cultivated relations with American merchants to diversify his financial holdings. Delano was, not surprisingly, one of the American merchants invited to sumptuous banquets at Houqua's luxurious mansion on Honam Island. These events provided opportunities for foreign and Chinese traders to interact in an informal and friendly environment.[12] With changes that were about to take place in the trade—much of which revolved around opium smuggling—maintaining relations within the Chinese community was of utmost importance.

9. Downs, *The Golden Ghetto*, 101–4.
10. Sarah Forbes Hughes, ed., *Letters and Recollections of John Murray Forbes*, 2 vols. (New York: Houghton and Mifflin, Inc., 1899), Vol. 1, 85.
11. William C. Hunter, *Bits of Old China* (London: Kegan Paul, Trench, and Co., 1885), 276–79; *The Canton Press*, 1837.07.15, p. 2, cols. 1–2.
12. Harvard Business School, Baker Library (HBL): Forbes family papers, series E. Robert Bennet Forbes papers, box 1, folder 20, Houqua to Robert Bennet Forbes, 1840.05.23; William Cameron Forbes, *Houqua: The Merchant Prince of China, 1769–1843* (Boston: Asia Publishing Company, 1940), 1–16; and John D. Wong, 'Global Positioning: Houqua and His China Trade Partners in the Nineteenth Century' (PhD diss., Harvard University, 2012).

Preparing for War

In 1835 Delano's relationship with Houqua was sorely tested as Russell and Co. began to supplement its legitimate trade in tea and porcelain with opium smuggling. Although British and other India-based merchants dominated the drug trade, Russell and Co. found a niche market in lower grade but cheaper Turkish opium.[13] This was about the same time that Qing officials in Beijing were considering legalizing the drug and were uncertain of how to deal with the great expansion of that illegal commerce. By 1836, it had been decided that legalization would not work and a series of new initiatives was launched to bring the trade under control.[14] Russell and Co. continued to trade in opium for the next couple of years, but the risks of getting caught had increased considerably until things came to a head in 1838. Alarmed by the drastic increase in opium addiction among ordinary Chinese, the Daoguang emperor (道光帝) in spring of that year ordered Chinese officials in Canton to seize chests of opium from Western merchants and put Chinese sailors involved in opium trafficking to death. When a Chinese official attempted to execute the owner of an opium den in plain view of the foreign factories, a group of British sailors intervened. Such bold action triggered a riot in which 8,000 Chinese civilians laid siege to the foreign quarter.

Delano helped to block the doors of the American factory and create barricades in anticipation of a prolonged siege. However, he also dispatched Gideon Nye Jr., and William Hunter across the rooftops and through the backstreets of the factory district to seek help from Houqua. The old Hong Merchant, in turn, convinced the Cantonese viceroy to dispatch militia troops to quell the siege. In return, Delano agreed that Russell and Co. would no longer deal in opium. The informal but effective alliance between Hong merchants and foreign traders had staved off disaster for the moment.[15]

In March 1839, the Chinese emperor dispatched Imperial Commissioner Lin Zexu (林則徐) to Canton to put a stop to the opium trade, through force if necessary. Lin arrested 1,700 Chinese opium dealers and confiscated 70,000 opium pipes in just six weeks. He also demanded that Western merchants sign an oath not to participate in the opium trade and to register a bond with the Chinese government to ensure their good behaviour. When British and American merchants played for time, Lin surrounded the foreign quarter with troops, cut off all supplies, and dismissed Chinese servants who worked in the factories until the foreigners surrendered

13. Martin Booth, *Opium: A History* (New York: St. Martin's Press, 1996), 35–50.
14. For a summary of the new initiatives put into place to stop the trade in opium in 1836 and after, see Paul A. Van Dyke, *The Canton Trade: Life and Enterprise on the China Coast* (Hong Kong: Hong Kong University Press, 2005), Chapter 7 'Flag Boats, Silver, Contraband and Rice'.
15. Peter Ward Fay, *The Opium War, 1840–1842: Barbarians in the Celestial Empire in the Early Part of the Nineteenth Century and the War by Which They Forced Her Gates* (Chapel Hill: University of North Carolina Press, 1997), 128–60.

their opium stores.[16] Revealing concern not merely for his Western colleagues but Chinese allies, Delano reported that Lin 'seems determined to suppress the trade and we are in an uncomfortable state of suspense as to whether he intends to carry his threats towards us and the innocent Hong merchants into effect or not'.[17]

Forced for the first time to live outside their traditional social and gender roles, Delano and the other men of Russell and Co. adapted creatively, if comically, to the situation. Robert Bennet Forbes cooked up ham and eggs that looked like 'shoe leather', only to be replaced by Delano who 'produced hardboiled eggs that resembled grapeshot and rice indistinguishable from glue'. The men also lit lamps, swept floors, and mended clothes to keep busy.[18] Many of the foreigners who traded at Canton were unaccustomed to housework or cooking so when the Chinese servants were removed; they had to fend for themselves, which, for some of them, would have been the first time in their lives to do domestic duties.

Delano, Forbes and their colleagues channelled their frustration into a petition to the United States Congress. Although 'believing in the sincerity of this government in their efforts to destroy the [opium] trade', the merchants claimed that this did not justify 'robbery committed upon British subjects here, nor for the detention of the persons, ships and property of those who are entirely disconnected from the obnoxious trade'. Only the intervention of a combined American-British-French fleet that could force the Chinese to sign a treaty providing for full diplomatic relations, fixed tariffs, bonded warehouses, open ports, and strictly enforced contract laws could save the merchants' livelihoods.[19] Although the petition triggered an intense debate in Congress, ultimately the spectacle of lost corporate profits gleaned largely from smuggled opium failed to generate enough public sympathy to endorse military intervention. As business associate George Russell reported to Delano from Boston, 'Popular feeling is in favor of the Chinese Govt. & the unaccustomed energy it has evinced in suppressing the opium trade has given rise to more admiration for it than sympathy for the foreign sufferers.'[20]

In a letter to his brother Franklin, Delano condemned the 'bullying and abuse' of the Chinese government and asserted that it was 'to be most devoutly prayed for that a powerful British force, aided by some Frenchmen and Americans, come here and give these people a few lessons upon practical good sense'. However, Delano merely wanted a show of force rather than an all-out war. He maintained that 'I would not like to see [the Chinese] cut to pieces right and left by a foreign force, for I believe that they would confess their inferiority immediately on the arrival of a fleet.'[21]

16. Fay, *The Opium War*, 128–60.
17. NBWMRLA: DFP, Warren Delano to Edward Delano, 1839.03.21.
18. Fay, *The Opium War*, 150–51.
19. *Congressional Globe*, 26th Congress, 1st Session (1840.03.16), 274–75.
20. FDRPL: DFP, George Russell to Warren Delano, 1839.10.09.
21. NBWMRLA: DFP, Warren Delano to Franklin Hughes Delano, 1839.05.13.

First Opium War

Throughout the spring and summer, Delano became increasingly involved in the opium trade. In an often quoted 1839 letter, Delano defended his action to his family and friends by invoking the same commercially oriented logic of his petition a month earlier.

> I do not pretend to justify the prosecution of the opium trade in a moral and philanthropic point of view . . . but as a merchant I insist that it has been a fair, honourable and legitimate trade; and to say the worst of it, liable to no further or weightier objections than is the importation of wines, Brandies & spirits into the U. States, England, &c.[22]

If moral blame were to be assigned at all, Delano suggested that the Chinese government bore ultimate responsibility. 'It must be apparent to everyone at all acquainted with the Chinese character and Chinese government that the opium trade could never have increased in amount as it has done in the past fifteen years without the fostering care of those in authority', Delano argued. [23] The use of such language suggested that Delano was attempting to defend opium smuggling on, of all things, his interpretation of Chinese culture. Delano, like many China traders, held a rudimentary understanding of Confucian concepts like familial piety. Just as a leading American businessman bore responsibility for the wellbeing of his family members and friends, the Chinese government, symbolized by the emperor, was accountable for the safety of his subjects. As Delano and many opium smugglers reasoned, if the emperor abdicated this responsibility through indifference and the use of corrupt officials, who at best turned a blind eye to the opium trade and at worst openly engaged in it, then where did the fault for the opium problem truly lie?

In June 1839, British Trade Superintendent Captain Charles Elliot reluctantly handed over 20,000 chests of opium to Chinese authorities and announced that all British subjects would leave Canton. With the departure of British merchants, there were now even more profits to be made from opium smuggling. Foregoing his pledge not to engage in opium trafficking, Delano began to increase imports into China, selling 8,000 chests of opium to Chinese merchants in a matter of weeks. Still angry at Chinese officials, Delano complained to his brother Franklin that 'Great Britain owes it to herself and the civilized world . . . to knock a little reason into this besotted people, and teach them to treat strangers with common decency'.[24]

The year 1840 represented a massive year of change for both Delano and the American expatriate community in Canton. As John M. Forbes reported to a colleague in London, 'I have arranged to admit Mr. Delano into Russell and Co. on 1 Jan'y 1840 and he is to be ready to help next summer.' Touting Delano as 'a very clever worker and a good worker', Forbes named Delano as his successor in the

22. FDRPL: DFP, Warren Delano to 'My Dear Brothers', 1839.04.11.
23. Ibid.
24. FDRPL: DFP, Warren Delano to Franklin Hughes Delano, 1839.09.04.

newly reformed Russell and Co.[25] Delano's investment in pursuing powerful friends and allies had paid rich dividends.

When Forbes departed for home several months later, Delano found himself not merely in charge of Russell and Co. operations in Canton, but also increasingly assuming a larger leadership role in the growing crisis with Chinese authorities over the opium trade. In February 1840, Peter W. Snow, American consul at Canton, departed for the United States due to ill health. On 23 April, the Chinese governor of Guangdong Province issued an edict acknowledging Delano as vice-consul. In fact, Delano had been carrying out many of Snow's duties unofficially for several months. However, the formal designation of *ling-sze* or 'controller of affairs' by the Qing government afforded Delano not merely oversight over all American trade in Canton, but also unparalleled access to Hong merchants and Chinese officials.[26] Aware of his growing influence, Delano boasted, 'We have a prospect of more stoppage of trade and more trouble than before. I'm in good health and ready for fight or anything else.'[27]

In April 1840, Delano tested the limits of his new authority by issuing a petition on behalf of the American merchant community to Commissioner Lin. Once again phrasing his requests bluntly in commercial terms, Delano related to Lin's fears gleaned from British newspapers that an imperial fleet with orders to blockade Canton would arrive in early June. As the United States was a neutral nation in this conflict, could not American vessels who only wished to pursue an 'honourable trade' proceed directly to Whampoa to unload their cargoes? If Lin did not release the American vessels, 'the English men-of-war once come at the appointed time, will prevent our ships leaving port, and they cannot return to their country, and our losses will be immense'.[28]

Lin was well aware of the role that Delano and other foreigners continued to play in the opium trade. He was more concerned with Chinese lives and national security and, like the US Congress and the American public, was in no mood to listen to the complaints of opium smugglers. The commissioner responded in a polite letter that confirmed that American traders still enjoyed free trade in Canton—only British ships were prevented from doing business. Lin dismissed reports of an approaching British fleet as mere rumours and speculation.

Lin ordered all incoming ships to be searched, but only those containing opium would be hindered from trading in Canton. He took Delano to task for complaining about lost profits. As the Chinese viceroy reasoned, 'since the time the British trade was stopped the profits which the Americans have received have been several

25. Russell and Company Papers, Library of Congress, 1839.01.12; *The Canton Press*, 1840.01.25, p. 1, col. 1; Tim Sturgis, *Rivalry in Canton: The Control of Russell and Co. 1838–1840 and the Founding of Augustine Heard and Co.* (London: The Warren Press, 2006), 75.
26. *The Canton Press*, May 2, 1840, p. 3, col. 1.
27. NBWMRLA: DFP, Warren Delano to Franklin Hughes Delano, 1839.05.13.
28. *The Canton Press*, 1840.05.02, p. 4. col. 3, p. 5 col. 1.

times doubled beyond those of former years. Whence then come these losses?' He concluded with a warning that 'if you do not know good from evil . . . and for the English, exaggerate their announcement, it is to be apprehended that you yourselves will afterwards regret.'[29]

Despite Lin's apparent nonchalance, a British expeditionary fleet arrived promptly at Canton and placed a blockade around the city in June 1840. Chinese military officials surrounded the British fleet with their own ships. Such a delicate standoff placed Delano in a difficult situation. He bore little love for the British, who had authored his family's financial difficulties during the War of 1812. Nevertheless, Delano had no sympathy for the Chinese officials who had repeatedly searched and held up Russell and Co. ships. For the moment, Delano, therefore, opted to pursue a dangerous game of alternately sympathizing with the British and with the Chinese authorities.

Delano had already purchased the 900-ton British ship *Cambridge*, which was stranded in Whampoa by the blockade. He then resold the ship to Commissioner Lin for use by the Chinese Navy.[30] Delano nevertheless refused to give into Chinese demands that foreign merchants put up bonds as proof of their good intentions. In a letter to the Chinese government, Delano responded that he tried in all cases to obey Chinese laws, except when they conflicted with American laws. To sign such a bond 'would call down upon me the severest censure from my own government, it will only remain for me, if it is persisted in, to leave the country'.[31]

In point of fact, no American state or federal law prevented US merchants from signing bonds with foreign governments. Nevertheless, Delano's bluff worked on several levels. It professed respect for Chinese laws and a willingness to accommodate Chinese interests. Delano also invoked the power of the American government, and hinted at the spectre of an international diplomatic incident should he be pressured into signing a bond. Furthermore, Delano's threat to leave Canton suggests his growing importance as a deal-broker, not just to American expatriates but also to Chinese officials.

As late as September 1839, Delano still believed that it was Great Britain's duty to bring China to its senses.[32] However, his attitude towards the Chinese changed drastically over the course of the war. On 7 January 1841, the British Navy began to shell two Chinese forts, Chuenpi and Taikoktow, which guarded the entrance to the Pearl River. Five days later Edward Delano, who had joined his brother Warren in Canton in 1839, toured the devastated fort filled with bodies of Chinese soldiers. 'Some—nearly all of the bodies I saw had received their death blows or shot in the head,' reported Edward. 'Many it appeared on the alarm rushed into the water, having no means of defence, and were there shot down by the sailors. What horrid

29. *The Canton Press*, 1840.05.02, p. 4. col. 3, p. 5 col. 2.
30. *The Canton Press*, 1840.02.01, p. 2, cols. 2–3.
31. *The Canton Press*, 1840.10.03, p. 2, col. 3.
32. FDRPL: DFP, Warren Delano to Franklin Hughes Delano, 1839.09.04.

butchery!' Eight months later, Warren noted 'some half a dozen of H. B. M.'s vessels of war have been committing atrocities in the vicinity of Canton, which has made it necessary for most of the foreigners to restrict to Whampoa'.[33]

Heeding the advice of their colleague George Russell, the brothers fled to the relative safety of Macao in January 1841 before returning to Canton via a Chinese barge several days later. With the same bravado characteristic of his earlier letters to Franklin, Warren brought along an arsenal of swords, shotguns, and revolvers. Freed for the moment of business and diplomatic concerns, Edward reported, 'Warren is full of life too and we enjoy ourselves.'[34] Disaster struck, however, when a Chinese sailor was accidentally killed while handling one of the loaded weapons that Warren had left cocked on the deck. Edward noted that the tragedy had 'saddened our hearts'. Delano, not wishing to face the Chinese legal system, and regretting his role in the death of an innocent man, visited the sailor's family in Canton to express his condolences and paid the victim's widow $200.[35]

Fearing that the British flotilla might launch an invasion of Canton, in March 1841, Commissioner Lin asked Warren Delano to meet with Captain Elliot in Macao and negotiate an end to the siege. Delano was the logical choice to make such an overture. In addition to his professional credentials, he was on particularly good terms with the British forces. In September 1840, Delano had helped secure the release of several British sailors captured by Chinese soldiers when their steamer, the *Madagascar*, sank 150 miles south of Hong Kong.[36]

Careful to maintain his ability to deal with both sides, Delano agreed to meet with the British in Macao, but unofficially. Failing to reach an agreement, Delano returned to Canton aboard a dispatch boat under a white flag of truce. He was, however, fired upon and captured by Chinese troops who delivered him to Military Assistant Governor Yang Fang (楊芳). Delano described Fang as:

> a decrepit looking man of the age of 74 years, with bleared eyes, and deaf as a haddock, who asked me some foolish questions, examined my clothing, hat, shoes and cane, expressed his surprise that my head was not shaved. He took my hands, examining them carefully, and smelling them, asked me to unbutton my shirt-bosom and show my hide, which I did, and he then pronounced me a good man, an excellent man, one of the best men he had ever known, and seizing a lousy, ragged dirty soldier, who stood within three inches of His Excellency, said I was "all the same as he."[37]

---

33. FDRPL: DFP, Edward Delano Journal, 1841.01.12; Warren Delano to 'Dear Brothers and Sisters', 1841.09.15. A graphic account of the destruction wrought by the British shelling of the Chinese forts can be found in Elma Loines, *The China Trade Post-bag of the Seth Low Family of Salem and New York, 1829–1873* (New York: Falmouth Publishing House, 1953), 86–88.
34. FDRPL: DFP, Edward Delano Journal, 1841.01.16 and 19.
35. FDRPL: DFP, Edward Delano Journal, 1841.01.17. See also George Russell to Warren Delano, 1839.10.09 and 23; 1841.03.08.
36. Fay, *The Opium War*, 326.
37. FDRPL: DFP, Warren Delano to Edward Delano, 1841.03.18.

As a native New Englander trained to eschew outward overt physical contact except by the closest friends or family members, Delano must have been repulsed by the examination. However, he may have also realized that Yang Fang's actions could be for the benefit of his followers. Although Fang was an imperial official, his troops were local militia bound to their commander by customs of deference. By requesting a physical examination, Yang could demonstrate that Delano was as well manicured, dressed, and clean as any Mandarin. Yang thus depicted Delano as someone whom the governor personally held in high esteem, as one would treat a close friend or family member. Delano was knowledgeable enough to bear the examination without complaint and wait until Qwang Chow Foo (Guangzhoufu 廣州府), Houqua, and Mowqua were able to secure his release. Yang then returned Delano to Houqua's office in a sedan chair, once again publicly highlighting the notion that Delano was an important individual.[38]

To return the favour, Delano forwarded an offer of a possible truce to Captain Elliot from Lin Zexu. In a break from his earlier entreaties to the US Congress and Commissioner Lin, Delano now sought to appeal to Elliot not just on the basis of trade considerations, but also on his personal relationship with Houqua. In particular, Delano noted that 'my general interest with trade in China, as well as my friendship for the Senior Hong merchant, prompts me to do all I can, to bring his countrymen to an early settlement of a business, which may otherwise work their downfall.'[39]

Securing Peace

Despite Delano's attempts at mediation, British soldiers continued to fight Chinese militia and civilians for control of Canton before evacuating in May 1841. Over the winter Delano tapped his friend and colleague Robert Bennet Forbes to help secure an appointment as Chief Consul for the United States. As he reminded Forbes, 'You know that I will make a good counsel, having had long experience with the Chinese and, from my great age, not liable to sudden outbreaks of passion.'[40] Delano failed to gain the position, which instead went to Forbes's nephew, Paul S. Forbes. Nevertheless, as acting US vice-consul, Delano played a leading role in the peace negotiations which accompanied the end of the First Opium War.

In March 1842 Commodore Stephen Kearny arrived on the Chinese coast aboard the USS *Constellation* to press the Chinese government for damages claimed by American merchants during the conflict.[41] As a show of good faith, Kearney had Delano forward a notice to the Qing officials 'that the government of the United

38. Ibid.
39. FDRPL: DFP, Warren Delano to 'Private' (presumed Charles Elliot), 1841.03.18.
40. FDRPL: DFP, Warren Delano to Robert Bennet Forbes, 1842.01.13.
41. 'Popular Portraits with Pen and Pencil: Lawrence Kearney, Captain, U.S. Navy', *United States Magazine and Democratic Review* 28 (1851): 266.

States does not sanction the "smuggling of opium"' on this coast under the American Flag in violation of the Laws of China. Furthermore, the US Navy would not give any aid or support to Americans arrested by Chinese authorities for trafficking in opium. Delano also published Kearney's proclamation in *The Canton Press* and *The Canton Register*.[42] As Delano informed Forbes, 'Kearney has notified all whom it concerns that if they go to smuggling opium in American vessels they must take care of themselves as he will not help them out of scrapes, if they get into any.' However, Delano also reiterated that Kearney had won the favour of Chinese officials and that the American delegation's visit to Canton 'will be productive of good to us here'.[43] The tactic worked, for in April 1842 Chinese Viceroy Aisin Gioro Keying (愛新覺羅耆英), referred to by Americans as Keying, agreed to meet with the Americans at Whampoa.

Delano accompanied Kearney and missionary Peter Parker, who served as translator, to Whampoa. Delano was amazed at the apparent sincerity and goodwill displayed by both American and Chinese officials at the talks, a stark contrast to his earlier quarrel with Commissioner Lin. As he remarked to Forbes:

> Commodore Kearny is in correspondence with the Chinese authorities, who evinced the most sincere desire to remain on peaceable and friendly terms with the United States of America. The communications from the Governor addressed to Commodore Kearney are written in a very respectful and proper language, and entirely different from anything you saw while you lived in China.[44]

In August, Kearny and Delano learned that British and Chinese diplomats had signed the Treaty of Nanking, which disbanded the Cohong and opened five coastal cities, including Canton, to Western trade. Moving quickly, the Americans negotiated with Keying for American merchants to receive the same rights as British subjects on Chinese soil, a measure that would be formalized two years later with the signing of the Treaty of Wanghia, the first diplomatic agreement between the United States and China.

The end of the First Opium War signalled not only a sea change in US-Chinese relations but also in Warren Delano's mindset. In May 1841, former President John Quincy Adams gave a famous speech to the Massachusetts Historical Society that supported the British war effort against China. Seeking to link the Opium War to British efforts to abolish the slave trade, Adams insisted that opium was 'a mere incident to the dispute, no more the cause of the war than the throwing overboard of tea in Boston Harbor was the cause of the American revolution'. Instead, 'the cause of the war is the kowtow—the arrogant and insupportable pretensions of China that she will hold commercial intercourse with the rest of mankind not upon

42. *The Canton Press*, 1842.04.01, p. 2 col. 3; *The Canton Register*, 1842.04.05, p. 2, col. 3.
43. FDRPL: DFP, Warren Delano to Robert Bennet Forbes, 1842.04.08.
44. FDRPL: DFP, Warren Delano to Robert Bennet Forbes, 1842.05.12.

terms of equal reciprocity, but upon the insulting and degrading forms of the relation between vassal and lord.'[45]

Upon learning of Adams's speech, Delano noted to Forbes that given their percentage of the world's overall population, 'the Chinese have far more right to claim more territory from the rest of the world than the rest of the world has to claim territory from the Chinese'. Furthermore, 'the Chinese have been led to look upon and to treat foreigners with contempt, more by the act of foreigners themselves than by any other cause, and you who have been to China, can say whether the whole body of foreigners visiting China are, as a body, capable of impressing any stranger with an idea of respect.'[46] By thus learning to see beyond mere financial concerns to larger considerations involving a growing respect for different cultures, group responsibility, and the importance of mutual respect, Delano had not only expanded his horizons but placed himself in an excellent position, with a solid reputation amongst the Chinese merchant community, to benefit from future trading opportunities in Asia.[47]

Returning to America

Armed with newfound diplomatic fame and over $200,000 in profit from the China trade, Delano began the long voyage back to America. Even at the height of the Opium War, Delano had expressed a desire to return home, marry, and purchase a large home in Connecticut or New York.[48] Before departing for America, Houqua threw a lavish banquet for his American ally. As Edward Delano recalled the meal included 'about 15 courses – bird's nest soup – sharkfins – pigeons' eggs – quail & sturgeon's lip, etc. We were 13 hours getting thro' with it. It is many years since Houqua has given a Chinese dinner at his own house and perhaps never before did he give to a friend the like of this.'[49] Amongst Western and Chinese merchants, Delano left behind a solid reputation as an attentive businessman and loyal ally. As fellow Russell and Co. employee James S. Prescott noted, Delano was 'the best friend I ever had'. Hinting at Delano's strong regard for personal connections, Prescott recounted, '[y]ou can have no idea how kind he was & the attention he always paid me & his wife too, [he] was one of the best creatures that ever lived'. Admitting that Delano 'is a man of strong prejudices', Prescott provided insight into Delano's social networking skills by insisting 'but when he takes, he is the best of friends'.[50]

45. John Quincy Adams, 'Lecture on the War with China', *Niles National Register* (1842.01.26), 326–30.
46. FDRPL: DFP, Warren Delano to Robert Bennet Forbes, 1842.05.12.
47. Tong Te-Kong, *United States Diplomacy in China, 1844–1860* (Seattle: University of Washington Press, 1964), 68–74.
48. NBWMRLA: DFP, Warren Delano to Joseph Delano, 1834.04.24 and 1836.10.16.
49. Forbes, *Houqua*, 1–16; and FDRPL: DFP, Edward Delano, Personal Diary, 1842.01.20.
50. Mystic, Connecticut, G. W. Blunt White Library (BW): Coll. 47, Collection of Howard W. Krumwiede, James S. Prescott to Henry W. Prescott, 1847.07.01.

In January 1843, Delano departed Canton bound for America. Upon arriving in New England, he quickly carved out a niche in Massachusetts upper-class society. This proved easy to do. After all, his fortune represented twice the normal 'sufficiency' which China traders usually brought back, more than enough to restore the Delano family fortune and standing in New England society. Upon arriving in Massachusetts, he courted and married Catherine Robbins Lyman, the daughter of a well-known judge whose social connections would in time prove a great benefit. In November 1843, the young couple, with Delano's younger sister Deborah in tow, departed for Macao, where they lived for three years. Although opium smuggling remained illegal under both Chinese and US law, only American authorities could charge Delano, an unlikely event given his status in the China trade. Under the treaty port system, Delano could now function as an equal with Chinese merchants, making the need for close friendships less important.[51]

Although Delano continued to increase his fortune, he and his family faced a series of disasters. The loss of their mansion Arrowdale to a fire, the death of their infant daughter Susan, and Deborah's contraction of tuberculosis forced the Delanos to return to the United States in 1846. The family initially settled into a townhouse in the fashionable Lafayette Square district of New York City. They lived several doors down from Delano's younger brother, Franklin, who had recently married Laura Astor, the daughter of John Jacob Astor, a key player in the China trade and one of the wealthiest men in America. Just as Delano had cultivated business associates in China, he now made use of the Astor family's business contacts throughout Asia. Delano also made acquaintances with Herman Melville, William Cullen Bryant, and Nathaniel Currier through services at the nearby All Souls Unitarian Church. By living in close quarters with friends, families, and business associates in the midst of an urban environment, Delano consciously or unconsciously recreated many of the same living conditions he had known in Canton and Macao, revealing ever-increasing skill in cultivating close friendships.[52]

Since both Warren and Catherine Delano had grown up in small New England towns, they wished to create the same experiences for their children. Delano also wanted to showcase his wealth and experiences in the China trade to potential business prospects through the building of a suitable mansion. In 1851, construction began on Algonac, a majestic summer home located in the scenic Hudson Highlands near Newburgh, New York. Although fashioned in a typical federal style, Algonac's interior boasted one of the best collections of Chinese artefacts in the United States. Chinese silk paintings hung in the entrance hall. Carved jade statues, teakwood screens, and a pair of cast-iron bells from a Buddhist temple gave the home the feel of Houqua's mansion in Canton. A Chinese gong summoned the family to dinner

51. Jan Pottker, *Sara and Eleanor: The Story of Sara Delano Roosevelt and Her Daughter-in-Law, Eleanor Roosevelt* (New York: St. Martin's Press, 2005), 10–14.
52. Ibid.

every evening. An oil painting of the old Hong merchant graced the library and was flanked by paintings of Delano and Lyman family members. Even Delano's master bedroom boasted a Chinese-crafted bedstead inlaid with mother-of-pearl. By adorning his house with souvenirs of the China trade, Delano could cultivate the image of a successful businessman, world traveller, and tasteful patron of the arts, in essence an American version of Houqua, with Algonac filling in for the Hong merchant's Honam Island mansion. Such refinement also served to distance Delano from the questionable source of much of this wealth.[53]

Like many China traders, Delano invested his profits from the China trade in various industrial projects including New York real estate, clipper-ship construction in California, and copper mines in Pennsylvania, Tennessee, and Maryland. He also became a local philanthropist, giving generously to the American Anti-Slavery Society and a local Unitarian Church. To both honour his ancestors and highlight his own lineage, Delano sponsored a fund to create a public cemetery in Fairhaven.[54]

Following years of financial success, the Panic of 1857 ruined Delano and forced him to return to China in 1860 to amass a new fortune through trading tea, porcelain, and, at times, opium. Delano arranged for his family to join him in Hong Kong in 1862. In 1866, Delano returned to the United States, his fortune and business reputation once more restored.[55]

Establishing a Legacy

Upon returning to Algonac, Warren Delano retired from Russell and Co. and resumed the life of a wealthy upstate New Yorker. He maintained a considerable stock portfolio, particularly in real estate and mining, but invested much more cautiously than he had in the 1850s. He also played the role of staunch paternalist with fresh enthusiasm, urging his son Warren Delano III to pursue an engineering degree at Harvard and giving him a position managing the family's mining concerns in Maryland. Delano also, somewhat reluctantly, gave his blessing to the marriage of his daughter Sara to an up-and-coming attorney (and Democrat) named James Roosevelt. Their son Franklin would go on to become the thirty-second president of the United States.

Warren Delano occasionally spoke of his experiences in the China trade to family members and friends, particularly his grandson Franklin, but he avoided public conversations and interviews on the subject. He did not have the moral

53. Peter Collier, *The Roosevelts: An American Saga* (New York: Simon and Schuster, 1995), 53.
54. *The Liberator*, 1850.11.01, p. 20, col. 1–2; *The Christian Register*, 1850.11.09, p. 29, col. 1; and *American Railway Times*, 1853.06.23, p. 2, col. 2. The links between China traders and industrialization in the United States is a topic of much recent debate, best discussed in James R. Fichter, *So Great a Proffit: How the East Indies Trade Transformed Anglo-American Capitalism* (Cambridge: Harvard University Press, 2010).
55. Pottker, *Sara and Eleanor*, 10–22.

convictions of Nathan Dunn, and had no qualms about trading in opium. While Dunn is a rather atypical example, Delano represents a typical trader who needed more than moral integrity to keep him away from the opium trade. The openness of Canton in carrying out trade also proved to be its weakness, because before 1836, it was relatively easy to become involved in contraband. With substantial profits to be made and little risk of getting caught, Russell and Co., as well as numerous others, had no reservations about participated in the trade. Delano and Dunn both returned to the States with a fortune of around $200,000 from the China trade, but the former was gotten largely from illegal trade and the latter exclusively from legal commerce. Had Delano been faced with sufficient deterrents he might also have gone the route that Dunn had chosen, and could have possibly returned home with the same fortune. This does not justify his actions, but in an environment where there are few restrictions to engage in contraband, it is logical to assume there will be an increase in that commerce. From Delano's example, one could argue that perhaps the Canton trade had been too open prior to 1836. During the period from 1858 to 1906, it was legal to import foreign opium into China and Delano returned again to the trade to restore his lost fortune.[56]

In 1898, Warren Delano died. An article in the *Daily Journal* remarked upon his ability to make and retain personal connections, describing him as:

> a man of quick perceptions, accurate judgment, indomitable will and possessed in a remarkable degree the rich endowment of common sense. Mr. Delano was gifted with an instinctive and a delicate sense of propriety as well as a strong amiable sensibility. He could tolerate bores and did, but not too often, or too long at a time.[57]

It is in this context that Warren Delano's China career is best understood. Growing up in a world where paternalism lingered and the impersonal, individualistic-driven market of the Gilded Age had yet to arise, Delano learned over time to pursue a career that intermingled ambition with personal connections and the ability to navigate amongst informal kinship- and friendship-based networks. Furthermore, by invoking the language of friendship, Delano could trade opium with Chinese merchants whom he viewed as personal allies without overly worrying about the effects of such products on ordinary Chinese. Such a mindset aided Delano in building two overseas fortunes and leaving a lasting legacy of profits and networking skills to his descendants. An examination of Delano's life accordingly points to the possibilities and realities of trade between Americans and Chinese in the early nineteenth century.

---

56. For the trade in opium in the Pearl River Delta from 1858 to 1906, see Ma Guang, 'Opium Problems in the Modern Pearl River Delta' (MA thesis, Dept. of History, University of Macau, 2010).
57. 'The Late Warren Delano, An Appreciative Biographical Sketch', *The Daily Journal*, 1898.01.28, reprinted in Frederic D. Grant Jr., 'Edward Delano and Warren Delano II: Case Studies in China Trader Attitudes Toward the Chinese, 1834–1844' (Honors thesis, Bates College, 1976), 149.

Conclusion

Paul A. Van Dyke

When we look at each of the individual chapters in this volume, it is often difficult to envision the importance of these private traders to the commerce as a whole. For the most part, their operations were miniscule compared to the large volumes of goods that each of the European East India companies purchased in China annually. The importance of the companies to the trade is much easier to qualify and quantify owing to the massive volumes of records that they left behind for us to examine. It is thus understandable that those enterprises have commanded most of the attention of scholars in the past; their work now constitutes many dozens of publications. It was, in fact, necessary for those studies to be done first, before we could begin to understand the roles that private investors played in the trade.

Taken as a whole, the micro studies presented here reveal some very significant contributions. First and foremost is that all of the men were welcomed in China regardless of the size or volume of their trade. As several of the chapters have shown (Hanser, Van Dyke, Schopp, and Hellman), China's open policy made it possible for private traders to channel large amounts of foreign capital into that market. Even though some of the companies such as the EIC tried to limit these private exchanges in Canton, it proved impossible to stop them because Qing officials guaranteed that all private traders would have access to the market that was equal to what the companies enjoyed. Despite the EIC's objection to these private traders, as time progressed, the large companies—like the Hong merchants—became increasingly more dependent on investments from these individuals to finance their operations in China.

As Mok shows in her chapter, the Chinese shopkeepers also had great freedom in carrying out their trade. The market was very competitive, which meant that quality of service and products became even more important over time, as the trade continued to grow. While it has been shown in recent studies that the Chinese Hong merchants were discouraged by Qing policies from leaving Canton and from expanding their operations abroad—which probably affected shopkeepers as well—those men nonetheless had great freedom to carry out their trade in China. The day-to-day business was left entirely up to the individual proprietors to manage, with little or no interference from government. Merchants might be asked to make contributions to officials from time to time, but how they conducted their businesses on a daily basis was left entirely up to them. Government officials only interfered in the conduct of trade if complaints emerged from customers, such as being cheated or treated unfairly.[1]

With these chapters being added to the historiographical literature, we can now say unequivocally that all of the East India companies, including the French, English, Dutch, Danish, Swedish, Ostend, Imperial, and Prussian would have been very hard pressed had they not had access to private capital to finance their operations. Their trade with China would have certainly been much hindered without those investments, to the point that fewer ships would have been dispatched. Some of the smaller companies would probably have quit the trade much earlier without the investments from private individuals. As those private interactions grew, China became the avenue through which Asian-based Europeans sought to transfer their funds back to Europe. If China had restricted private traders' access to its market as the large monopolistic companies had done in the ports they controlled in India and elsewhere, the flow of money across Asia and between Asia and Europe, would have been greatly hindered.

Although it has been argued that the high interest rates in China were detrimental to the Hong merchants and possibly to the sustainability of the trade in the long term, the attraction of earning profits from arbitrage channelled an enormous amount of foreign money into China, which in turn financed its growth.[2] Thus, in addition to the companies and the Hong merchants, we could rightfully say that the Canton trade in general would have turned out very differently without those private contributions. While there was money to be made in the commodity and usury sectors, not everyone came out successful in the long term. Hanser shows how dozens of Englishmen lost on their investments with Hong merchants. However, for many of those men the losses they incurred probably did not ruin them (even though they may have claimed this outcome). Many of the losers were undoubtedly hard pressed owing to the Hong merchants' inability to repay their money, but because it was common practice not to invest all of one's funds in one source, the losses were likely to have been only a fraction of their total wealth.

Several examples in this volume show that a fortune could be lost just as quickly as it took to gain it. Grubb, Dunn, and Delano all lost their fortunes after they left China, owing to unprofitable investments and other factors. Some men, such as

1. For the relationship between the Qing government and the Chinese Hong merchants and shopkeepers, see Paul A. Van Dyke, *Merchants of Canton and Macao: Politics and Strategies in Eighteenth-Century Chinese Trade*, Vol. 1 (Hong Kong: Hong Kong University Press, 2011); and Paul A. Van Dyke, *Merchants of Canton and Macao: Success and Failure in Eighteenth-Century Chinese Trade*, Vol. 2 (Hong Kong: Hong Kong University Press, 2016).
2. For many examples of how high interest rates in China contributed to the growth of the Canton trade, see Van Dyke's books. Paul A. Van Dyke, *The Canton Trade: Life and Enterprise on the China Coast, 1700–1845* (Hong Kong: Hong Kong University Press, 2005; reprint, 2007); Van Dyke, *Merchants of Canton and Macao*, Vols. 1 and 2.

Basilion, Metree, and de Constant, lost their fortunes as the result of war; others faced loss from the risks of sea, as shown in Hellman's chapter. Thus, even though there was money to be made in the China trade, there were risks involved, which might vary from one year to the next depending on the political situation in Europe and/or Asia at the time.

Schopp shows in her chapter that expenses could be very high in Canton, which meant that a large amount of money was needed up front, before one could engage directly in the trade. Van Dyke shows many individuals going to China from India and elsewhere, some of whom only had small amounts of goods to trade. But it needs to be kept in mind that those persons also needed money up front, over and above their investments in trade goods, in order to pay the rents and living expenses in Macao and Canton and their passages to and from China. If they ran short of money, then they might have to borrow from one of the foreign commission merchants operating in China until they sold their goods and acquired more funds. Or they might ask friends or relatives outside of China to send them money, in which case there would be a long delay.

Wills, Goldstein, and Hellman show us that a lot of non-commercial activity emerged as a by-product of the trade. There were a great number of intellectual exchanges with China. European botanists were eager to study the plants of Asia, and did much experimenting with different varieties. While the Qing government's openness to outsiders was predominantly commercial in nature at this time, and was not extended to missionaries, there were religious men who were employed in various aspects of the trade. The Swedish chaplain Pehr Osbeck wandered the countryside in his spare time to document the plants and animals he encountered; the American Nathan Dunn ordered and received a huge collection of artefacts concerning Chinese life and culture, which had nothing to do with the trade; the Swedes Grubb and Grill nurtured female companionship in Macao; and throughout the chapters we see a lot of socializing going on between groups and between foreign traders and Hong merchants. There were also excursions to the famed Fa-ti gardens and boat races in which both foreigners and Chinese participated. All of these activities point to a very lenient administration that allowed for pleasure and interactions outside of the day-to-day activities of trade. While the restrictions on the foreign community could vary from one year to the next and/or from one official to the next, on the whole, Qing officials understood that there needed to be room for socializing in order to make the trade viable in the long term.

As far as the experience of shopping in Canton is concerned, Mok shows us that the overwhelming majority of the foreign customers probably left China very satisfied with their purchases. While some men such as John Francis Davis had a rather low opinion of the Chinese shopkeepers, this was not the view of other customers. The great expansion of the trade itself and the increase of foreign visitors over time is testimony to Canton's popularity in global commerce. There were plenty of other places in the world where those men could go, but they invariably returned to

Canton. In fact, Mok shows us that shopkeepers tried to generate goodwill among patrons in order to build a good reputation within the foreign community and thereby increase their pool of repeat-customers. The Qing government's open policy of ensuring that everyone had equal access to the market (with the exception of the Russians and Japanese), combined with the accommodating and competitive spirit of the Cantonese merchants, earned the city the reputation of being a place where 'there is no part of the world where cargoes may be sold and bought, unloaded and loaded, with more business-like speed and activity'.[3]

It is these positive aspects of the trade that we have heard so little about from the history books of the twentieth century, mostly because that narrative has often been drowned out by the business activities and complaints of the large companies, by discussions of opium smuggling, and by the many reasons for the Opium Wars. There are exceptions, but previous scholars in general were not interested in what made the trade successful, but rather what led to its decline.[4] This approach—perhaps unintentionally but invariably—encased the history within a negative narrative. When failure is your ultimate goal, then you automatically look for all of the contributing factors that brought that about, such as unfair policies, overbearing restrictions, arrogant and greedy officials, unjust exactions, etc., all of which generate a negative impression. There is no room for discussions of positive things with such an approach, because those aspects do not support the desired outcome.

When we look at the individual and private experiences within the commerce, however, we begin to see a much different picture. The policies and practices of Qing officials' involved in managing the trade and the foreign community in Canton often showed great leniency and latitude for compromise. Hoppos, governor generals and other top officials in Canton might make use of harsh words and maintain strict demeanours in order to give the outward appearance of being an authoritarian ruler, but many of their actions (or inactions) show incredible patience when dealing with problems arising from the trade and/or within the foreign community. While there were some very strict officials who tried to force the foreigners into compliance such as Commissioner Lin Zexu, he and others like him were not representative of the Qing administration as a whole. From all of the examples presented here and in other recent studies that have been done on the trade, we see that forbearance was an underlying factor influencing the implementation of many of Qing's policies. This theme has only recently come to light and is one that we are only now beginning to understand.[5]

3. *The Saturday Magazine* (June 1838), Supplement, p. 250, quote by Mr. Macculloch.
4. For example, Christiaan Jörg's publication tends to be very positive, and he is not the only one. For one example, see Chrisiaan J. A. Jörg, *Porcelain and the Dutch China Trade* (The Hague: Martinus Nijhoff, 1982), which has some very lively accounts of social interaction in Canton.
5. For example, it has been recently shown that the management of the foreign factories in Canton actually became much more lenient over time, with foreigners purchasing, owning,

Cox shows us with his example of Warren Delano that contrary to what we normally read in the history books (that the trade was very restrictive), Qing policy may have been too lax in the management of the trade. There was so much freedom to engage in all types of commerce, including smuggling, that a huge contraband business emerged that ran parallel to the legal trade. As Hanser, Goldstein, Hellman, and Cox show, there were so few risks involved in trading opium before 1836, that many people were attracted to it. Officials on all levels were involved in opium. If officials had monitored and regulated the day-to-day transactions more closely, they could have been more successful in curbing these illegal transactions, before they reached crisis proportions.

Dunn refrained from trading in opium and returned home with a fortune that was about equivalent to what Warren Delano had earned from his opium business. If the risks of getting caught had been greater, Delano would likely have also turned to a more legitimate commerce. Moral convictions only worked with a small minority of traders. The majority of them needed something else to keep them away from smuggling, such as high risks that threatened profits and/or a high probability of getting caught, being charged and punished. Before 1836, there were no such effective deterrents in place.

While these chapters only represent a tiny fraction of the hundreds of private traders who ventured to China to try their luck in the trade, they nonetheless bring us one step closer to filling a void in our understanding. We now know that the private traders were central to both the success of the companies and to the Canton trade in general. Of course, they were also central to its eventual downfall and demise as well. As more studies are done on these men, we will likely learn many more new things about their interactions and the roles they played in the rise and fall of that commerce.

---

renovating and/or constructing their own buildings from the ground up. By the early 1800s, foreigners were even opened hotels and saloons in the foreign quarter to service the foreign community. Although all of this activity was illegal, it was tolerated because it helped to maintain peace and harmony within the foreign community. In the first half of the eighteenth century, such activities were unthinkable, but by the late eighteenth century, there was great leniency shown to foreigners in all of these activities. Paul A. Van Dyke and Maria Kar-wing Mok, *Images of the Canton Factories 1760–1822: Reading History in Art* (Hong Kong: Hong Kong University Press, 2015). See also Paul A. Van Dyke, 'The Hume Scroll of 1772 and the Faces behind the Canton Factories', *Review of Culture*, International Edition No. 54 (2017), 64–102, which has more discussion about foreign ownership and management of the buildings.

Bibliography

Electronic Databases

Adam Matthew Digital: 'China: Trade, Politics & Culture, 1793–1980: Sources from the School of Oriental and African Studies and the British Library, London', Sir George Staunton, 'Journal of a Voyage to China'.

URLs Cited

http://www.eah.geschichte.uni-freiburg.de/staff/wang-shuo (accessed 24 December 2016).

http://www.crommelin.org/history/Biographies/1763CharlesRussel/02-CharlesGovOfBombay.htm (accessed 5 January 2017).

http://euclidlodge158.com/documents/FreemasonryinChina.pdf (accessed 12 January 2017).

https://www.hrionline.ac.uk/lane/index.php (accessed 11 January 2017).

http://www.nhm.ac.uk (accessed 25 January 2017).

http://gallica.bnf.fr/ark:/12148/bpt6k1102726?rk=85837;2 (accessed 15 February 2017).

http://gallica.bnf.fr/ark:/12148/bpt6k1042673v?rk=21459;2 (accessed 15 February 2017)

http://gw.geneanet.org/pierfit?lang=fr&p=edmond&n=de+rothe (accessed 15 January 2017).

Archival Sources

(Listed alphabetically by country/city/repository/collection)

Belgium

Antwerp: Stadsarchief (Municipal Archive, SAA)

IC 5704, 5705, 5922

Ghent: Universiteits Bibliotheek (University Library, GHL)

Ms 1848–49, 1923, 1928, 1985 (VOC *dagregister* for 1791)

Denmark

Copenhagen: Rigsarkivet (National Archives, RAC)

Ask 879a, 999, 1024, 1144, 1183, 1206

France

Aix-en-Provence: Archives Nationales d'Outre-Mer (ANOM)
C.1.10–13, 15
E 358
La Courneuve: Centre des Archives diplomatiques, formerly Archives des Affaires Etrangères (AAE)
8MD Asie 16–17, 19
15MD Chine 16
Lorient: Service historique de la Défense (SHDL)
1P 305 L 70
2P 28-II.20, 34-I.11
Montigny-le-Bretonneux: Archives départementales des Yvelines
E 3056, Pierre-Louis-Achille de Robien
Nantes: Archives départementales de Loire-Atlantique
E 1245 François Terrien
Nantes: Archives municipales de Nantes
8Z 403–11, 502, and 508
Paris: Archives Nationales (ANP)
4JJ 131.31–32, 132.44

Holland

Middleburg: Zeeuws Museum
Grand Chops from 1817 and 1819, Inv. Nos. G02-005 and G0-006
The Hague: National Archives (NAH)
Canton (1.04.20) 17, 79, 84, 87–89, 97, 223–24, 226–33, 246–47, 256–388
Hoge Regering van Batavia (1.04.17, HRB) 80, 82, 95–136
RAB (2.01.27.02) 140–42
OIC (2.01.27.01) 193–98, 238A, 238Q
VOC (1.04.02) 4384, 4386, 4388, 4390, 4426, 4428, 8721

Hong Kong

Hong Kong Museum of Art: Accession nos. C1991.0001, AH1975.0001.

Indonesia

Jakarta: Arsip Nasional Republik Indonesia (ANRI)
Batavia Castle *dagregisters* (DR) 2516, 2555, 2559

Macao

Macao Archives:
Carl Smith Collection
Leal Senado 1760–1770

Spain

San Sebastián: Untzi Museoa-Museo Naval (UM)
Fondo Manuel de Agote (FMA), R630–638 Manuel de Agote Diarios 1787–1796

Sweden

Gothenburg: Maritime Museum (Sjöfartsmuseum) (GMM)
SMG 6131 *Lovisa Ulrica* Journal
Stockholm: National Library of Sweden (NLS), Manuscript Collection (MC)
Brefochhandlingarrörande Eric von Stockenström, IS 46
Diverse Mindre Räkningar & Conto Couranter Hållne Uti Canton Åren 1780–1787, 21
Letter to Eric Stockenström in Canton from Jean Abraham Grill 1784.01.02
Carl Rappe, 'Dagbok För Skeppet Rycksens Ständer På Resa till Surat Och Canton 1760–1762'
Fredric Christian Sternleuw, 'Utkast till En Beskrifning Om Mina Sjö-resor Upsat Af Mig Sjelf Frid. Crist. Sternlöw På Fogelvik År 1794'
Stockholm: Nordic Museum Archive (NM):
Godegårdsarkivet (GG). Ostindiska Handling F17: 1–7 (F17)

Taiwan

Taipei: National Palace Museum, 軍機及宮中當
26992, Memorial of Li Zhiying and Tu Ming'e to the Qianlong Emperor, dated 45/05/12 (15 May 1780).

United Kingdom

Edinburgh: National Library of Scotland
Melville Papers, No. 3385, letter dated 1788.11.04, from Cornwallis to Dundas, p. 162
London: British Library (BL), India Office Records (IOR)
Add MS 29210, Warren Hastings Papers
E/1/73
G/12/8–254
H/24, 155, 219, 411, 434
J/1/2
L/MAR/A/CXXIII
L/MAR/B/1H, 36C, 98C, 98E, 112B, 124B, 172G, 235B, 257A, 259B, 285LL, 322A, 390C, 397B, 404B, 407A, 408A, 420D, 437F, 438J, 450G, 452J, 469G, 482J, 486D, 489A, 490C, 499D, 530E, 535D, 544-I-M, 572B, 582D, 596A-B, 602-I, 603A, 603B, 607B, 614A, 614B, 619A, 622E, 626D, 646A, 665B, 700B, 715B, 776A, 800A
Mss EUR F331/19
R/10/7–8

United States

(Listed alphabetically by state/city/repository/collection)

Connecticut, Mystic Seaport: G. W. Blunt White Library (BW)
Misc. Vol. 552, Nathan Dunn Letter copybook 1829–1830
Coll. 47 Howard W. Krumwiede Collection
Delaware, Newark: University of Delaware Library (UDL), John R. Latimer Papers
Massachusetts, Boston: Massachusetts Historical Society (MHS), Shattuck Collection
Massachusetts, Cambridge: Harvard Business School, Baker Library (BL): Forbes family papers, series E. Robert Bennet Forbes papers
Massachusetts, New Bedford: New Bedford Whaling Museum Research Library and Archives (NBWMRLA), Delano Family Papers (DFP)
Massachusetts, Salem: Phillips Library, Peabody Essex Museum (PEM), Bryant P. Tilden MH-219 Journals 1815–1837 (typescript)
New York, Hyde Park: Franklin Delano Roosevelt Presidential Library (FDRPL): Delano Family Papers (DFP)
New York, Ithaca: Cornell University, Kroch Library
MSS HF. G44, John Gibson, 'Observations on the Manner of Trading at Canton'
Pennsylvania, Haverford: Haverford College Library, Quaker Collection (HC)
Pennsylvania, Philadelphia:
American Philosophical Society Library (APS)
Historical Society of Pennsylvania (HSP)
Albert Newsam Collection
Joseph Archer Letterbooks
Nelson B. Gaskill, 'Nathan Dunn' scrapbook, 'List of Philadelphia directories, 1802–42', Testimony against Nathan Dunn, 28 November to 5 December 1816, Minutes of the Philadelphia Monthly Meeting of Friends
Library Company of Philadelphia (LCP)
Am 1835 Dunn 2603.Q.14
McAllister Collection
Washington DC, Library of Congress (WLC)
Latimer Papers
Russell and Company Papers

Printed Sources and Unpublished Papers and Dissertations

(Listed alphabetically by author/editor's surname)

1831–2 Parliamentary Debates and Papers. Reports from Committees: eighteen volumes. Appendix to Report from Select Committee
'Art in China'. *The Bulletin of the American Art-Union* 7 (October 1850): 118–19.
'Popular Portraits with Pen and Pencil: Lawrence Kearney, Captain, U.S. Navy'. *United States Magazine and Democratic Review* 28 (1851): 266.
Adams, John Quincy. 'Lecture on the War with China, delivered before the Massachusetts Historical Society, December 1841'. *Chinese Repository* 11 (May 1842): 274–88.
———. 'Lecture on the War with China'. *Niles National Register* (1842.01.26): 326–30.

Affairs of the East India Company. Reports from Committees: 1831–2. Vol. 6. (London: The House of Commons, 1832), 462.

American Railway Times, 1853.06.23.

Aslanian, Sebouh David. *From the Indian Ocean to the Mediterranean: The Global Trade Networks of Armenian Merchants from New Julfa*. Berkeley: University of California Press, 2011.

Bannister, Saxe, trans. *A Journal of the First French Embassy to China, 1698–1700*. London: Thomas Cautley Newby, 1859.

Barber, John, and Henry Howe. *Historical Collections of the State of New Jersey*. Newark: Benjamin Olds, 1857.

Barrow, John. *Travels in China from Pekin to Canton*. London: Cadwell & W. Davies, 1806.

Basu, Dilip K. 'Asian Merchants and Western Trade: A Comparative Study of Calcutta and Canton, 1800–1840'. PhD dissertation, University of California Berkeley, 1975.

Bayly, C. A. *The Birth of the Modern World, 1780–1914*. Oxford and Malden, MA: Blackwell, 2004.

Blackman, Leah. *History of Little Egg Harbor Township, Burlington County, N.J., from Its First Settlement to the Present Time*. Camden, NJ: Proceedings . . . of the Surveyors' Association of West New Jersey, 1880.

Booth, Martin. *Opium: A History*. New York: St. Martin's Press, 1996.

Bowen, Huw. *Business of Empire: The East India Company and Imperial Britain, 1756–1833*. Cambridge: Cambridge University Press, 2006.

———. 'Privilege and Profit: Commanders of East Indiamen as Private Traders, Entrepreneurs and Smugglers, 1760–1813'. *International Journal of Maritime History* 19, no. 2 (December 2007): 43–88.

Briand, P. C. *Les Jeunes Voyageurs en Asie, ou Description Raisonnée des Divers Pays compris dans cette Belle Partie du Monde*. Paris: Chez Hivert, 1829.

Bruijn, Jaap R. *Commanders of Dutch East India Ships in the Eighteenth Century*. Woodbridge, Suffolk [England]: The Boydell Press, 2011.

Buckingham, James Silk. *The Eastern and Western States of America*, 3 vols. London: Fisher, 1842.

Bulletin de la Société des archives historiques: Revue de la Saintonge et de l'Aunis 19, no. 2 (1899).

Bulley, Anne. 'The Bombay Country Ships 1790–1833 with Lists of Captains and Nominal Owners'. Compiled by Anne Bulley, 1995, revised 1999. Unpublished manuscript, available in a folder on the shelves of the British Library in the Asian and African Studies Reading Room.

———. *The Bombay Country Ships 1790–1833*. Richmond, Surrey: Curzon Press, 2000.

———. *Free Mariner: John Adolphus Pope in the East Indies 1786–1821*. London: British Association for Cemeteries in South Asia (BACSA), 1992.

The Canton Press (1835–1844).

The Canton Register (1827–1843).

Caplan, Aaron. 'Nathan Dunn's Chinese Museum'. Unpublished research paper, History, University of Pennsylvania, 23 April 1986, courtesy of the author.

Carey, Mathew. 'Essays on the Public Charities of Philadelphia'. In *Miscellaneous Essays*, 153–203. Philadelphia: Carey & Hurt, 1830.

Carroll, John M. 'The Other "Inner Opium War": British Traders' Debates about Opium in the Canton Period'. Unpublished paper presented at Association for Asian Studies (March 2014).

Carter, Philip. *Men and the Emergence of Polite Society: Britain 1660–1800*. Harlow: Longman, 2001.

Ch'en Kuo-Tung. *The Insolvency of the Chinese Hong Merchants, 1760–1843*. Nankang, Taipei: Institute of Economics, Academia Sinica, 1990.

Cheong, Weng Eang. *Mandarins and Merchants: Jardine Matheson & Co., a China Agency of the Early Nineteenth Century*. London: Curzon Press, 1979.

The Chinese Repository. 20 vols. Canton: The South China Mission, 1832–1852.

The Christian Register, 1850.

Claeys, Thierry, and Yves Durand. *Dictionnaire biographique des financiers en France au XVIIIe siècle*. Paris: Editions SPM, 2009.

Clarke de Dromantin, Patrick. *Les réfugiés jacobites dans la France du XVIIIe siècle: L'exode de toute une noblesse "pour cause de religion"*. Pessac: Presses universitaires de Bordeaux, 2005.

Collier, Peter. *The Roosevelts: An American Saga*. New York: Simon and Schuster, 1995.

Commelin, Isaac, ed. *Begin ende Voortgangh van de Nederlantsche Oost-Indische Compagnie*. 2 vols. 1646. Facsimile reprint, 4 vols. Amsterdam: Theatrum Orbis Terrarum, 1970.

Congressional Globe, 26th Congress, 1st Session (1840.03.16), 274–75.

Conner, Patrick. *The China Trade, 1600–1860*. Brighton: The Royal Pavilion, Art Gallery & Museums, 1986.

———. *The Hongs of Canton*. London: English Art Books, 2009.

Conner, Patrick, and Anthony Hardy. *Paintings of the China Trade: The Sze Yuan Tang Collection of Historic Paintings*. Hong Kong: Hong Kong Maritime Museum, 2013.

Constant, Charles-Samuel de, and Louis Dermigny. *Les mémoires de Charles de Constant: sur le commerce à la Chine*. Paris: S.E.V.P.E.N., 1964.

Coolhaas, W. Ph., ed. *Generale Missiven van Gouverneurs-Generaal en Raden aan Heren XVII der Verenigde Oostindische Compagnie. 1713–1725*. Vol. 7. The Hague: Instituut voor Nederlandse Geschiedenis, 1979.

Cordier, Henri. *The Decorative Arts of the China Trade: Paintings, Furnishings and Exotic Curiosities*. Suffolk: Antique Collectors' Club, 1988.

———. *La France en Chine au dix-huitième siècle: documents inédits publiés sur les manuscrits conservés au dépôt des affaires étrangères, avec une introduction et des notes*. Paris: E. Leroux, 1883.

———. 'La mission de M. le chevalier d'Entrecasteaux à Canton en 1787: d'après les archives du Ministère des Affaires étrangères'. In *Bulletin de géographie historique et descriptive*. Paris: Imprimerie nationale, 1911.Crossman, Carl L. *The China Trade. Export Paintings, Furniture, Silver and Other Objects*. Princeton: The Pyne Press, 1972.

———. 'Le Consulat de France à Canton au XVIIIe siècle'. *T'oung Pao* 9 (1908): 47–96.

Cunynghame, Arthur. *An Aide-de-camp's Recollections of Service in China*. London: Saunders-Otely, 1844.

Dahlgren, E. W. *Les relations commerciales et maritimes entre la France et les côtes de l'Océan Pacifique (commencement du XVIIIe siècle)*. Paris: H. Champion, 1909.

The Daily Journal, 1898.

Dalton, Sir Cornelius Neale. *The Life of Thomas Pitt*. Cambridge: Cambridge University Press, 1915.

Davies, Stephen. *East Sails West: The Voyage of the Keying, 1846–1855*. Hong Kong: Hong Kong University Press, 2014.

Davis, John Francis. *The Chinese: A General Description of China and Its Inhabitants*. 2 vols. London: Charles Knight, 1836.

Dawson, Raymond. *The Chinese Chameleon*. London: Oxford University Press, 1967.

Dennys, N. B., Wm. Fred Mayers, and C. King. *The Treaty Ports of China and Japan: A Complete Guide to the Open Ports of those Countries, together with Peking, Yedo, Hongkong and Macao*. London: Trubner and Co.; Hong Kong: A. Shortrede & Co., 1867.

Dermigny, Louis. *Cargaisons Indiennes. Solier et Cie 1781–1793*. 2 vols. Paris: S.E.V.P.E.N., 1959–1960.

———. *La Chine et l'Occident: le commerce à Canton au XVIIIe siècle 1719–1833*. 3 vols. and Album. Paris: S.E.V.P.E.N., 1964.

Dobell, Peter. 'Travels in Kamchatka and Siberia'. *American Quarterly Review* 9 (March–June 1831): 52–81.

Dolin, Eric Jay. *Fur, Fortune, and Empire: The Epic History of the Fur Trade in America*. New York: W. W. Norton & Company, 2010.

———. *When America First Met China: An Exotic History of Tea, Drugs, and Money in the Age of Sail*. New York: W. W. Norton & Company, 2012.

Downing, A. J. *A Treatise on the Theory and Practice of Landscape Gardening*. New York: Wiley and Putnam, 1841.

Downing, C. Toogood. *The Fan-qui in China in 1836–1837*. 3 vols. London: Henry Colburn, 1838.

Downs, Jacques M. *The Golden Ghetto: The American Commercial Community at Canton and the Shaping of American China Policy, 1784–1844*. Bethlehem: Lehigh University Press, 1997. Reprint, Hong Kong: Hong Kong University Press, 2014.

Dunn, Nathan, and William B. Langdon. *"Ten Thousand Things Chinese": A Descriptive Catalogue of the Chinese Collection in Philadelphia*. Philadelphia: Printed for the Proprietor, 1839.

Edmonds, John W. *Origins and Progress of the War Between England and China: A Lecture Delivered Before the Newburgh Lyceum, December 11, 1841*. New York: Narine & Co., 1841.

Ekeberg, Carl Gustav. *Capitaine Carl Gustav Ekebergs Ostindiska Resa Åren 1770 Och 1771*. Stockholm: Henr. Fougt, 1773. Facsimile reprint, Stockholm: Rediviva, 1970.

Fairbank, John K. *China Watch*. Cambridge, MA, and London, England: Harvard University Press, 1987.

———. *Trade and Diplomacy on the China Coast: The Opening of Treaty Ports, 1842–1854*. 2 vols. Cambridge: Harvard University Press, 1953. Reprint, 1964.

Fan Fa-ti. *British Naturalists in Qing China: Science, Empire, and Cultural Encounter*. Cambridge, MA, and London: Harvard University Press, 2004.

Farrington, Anthony. *Catalogue of East India Company Ships' Journals and Logs 1600–1834*. London: British Library, 1999.

Fay, Peter Ward. *The Opium War, 1840–1842: Barbarians in the Celestial Empire in the Early Part of the Nineteenth Century and the War by Which They Forced Her Gates*. Chapel Hill: University of North Carolina Press, 1997.

Fichter, James. *So Great a Proffit: How the East Indies Trade Transformed Anglo-American Capitalism*. Cambridge, MA: Harvard University Press, 2010.

Forbes, William Cameron. *Houqua: The Merchant Prince of China, 1769–1843*. Boston: Asia Publishing Company, 1940.

Forjaz, Jorge. *Famílias Macaenses*. 3 vols. Macao: Fundação Oriente, Instituto Cultural de Macau, 1996.

Forster, John Reinhold, trans. *A Voyage to China and the East Indies, by Peter Osbeck. Together with a Voyage to Suratte, by Olof Toreen, and an Account of Chinese Husbandry, by Captain Charles Gustavus Eckeberg*. 2 vols. London: Benjamin White, 1771.

France, and Dernis. *Recueil ou collection des titres, édits, déclarations, arrêts, règlemens et autres pièces concernant la Compagnie des Indes orientales établie au mois d'août 1664: Précédé d'un Avertissement historique . . . par le sieur Dernis*, Paris: Impr. Boudet, 1755.

Frängsmyr, Tore. *Ostindiska Kompaniet: Människorna, Äventyret Och Den Ekonomiska Drömmen*. Höganäs: Bokförlaget bra Böker, 1976. Reprint, Höganäs: Wiken, 1990.

Frank, Caroline. *Objectifying China, Imagining America: Chinese Commodities in Early America*. Chicago: University of Chicago Press, 2011.

Friends' Weekly Intelligencer, 1844.

Froger, François, and Ernst Arthur Voretzsch. *Relation du premier voyage des François à la Chine fait en 1698, 1699 et 1700 sur le vaisseau "L'Amphitrite"*. Leipzig: Verlag der Asia Major, 1926.

Fu Lo-shu. *A Documentary Chronicle of Sino-Western Relations (1644–1820)*. Tucson: University of Arizona Press, 1966.

Furber, Holden. *John Company at Work: A Study of European Expansion in India in the Late Eighteenth Century*. Cambridge: Harvard University Press, 1948.

———. *Rival Empires of Trade in the Orient 1600–1800*. Minneapolis: University of Minnesota Press, 1976.

Gibson, James R. *Otter Skins, Boston Ships, and China Goods: The Maritime Fur Trade of the Northwest Coast, 1785–1841*. Seattle: University of Washington Press, 1992.

Godden, G. A. *Oriental Export Market Porcelain and Its Influence on European Wares*. London: Granada, 1979.

Goldstein, Jonathan. 'Cantonese Artefacts, Chinoiserie and the Formation of an Early American Image of the Chinese'. In *The Chinese American Experience: Papers from the Second National Conference on Chinese American Studies (1980)*, edited by Genny Lim, 255–56. San Francisco: The Chinese Historical Society of America and The Chinese Culture Foundation of San Francisco, 1984.

———. *Philadelphia and the China Trade, 1682–1846*. University Park, PA: Pennsylvania State University Press, 1978.

———. 'A Philadelphian Author Turns to China: Robert Waln, Jr., as America's First Sinologist'. *The American Asian Review* 21, no. 3 (Fall 2003): 187–203.

———. 'Philadelphia's Old China Trade and Early American Images of China'. *Pennsylvania Legacies* 12, no. 1 (May 2012): 6–11.

———. Review of James Fichter's *So Great a Profitt. International Journal of Maritime History* 23, no. 1 (June 2011): 367–68.

———. Review of Kendall Johnson's *Narratives of Free Trade: The Commercial Cultures of Early US-China Relations. Journal of Chinese Studies* 56 (January 2013): 356.

———. *Stephen Girard's Trade with China 1787–1824: The Norms versus the Profits of Trade.* Portland, ME: MerwinAsia Publishers, 2011.

Gould, Robert Freke. *The History of Freemasonry*. 1882.

Gowans, Alan. *Architecture in New Jersey*. Princeton: Van Nostrand, 1964.

Grace, Richard J. *Opium and Empire: The Lives and Careers of William Jardine and James Matheson*. Montreal: McGill Queens University Press, 2014.

Grant, Frederic D., Jr. *The Chinese Cornerstone of Modern Banking: The Canton Guaranty System and the Origins of Bank Deposit Insurance 1780–1933*. Leiden: Brill Nijhoff, 2014.

———. 'Edward Delano and Warren Delano II: Case Studies in China Trader Attitudes Toward the Chinese, 1834–1844'. Honours thesis, Bates College, 1976.

Grassby, Richard. *The Business Community of Seventeenth-Century England*. Cambridge: Cambridge University Press, 1995.

Gray, John Henry. *Walks in the City of Canton*. Hong Kong: De Souza, 1875.

Greeley, Horace. *Essays Designed to Elucidate the Science of Political Economy*. Boston: Fields Osgood, 1870.

Greenberg, Michael. *British Trade and the Opening of China, 1800–1842*. Cambridge: Cambridge University Press, 1951. Reprint, 1969.

Griffis, William. *China's Story in Myth, Legend, Art, and Annals*. London: Constable, 1911.

Grill, Johan Abraham. *Inträdes-tal, Om Orsakerna, Hvarföre Chinas Natural-historia Är Så Litet Bekant; Hållet För Kongl. Vetenskaps Academien*. Stockholm, 1773.

Guo Deyan 郭德焱. *Qingdai Guangzhou de Basi Shangren* 清代廣州的巴斯商人 [Parsee merchants in Guangzhou during the Qing dynasty]. Beijing: Zhonghua shuju, 2005.

———. 'The Study of Parsee Merchants in Canton, Hong Kong and Macao'. *Review of Culture*, International Edition No. 8 (October 2003): 51–69.

Gutzlaff, Charles. *China Opened*. 2 vols. London: Smith, Elder and Co., 1838.

Haddad, John Rogers. *America's First Adventure in China: Trade, Treaties, Opium, and Salvation*. Philadelphia: Temple University Press, 2013.

———. 'China of the American Imagination: The Influence of Trade on US Portrayals of China, 1820 to 1850'. In *Narratives of Free Trade: The Commercial Cultures of Early US-China Relations*, edited by Kendall Johnson, 57–82. Hong Kong: Hong Kong University Press, 2012.

———. *The Romance of China: Excursion to China in U.S. Culture, 1776–1876*. New York: Columbia University Press, 2008.

Haffner, Christopher. 'Eastern Masonic Frontiers Before the Union'. In *Transactions of Quatuor Coronati Lodge No 2076* 104: 1991.

Halgouët, Hervé, du. 'Pages coloniales. Relations maritimes de la Bretagne et de la Chine au XVIIIe siècle. Lettres de Canton'. *Mémoires de la Société d'histoire et d'archéologie de Bretagne* 15 (1934): 331–441.

Hallward, N. L. *William Bolts: A Dutch Adventurer Under John Company*. Cambridge [England]: Cambridge University Press, 1920.

Hanser, Jessica. 'Mr. Smith Goes to China: British Private Traders and the Interlinking of the British Empire with China, 1757–1792'. PhD dissertation, Department of History, Yale University, May 2012.

Hao Yen-p'ing. 'Chinese Teas to America—A Synopsis'. In *America's China Trade in Historical Perspective*, edited by Ernest R. May and John K. Fairbank, 11–32. Cambridge, MA: Harvard University Committee on American-East Asian Relations, 1986.

Harlén, Hans. *Stockholm Från A till Ö, Innerstaden*. Älvsjö: Brännkyrka hembygdsförening, 1998.

Haudrère, Philippe. *La Compagnie française des Indes au XVIIIe siècle*. 2 vols. Paris: Les Indes Savantes, 2005.

Haverford Alumni Association. *A History of Haverford College for the First Sixty Years of Its Existence*. Philadelphia: Porter and Coates, 1892.

He Sibing. *Macao in the Making of Early Sino-American Relations 1784–1844*. Macao: Cultural Affairs Bureau of the Macao S.A.R. Government, 2015.

———. 'Russell and Company, 1818–1891: America's Trade and Diplomacy in Nineteenth-Century China'. PhD dissertation, Miami University, 1997.

Hellman, Lisa. 'Everyday Life in Canton: The Case of the Swedish East India Company 1730–1830'. PhD dissertation, Department of History, Stockholm University, 2015.

Hinshaw, William. *Encyclopedia of Quaker Genealogy*. Ann Arbor, MI: Edwards Bros., 1936–1963.

Hughes, Sarah Forbes, ed. *Letters and Recollections of John Murray Forbes*. 2 vols. New York: Houghton and Mifflin, Inc., 1899.

Hummel, Arthur W. 'Nathan Dunn'. *Quaker History* 59 (1970): 34–39.

Hummel, Arthur W., and Nan P. Hodges, eds. *Lights and Shadows of a Macao Life: The Journal of Harriett Low, Travelling Spinster*. Redmond, WA: History Bank, 2002.

Hunt, Lynn, Margaret C. Jacob, and Wijnand Mijnhardt, eds. *Bernard Picart and the First Global Vision of Religion*. Los Angeles: Getty Research Institute, 2010.

———. *The Book That Changed Europe: Picart & Bernard's 'Religious Ceremonies of the World'*. Cambridge, MA, and London: Belknap Press of Harvard University Press, 2010.

Hunter, William C. *Bits of Old China*. London: Keegan, Paul, Trench and Co., 1885.

Isaacs, Harold. *Scratches on Our Minds: American Images of China and India*. New York: John Day, 1958.

Johnson, Kendall. *Narratives of Free Trade: The Commercial Cultures of Early US-China Relations*. Hong Kong: Hong Kong University Press, 2012.

Johnston, Patricia, and Caroline Frank, eds. *Global Trade and Visual Arts in Federal New England*. Durham: University of New Hampshire Press, 2014.

Jörg, Christiaan J. A. *Porcelain and the Dutch China Trade*. The Hague: Martinus Nijhoff, 1982.

Kaeppelin, Paul, and François Martin. *Les origines de l'Inde française. La Compagnie des Indes orientales et François Martin; étude sur l'histoire du commerce et des établissements français dans l'Inde sous Louis XIV, 1664–1719*. Paris: A. Challamel, 1908.

Kjellberg, Sven. *Svenska Ostindiska Compagnierna 1731–1813: Kryddor, Te, Porslin, Siden*. Malmö: Allhems Förlag, 1974.

Koerner, Lisbet. *Linnaeus: Nature and Nation*. Cambridge, MA, and London: Harvard University Press, 1999.

Koninckx, Christian. *The First and Second Charters of the Swedish East India Company (1731–1766): A Contribution to the Maritime, Economic and Social History of North-western Europe in Its Relations with the Far East.* Belgium: Van Gemmert Publishing Co., 1980.

Krieger, Martin. *Daufleute, seeräuber und Diplomaten. Der Dänische Handel auf dem Indischen Ozean (1620–1868).* Köln, Weimar, Wien: Bohlau Verlag, 1998.

La Barbinais Le Gentil, de. *Nouveau voyage autour du monde: enrichi de plusieurs plans, vuës & perspectives des principales villes & ports du Pérou, Chily, Bresil & de la Chine: avec une description de l'Empire de la Chine.* 3 vols. Amsterdam: Chez Pierre Mortier, 1728.

Lam, Otto Chun-Cheung. 'The 1819 Bank Note and Parsee Bankers in China'. *The Numismatic Chronicle* 164 (2004): 209–18.

Lampe, Evan. *Work, Class, and Power in the Borderlands of the Early American Pacific: The Labors of Empire.* Lanham: Lexington Books, 2014.

Lancaster, Clay. 'The Chinese Influence in American Architecture and Landscaping'. In *Nineteenth Annual Washington Antiques Show 1974* (catalogue), 92.

Lane, John. *Lane's Masonic Records*, Amity Lodge no. 225 https://www.hrionline.ac.uk/lane/index.php (accessed 11 January 2017).

Langdon, William B. *A Descriptive Catalogue of the Chinese Collection Now Being Exhibited at St. George's Place, Hyde Park Corner, London.* London: Printed for the Proprietor, First English Edition 1842, Eighteenth English printing 1843.

Latourette, Kenneth Scott. 'Voyages of American Ships to China, 1784–1844'. In *Transactions of the Connecticut Academy of Arts and Sciences* 28 (April 1927): 237–71.

Lauring, Kåre, 'Kinahandelen-et Spørsmål Om Finansiering'. In *Søfart, Politik, Identitet: Tilegnet Ole Feldbæk*, edited by Ole Feldbæk and Hans Jeppesen, 215–26. København: Falcon, 1996.

Lavollée, Charles. *Voyage en Chine.* Paris: Just Rouvier, 1853.

Lee, Jean Gordon. *Philadelphians and the China Trade, 1784–1844.* Philadelphia: Philadelphia Museum of Art, 1984.

Le Netrel, Edmond. *Voyage of the Héros: Around the World with Duhaut-Cilly in the Years 1826, 1827, 1828 & 1829*, trans. Blanche Collet Wagner. Los Angeles: Glen Dawson, 1951.

Le Pichon, Alain. *China Trade and Empire: Jardine, Matheson & Co. and the Origins of British Rule in Hong Kong 1827–1843.* Oxford: Oxford University Press, 2006.

Lespagnol, André. *Messieurs de Saint-Malo: une élite négociante au temps de Louis XIV.* 2 vols. Rennes: Presses Universitaires de Rennes, 1997.

The Liberator, 1850.

Lim, Genny, ed. *The Chinese American Experience: Papers from the Second National Conference on Chinese American Studies (1980).* San Francisco: The Chinese Historical Society of America and the Chinese Culture Foundation of San Francisco, 1984.

Lindgärde, Valborg, and Elisabeth Mansén. *Ljuva möten och ömma samtal: om kärlek och vänskap på 1700-talet.* Stockholm: Bokförlaget Atlantis, 1999.

Lindroth, Sten. *Kungl. Svenska Vetenskapsakademiens Historia 1739–1818.* Stockholm: Kungl. Vetenskapsakademien, 1967.

Ljungstedt, Anders. *An Historical Sketch of the Portuguese Settlements in China.* Boston: James Munroe and Co., 1836. Reprint, Hong Kong: Viking Hong Kong Publications, 1992.

Lockyer, Charles. *Account of the Trade in India.* London: S. Crouch, 1711.

Loines, Elma. *The China Trade Post-bag of the Seth Low Family of Salem and New York, 1829–1873*. New York: Falmouth Publishing House, 1953.

Love, Henry Davison. *Vestiges of Old Madras 1640–1800*. 4 vols. London, 1913. Reprint, New Delhi: Mittal Publications, 1988.

Lundblad, Stefan. *Hedersam handelsman eller verksam företagare: Den ekonomiska kulturens omvandling och de ledande ekonomiska aktörerna i Gävle 1765–1869*. Uppsala: Acta Universitatis Upsaliensis, 2007.

Mackerras, Colin. *Western Images of China*. Oxford: Oxford University Press, 1989.

Ma Guang, 'Opium Problems in the Modern Pearl River Delta'. MA thesis, Department of History, University of Macau, 2010.

Malleret, Louis. *Pierre Poivre*. Paris: École Française d'Extrême-Orient, 1974.

Manning, Catherine. *Fortunes à Faire: The French in Asian Trade, 1719–48*. Aldershot, Hampshire, Great Britain: Variorum, 1996.

Marshall, P. J. *Bengal: The British Bridgehead, Eastern India 1740–1828*. Cambridge: Cambridge University Press, 1987.

———. *East Indian Fortunes: The British in Bengal in the Eighteenth Century* Oxford [Eng.]: Clarendon Press, 1976.

Martineau, Alfred. *Dupleix et l'Inde française, 1722–1741*. Paris: Honoré Champion, 1920.

———. 'Quatre ans d'histoire de l'Inde française, 1726–1730'. *Revue de l'histoire des colonies françaises* (3rd trimester 1919): 5–72.

May, Ernest R., and John K. Fairbank, eds. *America's China Trade in Historical Perspective*. Cambridge, MA: Harvard University Committee on American-East Asian Relations, 1986.

Mayer, Brantz. 'China and the Chinese'. *Southern Quarterly Review* (July 1847).

———. 'A Nation in a Nutshell'. *Baltimore Literary Monument* 2 (1839).

———. *A Nation in a Nutshell*. Philadelphia: Brown, Bicking, and Guilbert, 1841.

McCabe, Ina Baghdiantz. 'No Network is an Island: Collaboration and Competition between Trade-Diaspora in the Early Modern Period'. In *Diaspora as a Resource: Comparative Studies in Strategies, Networks and Urban Space*, edited by Waltraud Kokot, Christian Giordano, and Mijal Gandelsman-Trier, 143–70. Berlin: Lit Verlag, 2013.

Mézin, Anne. *Les consuls de France au siècle des Lumières (1715–1792)*. Paris: Ministère des Affaires étrangères, Direction des archives et de la documentation, 1998.

Milburn, William. *Oriental Commerce; containing a Geographical Description of the Principal Places in The East Indies, China, and Japan, with their Produce, Manufactures, and Trade, including the Coasting or Country Trade from Port to Port; also the Rise and Progress of the Trade of the various European Nations with the Eastern World, particularly that of the English East India Company, from the Discovery of the Passage round the Cape of Good Hope to the Present Period; with an account of the Company's Establishments, Revenues, Debts, Assets, &c. at Home and Abroad*. 2 vols. London: Black, Parry, & Co., 1813. Reprint, New Delhi: Munshiram Manoharlal Publishers, 1999.

Miller, Stuart Creighton. *The Unwelcome Immigrant*. Berkeley: University of California Press, 1969.

Mok, Maria Kar-wing 莫家詠. 'Some Restrictions on Westerners in Canton in the First Half of the 19th Century: A Study Based on the Hong Kong Museum of Art Collection'. *Arts of Asia* 41, no. 4 (2011): 102–15.

———. 'Xiěshí yù xiǎngxiàng zhī jiān: Guǎngzhōu shāngguǎn jì huángbù bódì wàixiāo huà de shǐliào yìyì' 寫實與想像之間：廣州商館暨黃埔泊地外銷畫的史料意義 [Between realism and imagination: The historical meaning of Canton and Whampoa export paintings]. PhD dissertation, Department of History, Sun Yat-sen University, 2017.

Mok, Patrick Kin Wai. 'The British Intra-Asian Trade with China, 1800–1842'. PhD dissertation, Department of History, University of Hong Kong, 2004.

The Morning Herald (London), 1842.

The Morning Post (London), 1842.

Morrison, Eliza A., and Samuel Kidd. *Memoirs of Life and Labours of Robert Morrison Compiled by His Widow*. 2 vols. London: Longman, Orme, 1839.

Morse, Hosea Ballou. *The Chronicles of the East India Company Trading to China, 1635–1834*. 5 vols. Cambridge, MA: Harvard University Press, 1926. Reprint, Taipei: Ch'eng-wen Publishing Co., 1966.

———. *The International Relations of the Chinese Empire: The Period of Conflict, 1834–1860*. New York: Paragon Book Gallery, 1910.

Müller, Leos. 'Mellan Kanton och Göteborg: Jean Abraham Grill, en superkargörs karriär'. In *Historiska Etyder*, edited by Janne Backlund. Uppsala: Historiska institutionen, Univ., 1997.

———. '"Merchants" and "Gentlemen" in Early-Modern Sweden: The World of Jean Abraham Grill, 1736–1792'. In *The Self-Perception of Early Modern Capitalists*, edited by Margaret C. Jacob and Catherine Secretan, 125–46. New York: Palgrave Macmillan, 2008.

———. 'The Swedish East India Company-Strategies and Functions of an Interloper'. In *Small Is Beautiful? Interlopers and Smaller Trading Nations in the Pre-industrial Period*, edited by Jan De Vries and Philipp Robinson Rössner, 83–101. Stuttgart: Steiner, 2011.

Murray, D. Roy. 'Freemasonry in China'. In *United Masters Lodge No. 167*. Auckland, New Zealand (June 1989).

Nachmanson, August, and David Hannerberg. *Garphyttan: Ett Gammalt Bruks Historia*. Stockholm: Bonnier, 1945.

The National Gazette, 1821.

The New-Jersey Mirror and Burlington County Advertiser, 1844.

Noble, Charles Frederick. *A Voyage to the East Indies in 1747 and 1748*. London: T. Becket and P. A. Dehondt, 1762.

O'Brian, Patrick. *Joseph Banks: A Life*. London: C. Harvill, 1987; Chicago: University of Chicago Press, 1987.

Oliver, S. Pasfield. *The Memoirs and Travels of Mauritius Augustus Count de Benyowsky*. London: T. Fisher Unwin, 1898.

Önnerfors, Andreas. *Mystiskt Brödraskap-Mäktigt Nätverk: Studier i Det Svenska 1700-tals-frimureriet*. Lund: Lunds Universitet, 2006.

Osbeck, Pehr. *Dagbok Öfver En Ostindisk Resa Åren 1750, 1751, 1752*. Stockholm: 1757. Reprint, Redviva Publishing House, 1969.

Osterhammel, Jürgen. 'Britain and China, 1842–1914'. In *The Oxford History of the British Empire*, edited by Andrew Porter, Vol. 3. Oxford: Oxford University Press, 1999.

———. *Die Entzauberung Asiens: Europa und die asiatische Reiche im 18. Jahrhundert*. München: C. H. Beck, 1998.

Paris-Jallobert, Paul. *Anciens registres paroissiaux de Bretagne: Saint-Malo*, Fasc. 7, Vol. 8. Rennes: Plihon et Hommay, 1901.

Permanyer-Ugartemendia, Ander. 'La participación españolaen la economía del opioen Asia Oriental trasel fin del Galeón'. PhD dissertation, Universitat Pompeu Fabra, Barcelona, 2013.

Perry, John Curtis. *Americans and the Opening of the Pacific*. Westport, CT: Praeger, 1994.

Phipps, John. *A Practical Treatise on the China and Eastern Trade: comprising the Commerce of Great Britain and India, particularly Bengal and Singapore, with China and the Eastern Islands*. Calcutta: Baptist Mission Press, 1836.

Pondicherry (India), and Alfred Martineau. *Correspondance du Conseil supérieur de Pondichéry et de la Compagnie*, 1726–1730. Pondicherry: Société de l'histoire de l'Inde francaise, 1920.

Pottker, Jan. *Sara and Eleanor: The Story of Sara Delano Roosevelt and Her Daughter-in-Law, Eleanor Roosevelt*. New York: St. Martin's Press, 2005.

Poulson's American Daily Advertiser.

Pritchard, Earl H. *The Crucial Years of Early Anglo-Chinese Relations, 1750–1800*. New York: Octagon Books, 1970.

———. 'Private Trade between England and China in the Eighteenth Century (1680–1833)'. *Journal of the Economic and Social History of the Orient* 1, no. 1 (Aug 1957): 108–37.

———. 'Private Trade between England and China in the Eighteenth Century (Concluded)'. *Journal of the Economic and Social History of the Orient* 1, no. 2 (April 1958): 221–56.

Ptak, Roderich. 'Macau: Trade and Society, Circa 1740–1760'. In *Maritime China in Transition 1750–1850*, edited by Wang Gungwu and Ng Chin-Keong, 197–204. Wiesbaden: Harrassowitz Verlag, 2004.

The Public Ledger (Philadelphia), 1844.

Pugh, Richard. 'Charles Crommelin (1717–1788) A Governor of Bombay'. http://www.crommelin.org/history/Biographies/1763CharlesRussel/02-CharlesGovOfBombay.htm (accessed 5 January 2017).

Quenell, Peter, ed. *Prodigal Rake: Memoirs of William Hickey*. New York: E. P. Dutton, 1962.

Quiason, Serafin. *English 'Country Trade' with the Philippines, 1644–1765*. Quezon City: University of Philippines Press, 1966.

Quincey, de. *Confessions of an English Opium-Eater*. London: Taylor and Hersey, 1823.

Quincy, Josiah, ed. *The Journals of Major Samuel Shaw, the First American Consul at Canton. With a Life of the Author*. Boston: Wm. Crosby and H.P. Nichols, 1847. Reprint, Documentary Publications, 1970.

Ranshaw, Carol. 'Calendar of the University of Delaware Collection of the John Latimer China Trade Papers'. MA thesis, School of Library Science, Drexel Institute of Technology, 1953.

Records of Fort St. George. Diary and Consultation Book. 1700–1722. Madras: Government Press, 1922–1930.

Records of Fort St. George. Letters to Fort St. George. 1703–1704. Madras: Government Press, 1931.

Recueil de pièces utiles pour l'instruction de l'affaire de la Compagnie des Indes. Place of publication not identified: n.p., n.d.

Règlement touchant la Marine de la Compagnie des Indes, arresté en l'assemblée d'Administration. 1733–1734. Paris: L'Imprimerie royale, 1734.

Renouard de Sainte-Croix, Felix. *Voyage commercial et politique aux Indes Orientales, aux îles Philippines, à la Chine, avec des notions sur la Cochinchine et le Tonquin, pendant les années 1803, 1804, 1805, 1806 et 1807*. 3 vols. Paris: Archives du droit français, 1810.

Reports from Committees. 18 vols. East India Company's Affairs. Session 6 December 1831–16 August 1832, Vol. X, Part II, 'China Trade', 457–64.

Richards, Rhys. 'United States Trade with China, 1784–1814'. *The American Neptune* 54: Special Supplement (1994).

Romain, Alain. *Saint-Malo au Temps des négriers*. Paris: Karthala, 2001.

Rose, Sarah. *For All the Tea in China: How England Stole the World's Favorite Drink and Changed History*. New York: Penguin, 2010.

Rosenblatt, Helena, ed. *The Cambridge Companion to Constant*. Cambridge and New York: Cambridge University Press, 2009.

Russel-Wood, A. J. R. 'An Asian Presence in the Atlantic Bullion Carrying Trade, 1710–50'. *Portuguese Studies* 17 (2001): 148–67.

Saksena, Shalini. 'Parsi Contributions to the Growth of Bombay and Hong Kong'. *Review of Culture*, International Edition No. 10 (April 2004): 26–35.

The Saturday Magazine, 1838.

Schmidt, Benjamin. *Inventing Exoticism: Geography, Globalism, and Europe's Early Modern World* (Material Texts). Philadelphia: University of Pennsylvania Press, 2015.

Schopp, Susan E. 'The French in the Pearl River Delta: A Topical Case Study of Sino-European Exchanges in the Canton Trade, 1698–1840'. PhD dissertation, Department of History, University of Macau, 2015.

Schurz, William. 'The Royal Philippine Company'. *The Hispanic American Historical Review* 3, no. 4 (Nov 1920): 491–508.

Sellers, Charles Coleman. *Mr. Peale's Museum*. New York: Norton, 1980.

Shinn, Henry C. *History of Mount Holly*. Mt. Holly, NJ: privately printed, 1957.

Silliman, Benjamin. 'Chinese Museum'. *Niles' National Register* 55 (1839.02.16).

———. *Mr. Dunn's Chinese Collection in Philadelphia*. Philadelphia: Brown, Bickering, and Guilbert, 1841.

———. 'N. Dunn's Chinese Collection, at Philadelphia'. *American Journal of Science and Arts* 35 (January 1839): 391–400.

Simpson, Henry. *Lives of Eminent Philadelphians*. Philadelphia: William Brotherhead, 1859.

Sinha, H. N. ed. *Fort William-India House Correspondence*. Delhi: Published for the National Archives of India by the Manager of Publications, Government of India, 1957.

Smith, Carl T. 'An Eighteenth-Century Macao Armenian Merchant Prince'. *Review of Culture*, International Edition No. 6 (April 2003): 120–29.

———. 'Parsee Merchants in the Pearl River Delta'. *Review of Culture*, International Edition No. 10 (April 2004): 36–49.

Smith, Carl T., and Paul A. Van Dyke. 'Armenian Footprints in Macau'. *Review of Culture*, International Edition No. 8 (October 2003): 20–39.

———. 'Four Armenian Families'. *Review of Culture*, International Edition No. 8 (October 2003): 40–50.

———. 'Muslims in the Pearl River Delta, 1700 to 1930'. *Review of Culture*, International Edition No. 10 (April 2004): 6–15.
Smith, George. *The Use and Abuse of Free-Masonry*. London: Printed for the author and sold by G. Kearsley, 1783.
Smith, Robert C. 'Friend Dunn'. *Haverford College Publication Horizons* 67, no. 6 (Summer 1969): 8–13.
Sottas, Jules. *Une escadre française aux Indes en 1690. Histoire de la Compagnie royale des Indes Orientales, 1664–1719*. Paris: Plon-Nourrit et Cie, 1905.
Souder, Casper. *History of Chestnut Street*. Philadelphia: Sunday Dispatch, 1858.
Souza, George Bryan. 'Merchants and Commerce in Asia and the Portuguese Empire over the Long 18th Century'. *Review of Culture*, International Edition No. 34 (April 2010): 64–76.
———. *Portuguese, Dutch and Chinese in Maritime Asia, c. 1585–1800: Merchants, Commodities and Commerce*. Burlington, VT: Ashgate, 2014.
———. 'The Portuguese Merchant Fleet at Macao in the Seventeenth and Eighteenth Centuries'. In *Rivalry and Conflict: European Traders and Asian Trading Networks in the 16th and 17th Centuries*, edited by Ernst van Veen and Leonard Blussé, 342–69. Amsterdam: Amsterdam University Press, 2005.
———. *The Survival of Empire: Portuguese Trade and Society in China and the South China Sea, 1630–1754*. Cambridge: Cambridge University Press, 1986. Reprint, 2004.
Spencer, Alfred, ed. *Memoirs of William Hickey (1749–1775)*. 4 vols. New York: Alfred A. Knopf, 1921.
Steele, Charles C. *American Trade in Opium to China in the Nineteenth Century*. Chicago: University of Chicago Libraries, 1938.
Stivers, Mabel. 'Wax Figures in Old Museums'. *Old Time New England* 17 (July 1926): 44.
Sturgis, Tim. *Rivalry in Canton: The Control of Russell and Co. 1838–1840 and the Founding of Augustine Heard and Co*. London: The Warren Press, 2006.
Subramanian, Lakshmi, ed. *The French East India Company and the Trade of the Indian Ocean: A Collection of Essays by Indrani Ray*. Calcutta: Centre for Studies in Social Sciences, 1999.
Thampi, Madhavi. *Indians in China 1800–1949*. New Delhi: Manohar Publishers & Distributors, 2005.
———. 'Parsis in the China Trade'. *Review of Culture*, International Edition, No. 10 (April 2004): 16–25.
Thampi, Madhavi, and Shalini Saksena. *China and the Making of Bombay*. Mumbai: K.R. Cama Oriental Institute, 2009.
Thill, Joan. 'A Delawarean in the Celestial Empire'. MA thesis, University of Delaware, 1973.
Thorne, R. G., ed. *The House of Commons, 1790–1820*. London: Published for the History of Parliament Trust by Secker and Warburg, 1986.
Tiffany, Osmond, Jr. *The Canton Chinese* or *The American Sojourn in the Celestial Empire*. Boston: James Munroe, 1849.
The Times (1842–1851).
Tong Te-Kong. *United States Diplomacy in China, 1844–1860*. Seattle: University of Washington Press, 1964.
Torén, Olof. *En Ostindisk Resa*. Stockholm: Tiden, 1961.

Tripathi, Amales. *Trade and Finance in the Bengal Presidency, 1793–1833*. Calcutta: Orient Longmans, 1956.
Vale, A. M. Martins do. *Os Portugueses em Macau (1750–1800)*. Macao: Institvto Portvgvês do Oriente, 1997.
Van Dyke, Paul A. *The Canton Trade: Life and Enterprise on the China Coast, 1700–1845*. Hong Kong: Hong Kong University Press, 2005. Reprint, 2007.
———. 'The Hume Scroll of 1772 and the Faces behind the Canton Factories'. *Review of Culture*, International Edition No. 54 (2017), 64–102.
———. *Merchants of Canton and Macao: Politics and Strategies in Eighteenth-Century Chinese Trade*. Vol. 1. Hong Kong: Hong Kong University Press, 2011.
———. *Merchants of Canton and Macao: Success and Failure in Eighteenth-Century Chinese Trade*. Vol. 2. Hong Kong: Hong Kong University Press, 2016.
———. 'Port Canton and the Pearl River Delta, 1690–1845'. PhD dissertation, Department of History, University of Southern California, 2002.
———. Unpublished ship list.
Van Dyke, Paul A., and Cynthia Viallé, comps. *The Canton-Macao Dagregisters*. 1762. Macau: Macau Cultural Institute, 2006.
———, comps. *The Canton-Macao Dagregisters*. 1763. Macao: Macao Cultural Institute, 2008.
Van Dyke, Paul A., and Maria Kar-wing Mok. *Images of the Canton Factories 1760–1822: Reading History in Art*. Hong Kong: Hong Kong University Press, 2015.
Van Heslinga, E. S. van Eyck. *Van Compagnie naar Koopvaardij, De scheepvaart verbinding van de Bataafse Republiek met de koloniën in Azië 1795–1806*. Amsterdam: De Bataafsche Leeuw, 1988.
Veyssière, Marion. 'Les voyages français à la Chine: Vaisseaux et équipages, 1720–1793'. Diplôme d'archiviste paléographe, Ecole nationale des chartes, Paris, 2000.
Viallé, Cynthia, and Paul A. Van Dyke, comps. *The Canton-Macao Dagregisters*. 1764. Macau: Macau Cultural Institute, 2009.
Vienne, Marie-Sybille de. *La Chine au déclin des Lumières: l'expérience de Charles de Constant, négociant des loges de Canton*. Paris: Honoré Champion, 2004.
Waln, Robert. *China; Comprehending a View of the Origins, Antiquity, History . . . &c of that Empire to which is Added a Commercial Appendix*. Philadelphia: Published by the Author, 1825.
Wang Gungwu, and Ng Chin-Keong. *Maritime China in Transition 1750–1850*. Wiesbaden: Harrassowitz Verlag, 2004.
Wang Shuo 王碩. 'Wu Bingjian and His Friends: The Relations Network of a Chinese Merchant in the Early 19th Century'. PhD dissertation, East Asian History, University of Freiburg, forthcoming.
Wathen, James. *Journal of a Voyage in 1811 & 1812 to Madras and China*. London: J. Nichols, Son, and Bentley, 1814.
Watson, Ian Bruce. *Foundation for Empire: English Private Trade in India 1659–1760*. New Delhi: Vikas, 1980.
Webster, Anthony. *The Twilight of the East India Company: The Evolution of Anglo-Asian Commerce and Politics, 1790–1860*. Woodbridge: Boydell Press, 2009.
Wei Yuan 魏源. *Hai Guo Tu Zhi* 海國圖志. 1841.
Wetmore, James. *The Wetmore Family of America*. Albany: Munsell and Rowland, 1861.

White, Ann. 'The Hong Merchants of Canton'. PhD dissertation, University of Pennsylvania, 1968.

Whitehill, Walter Muir. *The East India Marine Society and the Peabody Museum of Salem: A Sesquicentennial History*. Salem, MA: Peabody Museum of Salem, 1949.

Wills, John E., Jr. 'Functional, Not Fossilized: Qing Tribute Relations with Đại Việt (Vietnam) and Siam (Thailand), 1700–1820'. *T'oung Pao* 98 (2012): 439–78.

———. 'What's New? Studies of Revolutions and Divergences, 1770–1840: A Review Article'. *Journal of World History* 25, no. 1 (2014): 127–86.

Wilson, Dick A. 'King George's Men: British Ships and Sailors in the Pacific Northwest-China Trade, 1785–1821'. PhD dissertation, Department of History, University of Idaho, 2004.

Wines, Enoch. *A Peep at China in Mr. Dunn's Chinese Collection*. Philadelphia: Printed for Nathan Dunn, 1839. Reprinted in *Sermons Collected by the American Sunday School Union* 3: 27 (n.d.) and in *Chinese Repository* 8 (March 1840): 583.

Wong, John D. 'Global Positioning: Houqua and His China Trade Partners in the Nineteenth Century'. PhD dissertation, Harvard University, 2012.

———. *Global Trade in the Nineteenth Century: The House of Houqua and the Canton System*. Cambridge: Cambridge University Press, 2016.

Wood, William. *Sketches of China with Illustrations from Original Drawings*. Philadelphia: Carey and Lea, 1830.

Yvan, Melchior. *Inside Canton*. London: Henry Vizetelly, 1858.

Zhao Gang. *The Qing Opening to the Ocean: Chinese Maritime Policies, 1684–1757*. Honolulu: University of Hawai'i Press, 2013.

Zhou Xiang 周湘. 'Qingdai Guangzhou yu Maopi Maoyi' 清代廣州與毛皮貿易 [Guangzhou and the maritime fur trade during the Qing dynasty]. PhD dissertation, Department of History, Zhongshan University, 1999.

Contributors

Thomas H. Cox is an associate professor of history at Sam Houston State University. After receiving his PhD from SUNY-Buffalo, Dr. Cox published *Gibbons v. Ogden, Law, and Society in the Early Republic* (2009). He is currently completing a biography of Warren Delano, an American merchant in China.

Jonathan Goldstein (PhD in East Asian History, University of Pennsylvania, 1973) has been a research associate of Harvard University's Fairbank Center for Chinese Studies since 1985 and a professor of East Asian history at the University of West Georgia since 1981. His books include *Philadelphia and the China Trade* (1978), *Stephen Girard's Trade with China* (2011), *America Views China* (1991), *Jewish Identities in East and Southeast Asia* (2015), *The Jews of China* (1999/2000), and *China and Israel* (1999; Chinese ed. 2006; Hebrew ed. 2016).

Jessica Hanser is an assistant professor of history at Yale-NUS College in Singapore. Her research explores cross-cultural trade, diplomacy, and British imperial expansion in China during the eighteenth century. Her book monograph, *Mr. Smith Goes to China*, follows the lives of three Scottish traders, all named George Smith, to explore the eighteenth-century origins of Britain's economic and political relationship with China.

Lisa Hellman is a postdoctoral scholar at Freie Universität Berlin. She received her PhD at Stockholm University on the everyday life of Europeans in eighteenth-century Canton, and has since then worked at the University of Tokyo. She works in the intersection between cultural, maritime, and global history, with a focus on early modern Central and East Asia, and has published in five languages about how intercultural interaction changed the lives of the men and women involved.

Maria Kar-Wing Mok is a PhD candidate at Sun Yat-sen University, Guangzhou, and curator (Modern Art) at the Hong Kong Museum of Art. Her research focuses on Chinese export paintings and the nature of commodity art in the China trade. She co-authored *Images of the Canton Factories 1760–1822: Reading History in Art* (2015) with Paul A. Van Dyke.

Susan E. Schopp is an independent scholar who holds graduate degrees in art history from the Ecole du Louvre and a PhD in history. Her current research focuses on the French Canton trade. In 1997, she identified the wreck of the English East Indiaman *Earl Temple*. She is also a member of the crew of *Friendship of Salem*, a fully operational reconstruction of an American East India ship.

Paul A. Van Dyke is a professor of history at Sun Yat-sen University, Guangzhou, and author of *The Canton Trade: Life and Enterprise on the China Coast* (2005) and *Merchants of Canton and Macao* Vols. 1 and 2 (2011 and 2016).

The late **John E. Wills Jr.** (d. 2017), 'Jack' to all his friends and colleagues, was professor emeritus at the University of Southern California and authored many books and articles on Chinese, Asian, and Global history, with a specialty in Sino-Western relations. He was a prodigious writer and is considered to be one of the founding fathers of global and maritime history.

Index

www.ingramcontent.com/pod-product-compliance
Ingram Content Group UK Ltd.
Pitfield, Milton Keynes, MK11 3LW, UK
UKHW021838100926
8556IPUK00004B/427

9 789888 390939